Acts of Cruelty
Australia's Immigration Laws
and experiences of people seeking protection
after arriving by plane
—
Aileen Crowe

Dedication

This narrative is dedicated to the thousands of Australians
who have reached out to 'the other', the stranger with a different skin colour, different cultural practices, different religious beliefs and different, often unimaginable life experiences; to the many who have risked the safety of their own familiar lives in developing enduring friendships with people who were once complete strangers;
to those who have truly become citizens of the universe.

Acknowledgments

My deepest gratitude is extended to the heroes who have given this book life. The people who have taken enormous risks to reveal their deepest secrets, with all the unbearable pain that materialised during the sharing of their life experiences. Even called here by pseudonyms, they know who they are.

I could not have persevered over the past twenty or more years without the enduring emotional and intellectual support of Ngareta Rossell, a born journalist, who can sniff out injustices and get the stories into the public arena; Trish and John Highfield with their passion and tears for those so terribly mistreated by our governments and the systemic cruelty, and their unlimited determination to influence the minds and hearts of politicians; Zeena Elton who skilfully provided constructive criticism and, along with Dr Eileen Pittaway AM, inspired me to commence my study of the refugee determination process in the first place; and Marlene Hixon a fellow Franciscan nun with her skill of dropping by to propose yet another challenging idea.

This manuscript has been brought to life by editor, Pamela Hewitt, in such a way that the truths told are richer and more compelling than in my original text; and Peter and Morella Van Hees who read patiently, even while being confronted with so many typos. I also wish to acknowledge Sally Gardner, co-editor, Palaver, for her sensitivity and openness in our endeavours to tighten up the text. Our conversations opened up new horizons.

Aileen Crowe

Acts of Cruelty

Australia's Immigration Laws
and experiences of people seeking protection
after arriving by plane

Acts of Cruelty
Australia's Immigration Laws
and experiences of people seeking
protection after arriving by plane
A Palaver Book
Copyright © 2022 Aileen Crowe
All rights reserved.
No part of this book may be
reproduced, stored in a retrieval
system, or transmitted by any
means, electronic, mechanical,
photocopying, recording, or
otherwise, without written
permission from the publisher or
author except in the case of brief
quotations embodied in critical
articles or reviews.
ISBN: 978-0-6455881-0-1

For additional information,
bulk or educational purchases,
and other resources, please
contact Ethica Projects, Pty. Ltd.
c/o Paul Komesaroff:
paul.komesaroff@monash.edu
First Palaver edition
published May 2022
Design: Ian Robertson
Typefaces: Tiempos, FGrotesk

www.palaver.com
Palaver is an imprint of Ethica
Projects, Pty. Ltd.
10 Barnato Grove Armadale
Victoria 3143 Australia

Disclaimer
1. This work should not be construed as the publisher or author giving legal or other advice or services.
2. No person or entity should rely on the information contained in this work without first obtaining independent advice from a qualified professional person.
3. To the extent permitted by law, neither the publisher nor the author is responsible for, makes any representations or warranties whether expressly or impliedly, as to:
(a) The results of any action or omission by any person or entity who relies on the whole or any part of this work; or
(b) The completeness or accuracy of the information contained in this work.
4. To the extent permitted by law, the publisher and the author and each of them disclaims all and any liability for the consequences of any act or omission including but not limited to any negligent act or omission by any person or entity who relies on the whole or any part of this work.

Contents

Foreword *7*
The Honourable Michael Kirby AC CMG

Introduction and Welcome *16*

1. Arriving with fragile dreams *29*
2. The 'Australian way' with visas *44*
3. Surviving while waiting *56*
4. The assessment decision *65*
5. Reviewing a negative assessment decision *72*
6. Consequential errors *86*
7. Consequences of discriminatory policies *91*
8. The impact of a successful court challenge *96*
9. An inquisitorial process *105*
10. The court examines tribunal reviewers' decisions *115*
11. Politics and power *127*
12. Playing God: The minister's non-reviewable powers *132*
13. Pushing back against ministerial power *147*
14. A humanitarian visa story *157*
15. Exceptions: historical and contemporary *175*
16. Contested boundaries: the court and the parliament *184*
17. Cultural erosion: systemic discrimination *195*
18. If only: achieving fairness *203*
19. A society in peril: privilege and injustice *208*

Appendix *216*
Visa history of participants
Choices facing asylum seekers at each stage of the process

Glossary *218*
Bibliography *221*
Index *225*

Rally in support of freeing refugees detained as 'security threat', Sydney 2013.

Foreword

The Honourable Michael Kirby AC CMG

This is an uplifting book. It tells the story of human endeavour to help people tackle the challenges of the Australian legal system, as it applies to non-citizens arriving by planes with valid entry visas but who thereafter claim protection under the Migration Act 1958, on grounds expressed in the Refugees Convention 1951.

The special animosity that many Australians feel towards those who arrive on boats, making claims for refugee status without benefit of appropriate entry visas is told in other books and in countless administrative, tribunal and court decisions. This book is about a different cohort. But many of the obstacles and legal complexities recounted in these pages will remind the reader of the special animosity reserved for 'boat people' who arrived by sea.

Against their arrival, the Australian Parliament, and politicians of otherwise different persuasions, united to erect especially high barriers because of the spectre raised of little boats drifting towards their continent, their country, presenting a contemporary apparition of the 'yellow hordes' who terrified us in earlier centuries.

Those who arrive on planes present different challenges. Of necessity, they will arrive with visas. Those visas would have been checked by airline staff, both for validity and duration, because an airline carrying passengers not in possession of valid visas to enter Australia incur obligations themselves: ordinarily to take the arrivals away, sometimes with severe penalties for their mistake. Nonetheless, the enormous queues of new arrivals at Australia's international airports present different but acute problems in their cases. The arrivals have to be processed quickly. Very soon, they are, for the most part, merged in the Australian community. Without internal passports' or identity inspections, many who arrive may be absorbed and disappear from official scrutiny until something extraneous brings them to notice.

When, after their initial arrival, the immigrant carried by an airline claims refugee status, many of the same obstacles as those faced by the boat people are confronted. They are denounced as 'queue jumpers'. They are condemned as 'economic immigrants', not refugees. They are accused of having falsely obtained their short-term entry visas, generally as tourists. They should be expelled. But before expulsion, if they contest that result and persist with the assertion that they are 'refugees', they face very similar challenges to the 'boat people'. Those challenges, and the legal hurdles they have to confront, are described in this book. The description conjures up a special part of Hades, as portrayed in Dante Alighieri's *Divine Comedy*.

Crowe's thesis is that, in order to deter and repel most of the applicants who seek refugee status (and thereby to discourage other foolhardy souls who might be tempted to follow in their footsteps), complex and often harsh legal procedures have been put in place. As she describes them, the procedures produce 'a toxic immigration culture sanctioned by parliament, a culture that allows systemic cruelty to operate'.

Initially, the author had no particular knowledge of, or experience in, Australia's legal system for the protection of those who seek to establish refugee status. She was a nun of the Catholic Church. Her work was substantially in other fields of need. All this changed when a community social worker telephoned her office in the late 1990s seeking help for a family in a desperate situation. Drawing on her experience as a teacher and pastoral assistant in Papua New Guinea, the author responded intuitively. One thing led to another. Soon she was in the thick of seeking to help those claiming protection as refugees.

This experience brought her directly into contact with the mechanics of the bureaucratic and legal system put in place to decide, in each individual case, the merits or demerits of the application. The new desperation also brought her into close contact with the operation of Australia's independent tribunals and courts, the latter including the High Court of Australia, established under the Constitution. Because, at the time of which the author is writing, I was serving as a Justice of the High Court of Australia, I was also coming into contact with cases of the kind she describes, likewise at first, without a great deal of experience in that area of the law. In my case, the experience was presented at the peak of the pyramid of bureaucratic, tribunal and judicial responses to refugee applicants. But Sister Aileen, was down in the engine room. She was dealing up close and personally with real people. Cases, for her, were not mediated through learned counsel and distinguished judges and Ministers of the Crown. Cases came to her as people looking for urgent help with shelter, food and advice. Their predicaments motivated a rapid understanding of the vital necessity of pursuing the complex game of bureaucratic Snakes and Ladders put in place by law to decide the merits of the applications that she attempted to support.

Fortunately, Sister Aileen's experience 'as a woman in the Catholic Church' had exposed her to an experience, as she puts it, of 'powerlessness in many ways and on many occasions'.

Those who were seeking recognition of their claim to refugee status commonly suffered 'diminished power, especially when confronting immigration officials and others in positions of authority'. But what the clients lacked in confidence and determination, Sister Aileen could endeavour to supply. She did so, 'unashamedly us[ing] my dominant, white woman, Catholic nun power when accompanying people seeking protection in their interactions with the immigration department'.

Sister Aileen thus takes the reader through the often baffling, frequently discouraging and commonly frightening world of officialdom that Australia has in place to process a person's claim to being a refugee. The book is full of the system's seemingly irrational requirements. Such as the imposition of obligations to pay significant fees for government services whilst at the same time being forbidden to engage in work to earn the money vital for that purpose, not to mention for bare survival. Sister Aileen pulls no punches in describing what she sees as the injustices, irrationality, illogicality and plain error of the system she came to know and sometimes to operate. I cannot judge the justice of her complaints in individual cases. But I can empathise with her despair at many aspects of the system created, in the name of the Australian people, to impose a kind of litigious torture on desperate and vulnerable people.

Even in the small area of the refugee litigation that was viewed by a High Court Justice, there were features difficult to comprehend and almost impossible to explain, let alone justify. At the time of which Sister Aileen is writing, part of the burden of refugee applications was shifted into the High Court of Australia. This happened because other remedies were excluded by Acts of the Australian Parliament. However, the High Court unanimously determined that the Parliament could not exclude the supervisory role of the courts to ensure that officials stayed within power and exercised their jurisdiction according to law.

The consequence usually obliged the unfortunate applicants seeking redress to demonstrate a peculiar qualification for relief, namely 'jurisdictional error'. This was a highly technical expression, not always understood by judges and lawyers themselves. To explain to a self-represented applicant, struggling in a special leave application before the High Court the meaning of jurisdictional error was an exquisite burden to place on the judge, let alone the litigant. When it had to be attempted, usually through the fog of linguistic limitations, it sometimes approached the farcical. Little wonder, therefore, that eventually the High Court of Australia shifted the great bulk of such applications to be determined 'on the papers', without the pain and embarrassment of oral exchanges with the applicants. However, this meant, in many cases, that the court did not enjoy the benefit of an effective contradictor to the experienced and talented advocates who would contest and seek to repel the arguments of the applicants. The factual merits of the predicaments of the applicants all too often disappeared as the judges and lawyers tackled their special task. If they were heard at all, they were heard quarrelling over the elusive and mysterious 'jurisdictional error' concept that meant nothing to the applicants although it was absolutely critical to the outcome of their dreams to stay in Australia, their chosen land of refuge.

In every generation in the history of Australia, wrongs have occurred and many of them have been carried into effect by the law. At the outset of the penal settlement at Port Jackson in 1788, there were elements in the law that were admirable. But also, elements that we can now see as discriminatory and unjust. Thus, Governor Phillip brought with him the King's commission forbidding slavery in the Great South Land. Formally, Aboriginals were treated equally to 'white' people when charged with criminal offences. However, Indigenous Australians were denied recognition of their land rights, with consequences disastrous for their economic interests. That inequality was not finally addressed until the 1992 decision of the High Court in Mabo v Queensland [No.2]. Women also suffered great inequality in Australia's law. They enjoyed equal suffrage in federal elections after 1902, in some states later. However, until 1983, a married woman's application for an Australian passport had to be authorised by her husband. Many injustices remained for women until more recent times. Similarly, the White Australia Policy was not finally abolished until 1973.

Sister Aileen suggests that some of the deep anxieties that explain hostility in Australia towards those who claim protection as refugees can be traced to the same racial attitudes as earlier gave rise to White Australia – a fear of difference and of the other, especially if they look different or have a darker skin colour. Likewise, the hostility toward sexual minorities (LGBTIQ+) existed for more than two centuries in Australia. Effectively, they have remained until very recent times. Each of the foregoing sources of inequality and injustice would justify a book as detailed, and as bitter, as the present book on refugee applicants. Every such book would identify heroes like the author of this book. But also, opponents who took a long time seeing what later generations regarded as obvious.

Correctly, in one of her final chapters, Sister Aileen invokes the special sensitivity exhibited by Pope Francis in his message for the celebration of the World Day of Migrants and Refugees 2014. He wrote:

> While it is true that migrations often reveal failures and shortcomings on the part of states and the international community, they also point to the aspiration of humanity to enjoy a unity marked by respect for differences, by attitudes of acceptance and hospitality ... and by the protection and advancement of the dignity and centrality of each human being.

Long before these Papal words were written, it is clear that Sister Aileen was searching for the same path of kindness that would unlock the doors of legal technicalities that sometimes bar the way of those who seek protection in Australia on the ground of refugee status.

As she is quick to point out, she is not a lawyer. Nor is she a governmental official. She perhaps does not fully understand the meaning and suggested constitutional reasons for 'jurisdictional error'. I, myself, when a judge, was sometimes uncertain about that phrase and its elusive nuances.

However, Sister Aileen has never forgotten the central message of the religion that had nurtured her, and indeed of all global faiths, confronted with the claims of the vulnerable stranger who needs protection and a new life where that claim can be justified. She certainly knows the human urgency of shelter, food and advice about access to essential rights. She knows the rational necessity of financial help, especially for those, themselves, forbidden to work. She knows the frustration of Australia's many legal obstacles when the human merits seem to cry out for relief in the name of simple justice.

Just as today, we look back on the way our legal system has dealt with Aboriginals, non-white immigrants, women, gays and others, so in the future, I suspect, we will look back at the present time with disappointment at the way our generations have dealt with refugees and those who claim the protection promised for that status. When that time comes, and in a new enlightenment, people like Sister Aileen Crowe will be celebrated. They will be honoured among the righteous of the Australian nation.

Sydney 21 February 2021

The Honourable Michael Kirby is former Justice of the High Court of Australia (1996–2009); President of the International Commission of Jurists (1995–8); Co-Chair of the International Bar Association Human Rights Institute (2017–21).

12 \ Acts of Cruelty

Conservative Murdoch press claims luxurious refugee detention centre facilities at Woomera (SA) and Villawood (NSW), amongst others.

Teachers for Refugees, Melbourne rally 2016, State Library, Swanston Street.

Introduction and welcome

This is a book born out of more than twenty years, from the turn of this century, of assisting people who arrive by plane seeking to be legally accepted into Australian society. My intention in writing this book has been to explore how and why an immigrant country like Australia, with its signature firmly planted in the 1951 Geneva Convention on the Status of Refugees, uses cruel and discriminatory laws to open doors with one hand and close them with the other. One way to discover the roots of these policies is to explore, as I have done, the processes by which immigration decisions are arrived at.

The book documents the experiences of a number of families and individuals who arrived in Australia seeking its protection. It was my privilege to support and, for long periods of time, to become part of the lives of these people as they took the difficult journey through Australia's notorious immigration and refugee determination processes.[1]

Many, perhaps most, Australians may think that refugees who don't come through Australia's refugee resettlement program are 'queue jumpers', economic migrants or not real refugees. In fact, a variety of circumstances cause people to flee violent situations. In some countries, unscrupulous governments no longer control law and order. This makes it difficult for human rights to be upheld when certain people need to be protected. The 1951 Convention Relating to the Status of Refugees and 1967 Protocol should provide sanctuary to those at risk and in danger and who, because of a rupture within their country of origin, are 'compelled to leave their homes'. The core principles for the international protection of refugees are that the latter are to be afforded a 'legal, political and ethical significance' which reaches beyond their specific circumstances.[2] A refugee, according to the Convention, is a person who is outside their country of nationality or their usual country of residence when they seek protection and who is either unable or unwilling to return to, or seek the protection of, that country due to a well-founded fear of being persecuted for reasons of race, religion, nationality, membership of a particular social group, or political opinion.

It is important to recognise that a refugee can be a person arriving by plane seeking protection in a country, even when there has been no mass exodus or civil war in their own country. Unlike people arriving by boat, the people whose stories are recounted in this book came by themselves, individually or in a family group, and they came with legitimate visas.[3]

They were not detained when they entered Australia and, unlike refugees in the settlement programs, they were not met at the airport and assisted in their adjustment to a new culture. They had to establish themselves in Australian society with little or no support. This meant that they needed to learn how to submit their claims for protection without the assistance of any government program. Thus, they needed support from advocates like me.

Initially, I knew little of the plight of refugees and people seeking protection in Australia – in the same way that, when I first arrived as a teacher in Papua New Guinea in 1970, I myself knew nothing of its culture and languages. Thus, when I became acquainted with the people seeking protection in Australia whom you will meet in this book, I was familiar with their sense of acute disorientation and powerlessness in an unfamiliar socio-political environment.

As a woman in the Catholic Church, I have experienced powerlessness on many occasions. I have learnt that regardless of their gender, people seeking protection have diminished power, especially when they are confronted by Australian immigration officials. I am not a migration agent or a lawyer but, as a nun, it has always been my challenge to be able to redirect the power generously bestowed on me because of my position in the church.[4] I was able unashamedly to use my dominant, white woman, Catholic nun power to be beside people as they trod the tortuous path that the immigration department plots for them.

In the late 1990s, I received a call from community social worker, Isabel who was seeking help for a family. The family's rent was due. They were living on a diet of cheap noodles. By that time, I knew well that the most important thing to do, to be of help in such situations, was to approach each family and situation intuitively.

Soon after I had helped that first family, the rumour mill began turning. People from different walks of life and religious backgrounds came to know me. Community whispering is part and parcel of daily life. 'So and so suggested I contact you', would greet me as soon as I picked up the phone. There was no need to advertise my activities and I accepted no payment.

---

1. As a pastoral carer and former teacher, my involvement in the determination process was but one element of my support. Because, for these people, almost everything was foreign and there was no extended family to rely upon, I participated in attendances at births, weddings, funerals, helping to complete in English the seemingly endless forms for Centrelink and schools, CVs for job applications, references, traffic infringements and court appearances on other matters, hospital visits, tutoring university students, and babysitting.
2. Türk, V & Nicholson, F, 2003, 'Refugee protection in international law: an overall perspective', in E Feller, V Türk & F Nicholson (eds), *Refugee Protection in International Law: UNHCR Global Consultations on International Protection*, University Press, Cambridge, pp 3, 6.
3. Visitor visas, special visas for international sports events or international conferences, tourist visas or student visas.
4. As a Franciscan nun I belong to Franciscans International, a United Nations accredited NGO.

I quickly discovered that culturally disoriented people suffer physical, psychological and emotional trauma.[5] I realised that I was learning the complexities of seeking protection in Australia together with them. My immediate concern was that families were in danger of being returned to the place of their original persecution.[6] But I, and they, were yet to realise how long the road ahead was to be.

People were sometimes directed to me as a last resort. They may have been assessed and refused protection. There may have been no further visa for them to apply for. Lawyers could no longer assist them because the immigration assessments had been completed. They and their families had been locked out of the system and were in trouble. By this time and for the most part, they would have sparse savings, no bank account and no legal permission to earn a living.

After all claims are rejected, the person's only option is to make a personal plea to the immigration minister to intervene. When receiving a negative decision at the tribunal or court, and upon the immigration minister refusing to intervene, they were expected to leave Australia. Many ignored the directive and stayed. Why would anyone go back to the dangers and precariousness from which they'd fled?

Not all the people I met were seeking Australia's protection, some had had their visas refused. On two occasions, a family member with a disability had been categorised as an economic liability for Australia. Women on temporary visas who bore children to Australian citizens were in danger of being deported without their child; women escaping domestic violence were threatened with losing their temporary visas. To be fair, some laws have since changed to accommodate emerging immigration needs, but other laws remain permanently fixed or have been transformed into something more punitive or rigid.

One thing I learnt was that people seeking protection do so for different reasons. Some search for ways of remaining legal. Others live in the community illegally, like the many thousands of people who overstay their visitor, tourist or student visas. It doesn't take long for the stay to run into months, even years. In some cases, negotiations can go on for over ten years until that magic day when the minister decides to intervene. In

---

5. Mackenzie, C, McDowell, C & Pittaway, E, 2007, 'Beyond "Do No Harm": the challenge of constructing ethical relationships in refugee research', *Journal of Refugee Studies*, vol. 20, no. 2, pp.299-319; Wilson, J.P & So-kum Tang, C (eds), 2007, *Cross-Cultural Assessment of Psychological Trauma and PTSD*, 1st edition, Springer Publishing Company, USA.
6. See Glendenning, P, Leavey C, Hetherton, M & Britt, M, 2006, *Deported to Danger II: The Continued Study of Australia's Rejected Asylum Seekers*, Edmund Rice Centre, Sydney, which documents the fate, sometimes murder, of asylum seekers returned to their country of origin.

this instance, not all negotiations end happily. From my position I could see with open eyes how this continual denial of justice effected a person's mental health and that of their family. To this day the situation remains on-going, a crippling fact of life for those seeking to find a new life, a fact seldom acknowledged or discussed.

~~~~~~~~

I began my own journey by researching the way the decisions are made. I ended with a PhD and a clearer perception of the Migration Act, along with a greater understanding of the cruelty of an Australian government whose policies so adversely affect so many lives. This book represents my aim to convey to a wide public how this cruelty continues to effect contemporary Australian society. I draw substantially on the qualitative research that formed the basis of my doctoral thesis.

Most of my interactions with the families took place in the security of their homes. They were cautious about whom to trust. If someone needed an interpreter this was usually another member of the family rather than a professional not related to them. I was often invited to stay for a meal. I saw this as an opportunity for debriefing, especially after a negative immigration decision had been received. At all times, I have considered people's rights, interests and wishes in reporting and recounting personal information.

In the early chapters of this book, the reader is invited to walk beside people from a variety of countries as they experience the system. These early chapters explore the lives of the people before they arrived in Australia. What were the bases of their claims for protection? Why did they flee? What drove them from their homes? What forced them to leave personal possessions, businesses, employment and, most of all, family behind? What was the driving force that motivated them to start a new life in a new country where everything was different – culture, climate, language, laws, especially immigration laws? What bridges do they have to cross to be accepted into Australian society?

Subsequent chapters follow visits to the compliance office, the journey through the immigration system of assessment of claims resulting in a negative decision, reviews at the tribunal, and appeals in the court. The first step is to become legal. The Compliance Office is where temporary visas are granted. This is when we would begin to work together towards the possibility of engaging the minister to use their intervention powers.

Subsequently, from chapter 11, I examine the 'God power' of the minister in the context of the fluid development of the Migration Act, the role of parliamentarians in their creation of laws designed to punish and exclude, and the tension between the parliament and the court.

Overall, I have attempted to avoid what I call 'immigration jargon and legalese'. Jargon and legalese not only strip a person of their uniqueness, it reinvents them as products to be processed and marketed as either a deportee (by deporting them the government claims to protect Australia's borders) or as participants in a very public official citizenship ceremony (used in promoting our much-touted multicultural society). In reality, the person, be they 'deportee' or 'grateful participant' merely wants a place in which to live normally in a safe and caring society.

For me, people's applications for protection ought not to be 'processed' like a box of tomatoes, subjected to a series of actions, ending crushed in cans of sauce. Every situation is unique, as are the people whose claims of persecution are examined and assessed either as being in need of Australia's protection, or not. I deliberately avoid the term 'asylum seeker' because some*one*, the person seeking protection is not some*thing*.

Similarly, when a person is objectified as 'the Applicant' they lose their personal identity. Because they come from a different country, as my ancestors did, this does not negate the fact that they are entitled to the same respect and Human Rights standards as I or any assessor is entitled to. The same goes for the word 'delegate'. When an assessor is objectified as 'the Delegate', 'the Member' or 'the Court' they are distanced from accountability for their decision. The end result of 'the process' or this system is a group of traumatised people – more traumatised even than when they first arrived.

'The Applicant' is a person like you and me, a neighbour, a person in the checkout queue at the supermarket, the driver at the traffic lights. 'An Applicant' is not an object without a name, devoid of deep feelings, or without agency.

Similarly, the term 'client' creates a distance between the 'haves' and the 'have-nots': the person who has the power to grant a future free of debilitating persecution, and the person who has a sense of powerlessness when confronted by frightening authority figures and a distorted and sometimes dishonest system. The person seeking protection is not a customer shopping around for a bargain but, rather, is persistently seeking fairness and justice. 'Cases' are claims about particular circumstances calling for careful examination according to International Human Rights standards.

The later part of this book is a call for parliamentarians, policy makers and some journalists to reimagine their roles in a society beset with illogical fears. Some people with authority in our society foster fear. Others pretend to 'keep us safe' from the terrible dangers – of living next door to people like ourselves – by promulgating cruel and unjust laws.

It is my hope that you, the reader, might come to understand people seeking protection as friends or neighbours as you accompany them in their struggle to navigate and face the refugee determination system. Walking in the shoes of the person seeking Australia's protection, the reader will also know the uninhibited elation when a permanent visa is granted. You might also experience incredible relief – because the fear of deportation and further suffering at these times can evaporate, to be replaced by a deep sense of gratitude and optimism for the future.

Yet again, the reader is granted the privilege of accompanying the advocate in exploring the tension experienced by ethical government officials having to abide by unfair policies that inevitably create a toxic, competitive work environment. We also observe the inability of parliamentarians to honour international obligations and the ruthless laws introduced and passed by themselves and their colleagues.

In struggling with this unfair system, I have reached out to the global consultations on international protection of the United Nations High Commissioner for Refugees (UNHCR).[7] These papers were published in 2003 at approximately the time this cohort of people arriving by plane were having their protection claims assessed.

Australia's contemporary exclusionary policies and practices are a continuation of a profoundly racist past. Parliament's treatment of contemporary refugees is an extension of the exceptions introduced long ago. Australia's Constitution was formed after 113 years of the coexistence of people of two very different cultures, each believing in their own sovereignty. Australia's Constitution 'excepted' (a legal term for excluded) the original owners of the land, denying their sovereign rights and excluding them from legal protections granted to British Australians, grounding the Australian legal system in discriminatory and exclusionary policies and practices. This legal exception was extended to non-British people in 1901 and a further 72 years of exclusionary policies and practices ensued. For 185 years, Australian parliaments legally excluded sovereign people who were either Indigenous to Australia or non-European. Australian cultural and legal practices in the almost five decades since the abandonment of the White Australia Policy have been influenced by historical exclusion. It permeates legislation about people seeking protection who arrive by plane.

The Australian Government is a signatory to the Refugees Convention and proud of its adherence to human rights. Nevertheless, the government's treatment of people seeking protection is a cause of deep

---

7. Feller, E, Türk, V & Nicholson, F (eds), 2003, *Refugee Protection in International Law: UNHCR's Global Consultations on International Protection,* University Press, Cambridge.

concern to many refugee advocates, human rights and refugee lawyers and members of civil society. While there is a very public focus on the inhumane treatment of people seeking protection who arrive by boat, people arriving by plane seeking protection often pass unnoticed.
The challenge to look deeper into ourselves as we explore together the roots of our exclusionary Australian society prompts us to consider the possibilities available to us to take responsibility for our past discriminatory and destructive policies and practices and to engage in more effective and appropriate ways of embracing people not like ourselves. These are presented towards the end of the book. I finish with a warning about the risks to Australian society of its ongoing acceptance in their name of deep discrimination and injustice.

~~~~~~~~

There are many people in addition to those I supported through the immigration process who have contributed to this book. As a female researcher, I was motivated by RK Bergen, who suggested that feminist research involves 'passionate scholarship' where 'researchers are allied with those being studied and work with great devotion to eliminate oppressive social structures'.[8] I stand alongside some formidable women working at the coalface in this field, women diligently striving to persuade decision-makers that people seeking protection deserve to be welcomed to Australia. A few who come to mind are Louise Newman, a developmental psychiatrist who is passionate about addressing the government's lack of care for children and their parents who seek protection; and Trish Highfield, an early childhood educator, who is outstanding in her forthright, unwavering and tender support of child detainees. Very few immigration department employees have not faced Trish's outrage at the cruel treatment of people seeking protection in detention camps or the community, in Australia or banished to nearby ill-fated islands. Ngareta Rossell, is an insightful, experienced journalist, who has educated the media and fostered relationships with reporters, documentary and film makers. She shares the tremendous amount of data amassed through her experiences advocating, visiting detention camps, observing tribunals and negotiating with overseas consulates. Other journalists and writers who contributed are Margot O'Neil, Heather Ewart, Cynthia Banham, Yuko Narishuma and Rosie Scott, who was president of PEN (an international organisation of Poets, Essayists and Novelists). Zeena Elton is another dedicated researcher who, as head of Research at the Edmund Rice

---

8. Bergen, R K, 1993, 'Interviewing Survivors of Marital Rape' in C M Renzetti & R M Lee (eds), *Researching Sensitive Topics*, SAGE Publications, Newbury Park, London, p.203.

Centre, authored 'Debunking the Myths about Asylum Seekers' in 2001. Eileen Pittaway and Linda Bartolomei at the Centre for Refugee Research at University of New South Wales (UNSW) put me in touch with the bigger picture of women in refugee camps throughout the world. The indefatigable Frances Milne founded Balmain for Refugees and fought tirelessly for justice for people in the Villawood detention camp. Virginia Walker established the Bridge for Asylum Seekers Foundation to support those who were forbidden by law to earn a living. Then there is Freddie Steen in Brisbane, Sister Brigid Arthur and Pamela Curr in Melbourne, and Bernadette Wauchope in South Australia.

Unsurprisingly, it emerges that it is past and present elected members of parliament who must take responsibility for the systemic and cruel discrimination that has inhabited our law for far too long. And again, it is these parliamentarians who have the power to commit to a more inclusive way of governing all people living in Australia, not merely Australian citizens. If only they had the will power! It is also up to the courts to challenge discriminatory laws and protect their power to judge all people living in Australia equally and to resist any attempt by the government to usurp this power. It is up to all of us to work towards overcoming our fear of 'the other'. This is achievable, especially if public voices including journalists resist discriminatory language and move out of their comfort zone to positively report on people of unfamiliar cultures and practices.

Just as everything in the environment is interdependent, we are people of one world dependent upon each other economically through international trade, movements of peoples through migration and tourism, as well as international protections through treaties and obligations regarding peoples' rights. We dwell in Australia but live in one world. Welcome to global citizenship.

~~~~~~~~

To protect their privacy, all names of people seeking protection and their assessors and reviewers, lawyers and advocates have been changed or replaced by particular titles, as in 'the judge'. I have deliberately avoided including real names, dates or other details that might expose the people seeking protection mentioned in this book, not only because of their right to privacy, but also because the story is not primarily about them, individual assessors, reviewers, judges, or me. It is about unjust, unfair policies and procedures. It exposes historical systemic cruelty currently experienced by people seeking protection, their advocates, and all the ethical, fair-minded decision-makers caught up in this dishonourable system constructed by parliamentarians without the constraints of a Bill of Rights.

For convenience and consistency, the minister's title is abbreviated because, over the years during which my research took place, the Department of Immigration changed its name numerous times. I also abbreviate the Immigration Review Tribunal (IRT), Refugee Review Tribunal (RRT), the Migration Review Tribunal (MRT) and the Administrative Appeals Tribunal (AAT). For simplicity I simply use 'the tribunal'.

~~~~~~~~

'Let Them Stay' rally, Melbourne 2016.

Author with father and two sons having received their Australian citizenship, Sydney 2019.

Relief after the long fight for protection, Sydney 2015.

1. Arriving with fragile dreams

As I arrived at the gate of the small brick duplex, a woman was farewelling a grateful middle-aged man. Amora, a young four-foot-something lady, explained that she'd met the gentleman in the shopping mall and he looked so lonely. He was homeless. She invited him home for a hot meal. Somehow, she'd found it within herself to share her sparse noodles with a stranger.

We walked down the dark, narrow passage to the tiny dining room. Marco, Amora's husband, a man more than six feet tall, stood to greet me. Angelica, the youngest of the two children interrupted our conversation at regular intervals to ensure she retained her mother's attention.

Sitting in the family home in the warmth of their kitchen allowed the couple to open up, gradually. At first, they were guarded, suspicious of this stranger who had entered their unpredictable lives. They feared their situation and their location would be leaked into the community, where someone would forward their whereabouts to the government they'd fled. Both were reticent. Amora spoke perfect English – self-taught. Marco relied on her to interpret. After they were assured that I was under an obligation to observe strict confidentiality, and promises had been made that nothing that they felt was too dangerous would be included in the final drafting of their request to the minister, they began to relax.

Nothing that would identify Marco if government officials back home happened upon the case could be exposed. What was said that day was horrifying and made me determined to participate in their struggle to remain in Australia. Across the table was a strong, tall man sobbing. It really scared me. How could things have come to this?

As part of his work, Marco was responsible in his country of origin for dismantling a cocaine laboratory owned by a parliamentary member. Drug barons there were powerful and above the law. Marco couldn't get police protection. He fled to London where he met Amora, then a student. When they thought it safe to do so, they returned to their country of origin. But Marco began to be pursued. Amora's pregnancy was nearing full term. They fled back to London but were turned around at the airport. During their return flight, Amora's waters broke and the plane had to make an emergency landing. It was Amora's first pregnancy and she was terrified. Soon after baby Emilano was delivered, they were on the plane again, destined for the country they had fled.

It was too dangerous to stay. They travelled from one nearby country to another, only able to obtain three-months visas in each place. Eventually, they returned to their original country and bought an isolated farm. Peace reigned for a short period and two more children were born.

Then Marco was located. He fled down the nearby river while his father confronted the intruders. Soon after, his father suffered a heart attack and died. They had to get away, a long way away. They chose Australia because of the distance. They also judged Australia to be serious about protecting human rights.

Their last few dollars were spent on train tickets from the airport to Sydney's Central Station. Amora and Marco walked the streets with two young children and a three-month-old baby. They slept in Redfern Park and for the first few days, Indigenous people in the area brought them food. While walking one evening, they heard familiar music and knocked on the stranger's door. They were made welcome. Soon after, they were put in touch with the St Vincent de Paul Society which helped them with social and legal needs.

Marco explained that, when they arrived at the flat the lady from the Saint Vincent de Paul Society had rented for them, 'she thought we were going to bring a removal truck or something and we arrived with our backpacks as our luggage. We didn't even have blankets'. For food, Marco and his family relied on the Chinese market where 'it was very, very cheap and we used to buy at the last minute, the fruit, everything, so they gave it to us even cheaper'.

Emilano, the six-year-old, arrived home from school and Amora suddenly had other things on her mind. The child was asthmatic and needed mum's attention. Marco was not allowed to work, yet the bills had to be paid. He was not yet forty, strong and healthy. He wanted to work. Before I left, I assured Amora and Marco they would receive a regular allowance for their living costs.

This was my first encounter with a family who had arrived by plane seeking Australia's protection. I'd been to Villawood detention camp many times and heard many stories of people who came to Australia on leaky boats. But arriving by plane was a different story.

By the time he submitted his protection application, eighty-two of the eighty-four students in Marco's graduating year in his home country were dead and another died soon after. I was convinced of his need for protection. In a country well known for its corruption, Marco had valid grounds to claim persecution based on membership of a particular social group, his political opinion and the refusal of the state to protect him.[9]

~~~~~~~~

It was late November at a Christmas party with a group of friends including Ngareta, a journalist. When another guest, lawyer Patrick Peacot, heard I was a Catholic nun, he approached me with an air of great expectancy. Here was someone he was confident would be able to help one of his clients. He asked if I could get Mikhaila into a school. At almost eight years old she had never been to school. He wrote down the address and phone contact, and I assured him it wouldn't be too difficult.

How wrong I was.

The first step was to visit the parents, Sabina and Vasyl, in the comfort of their home, which had been bequeathed to them by an elderly aunt. We patiently waited until the children next door finished teaching Mikhaila the maths and spelling they had learnt at school that day. Mikhaila was our interpreter. Her parents weren't allowed to earn a living. They sometimes noticed a man in a white car parked all day across the road. They imagined they were being watched to see if they were creeping out to go to work. Frustrated by this scrutiny, they rang the police. They explained there was a child in the house and they were frightened by this mysterious presence.

The car never appeared again.

When Sabina and Vasyl approached the local Catholic school, the principal was horrified to hear that Mikhaila couldn't attend. It wasn't that the government didn't allow Mikhaila to go to school but, rather, made it impossible. School fees for people without permanent visas were based on those set for overseas students. About $6,000 per year in primary school. On top of this, the government had recently introduced a penalty for schools accepting children on bridging visas without permission to study.

Principals had allowed some children to attend but didn't mark them on the roll. Accordingly, they weren't enrolled! I was proud of this creative handling of moral obligations in the face of cruelly deficient government policy. But even this choice was made difficult by the threat that it would take a substantial sum from the school's budget.

The school principal contacted the Catholic Education Office for guidance and was told that taking Mikhaila wasn't possible. The system was having difficulty coping with the many South Sudanese children who had recently arrived. She was bitterly disappointed and somewhat ashamed.

Mikhaila had learnt English by watching ABC children's programs. As a five-year-old, she had interpreted for her parents when they renewed their visas on a three-monthly basis. She had prevented officers from detaining her mother and herself by deliberately throwing a tantrum in the compliance office when officers led her father away. Not a child to be reckoned with.

9. Aleinikoff, T, 2003, 'Protected characteristics and social perceptions: an analysis of the meaning of "membership of a particular social group"', in Feller et al (eds.) *Refugee Protection in International Law*, op. cit., pp. 263-311; Edwards, A, 2003, 'Age and gender dimensions in international refugee law', in E Feller et al, pp. 46-80.

Mikhaila was not a Roman Catholic, but a member of the Eastern Rite Catholic Church. After being rejected by three different Catholic schools, she was asked if she would be prepared to go to a public school. She replied, 'My church is as good as your church'. I was taken aback. Her confidence was challenging. Where to turn now? I called and left a message for Bishop David Cremin, the bishop responsible for education in the Archdiocese. He soon responded, concerned that I sounded disturbed. I told him I was. After I had explained, he said, 'Leave it to me'.

During the final week of the school term, the principal of the local Catholic school interviewed Mikhaila. Happily wearing school hat, blazer and backpack, she left the principal's office looking forward to the opening of the school in the new year. We went straight to buy school shoes and workbooks for her to practise writing in English over the holidays. On the first day of the school year, there were tears in her mother's eyes as Mikhaila entered the Grade 3 classroom. Her very first day in a classroom, in a real school.

Mikhaila's early childhood had been spent confined to a tiny unit. Her mother had been too afraid to allow her to play in the common courtyard for fear she would be abducted. Vasyl and Sabina were seen as wealthy because they had visited her mother's sister in Australia, all expenses paid. Vasyl, a lift mechanic, was constantly harassed. He bore a scar as a result of one of the attacks. He was easy prey as he rode his bicycle to and from his work. He had a car, but the authorities refused to register it. The two older children were also in danger. Their father was regularly told that something 'could happen' to one of his children. Corrupt officials could access information about where people lived, the type of dwelling they owned, and those wealthy enough to register vehicles. Vasyl and Sabina were constantly followed in shopping centres and at the markets. When the harassment became unbearable and Sabina became hyper nervous, Vasyl, Sabina and Mikhaila departed for Australia one last time. They were heartbroken when the authorities wouldn't provide visas for their two teenage children, Yeva and Maxim. Leaving their children behind wasn't easy. 'It was a terrible day', Vasyl said. He reflected that they 'were hoping that we go all together but we had no choice. We decided better we go three of us. It might be it was a bad decision'.

Vasyl had a valid claim for political persecution because he was repeatedly attacked, threatened and intimidated by authorities, and the state was implicated in the extortion. Also, he could have been recognised as a member of a particular social group (people returning from overseas and perceived to be wealthy) who are persecuted. According to the Canadian Immigration Refugee Board, Vasyl's wife and child could have had a separate claim as a member of a particular social group (family) whose husband/father was persecuted.[10] While persecution may be defined

> as the sustained or systemic violation of basic human rights demonstrative of a failure of State protection, the refugee definition does not require that the State itself be the agent of harm. Persecution at the hands of "private" or non-State agents of persecution equally falls within the definition. The State's inability to protect the individual from persecution constitutes failure of local protection.[11]

There was a genuine reason to investigate Vasyl and Sabina's protection claims.

~~~~~~~~

The phone rang. It was Edward, the interpreter who would bring a jar of honey from his hives each time we met at the compliance office or the review tribunal. I could accept gifts from Edward because I wasn't helping him. As a pastoral carer, I wasn't permitted to accept remuneration for any immigration assistance given to people seeking protection. This was great, because the government's position could always be argued when grateful, dignified people seeking protection wanted to make a contribution. Although they were managing on a pittance, they had their pride.

Edward was anxious and treading cautiously. He knew I was bogged down preparing a family's claims to take to the United Nations Human Rights Committee (UNHRC). He mentioned a young family who were packed and ready to go back to their country of origin. When they rang to say goodbye, he had begged them to wait, telling them he knew someone they should see before they took that dangerous step.

Standing in the tiny, cramped kitchen chatting to Zofia with her poor English, I noticed a burning candle in the corner of the stone bench. I asked about it. 'That's baby Natalka', Zofia responded with tears in her eyes. I was taken aback. On closer examination, I saw a small urn containing Natalka's ashes. Zofia and Olek's applications for protection had been rejected. They were terrified about returning to their home country. They were now in Australia without a legitimate visa, and were hesitant about burying baby Natalka here when they didn't know what their future might be.

It breaks my heart to recall the story they told me.

Zofia's waters broke, and Olek rushed her to the emergency department of a large suburban hospital. She had no Medicare card. Because of her

---

10. Canadian Immigration Refugee Board (CIRB) 1991, 'Membership in a Particular Social Group as a Basis for a Well-founded Fear of Persecution: Framework of Analysis', *Refworld*, https://www.refworld.org/docid/3ae6b32510.html. Accessed 2022.
11. Haines, R, 2003, 'Gender-related persecution' in E Feller et al, p332.

situation, she hadn't attended a prenatal clinic, but as a 42-year-old gynaecologist, she was confident she was carrying a healthy baby.

Because of her age, the delivery was drawn-out and difficult. After far too long a labour, a doctor was called and he performed a forceps delivery. Not a caesarean section, a practice with which Zofia was familiar, having performed many herself. The otherwise healthy baby was born brain dead. The parents sat with their baby daughter for eight days. The machines were turned off and the parents set about the unenviable task of preparing her funeral.

Initially, Olek had to carry Zofia up the stairs to their first-floor unit. She went into deep depression. Zofia needed corrective surgery because the procedure damaged her body, including her bladder. She took months to recover, physically and mentally.

Prior to coming to Australia, Olek had owned a trucking business. When moving goods from his home country to Europe he encountered many road-blocks. At each of these, the officials would climb aboard the truck and take whatever they wanted. Needless to say, by the time he reached his destination, the truck delivered fewer goods. Zofia described waiting for Olek to return from these regular European trips. She was so worried about his safety that she was 'like a tiger pacing back and forth in a cage' – a seventeen square metre studio.

With both parents working and home telephone numbers in the public domain, children at home alone after school were also victims of harassment. Daryna had regular phone calls demanding the whereabouts of her parents and threatening to kill her father. Zofia would arrive home from work to find Daryna shaking with fear, crying. For security, Zofia sent Daryna to live with her estranged husband.

The corruption in Olek and Zofia's country of origin was rated as one of the highest in the world. Despite this, his business flourished until extortionists discovered his prosperity. They then began demanding 'protection' money. It wasn't much in the beginning. When they demanded more than he was earning, he couldn't satisfy their requests. He was regularly beaten, and hospitalised on more than one occasion. He arrived in Australia with his ankle in plaster, his bones crushed in the final attack.

Olek had a prominent scar on his face, stretching from the corner of his mouth and almost reaching his ear.

Not long after arriving in Australia, Kalyna was born. Olek and Zofia's application for protection was refused and so they submitted an application for baby Kalyna on the basis of persecution of a family member.

Their grounds for persecution were valid in that Olek was a member of a particular social group of persecuted businessmen. A 'social group' claim may be established either by showing that the extortionist's actions are based on the businessman's occupation, and the state is unable or unwilling to provide protection against such conduct or that, whatever the reasons for the extortionist's actions, the state is unwilling to protect the businessman because of his occupation.[12]

Zofia had not fully recovered from the traumatic birth of their second daughter, Natalka, when I met her in that tiny kitchen. There is much more to their story.

~~~~~~~~

I was expecting to meet a couple who had been referred to me.

Upon my opening the door, three strapping young fellows all over six feet tall walked in. Bemused, I asked the whereabouts of the couple. As they filed into the living room, in came Naldo and Maita, whose sons had outgrown them. Scrambling to find enough chairs, I wondered if these bodyguards were necessary. They thought so. Their parents had been assured that somebody would be able to help them many times before but, alas, they had not been able to gain Australia's protection. The sons had come to 'suss out' the situation. Was I genuine, or was I going to rip them off, too? They sat quietly and suspiciously as I chatted to their parents.

There was a daughter too, but she didn't come. Valentina was close to giving birth to her first child. She was seeing a psychologist. She couldn't cope with the thought of delivering her first-born baby without the assistance of her mother. Valentina was so scared that her mother would be taken away from her in yet another hour of need. She had been separated from her parents before.

Valentina had arrived in Australia as a teenager. High school had been difficult. She constantly worried that, when she returned from school, her parents wouldn't be there to greet her. She had seen incidents on the news where adults were dragged from their workplaces and taken off to the detention camps. This could happen to her parents, and what would she do then? Valentina started missing days at school and spent hours at home in the shower because this was her 'comfort zone'. Naldo and Maita could not offer her much comfort because they had no idea what would become of them.

Australia's protection was not forthcoming.

In their home country, Naldo and Maita's son had held a position in a government office and uncovered government officials complicit in the trafficking of women and girls. He had made this known to people further up the chain of authority. He was told that if he continued the investigation, 'there would be consequences'.

12. Aleinikoff op. cit., p.303.

Naldo's son was given the option to move to another city. There, the security was no better. Vandalism was an intimidatory tool. Then came ongoing, persistent, subtle, terrifying persecution. Valentina would never forget waking up with a piece of glass on top of her head. She had become so afraid that Naldo and Maita sent Valentina and a brother to live with their grandparents. The police were uncooperative, demanding the names of the vandals breaking the windows of their house in the early hours of the morning. Maita found this a ridiculous request. As if such people would identify themselves. Naldo reported seeing 'one blue car, one four-wheel drive or something like that. Old car, but nothing else'. Eventually, Naldo and his family sold everything and left the country they loved.

Their claims were valid because state authorities were complicit in illegal activity resulting in inaction on the part of authorities. The persecution was tolerated and/or condoned by authorities who were either unable or refused to offer adequate protection.[13] Where 'harm is threatened by the police or military of a country, or where the national government actively sponsors or supports the persecutory activities of a theoretically independent agent, there should be a strong presumption against finding an Internal Protection Alternative'.[14] It was not safe to relocate internally.

Despite their being found not to be in need of protection, the four children, at different times and through different circumstances, gained permanent visas. They were all adults by now and, perhaps, in normal circumstances, they would not be dependent on their parents. The boys were not a worry, but it was incumbent upon Naldo and Maita to remain in Australia to care for their daughter, who was psychologically fragile.

I promised them nothing.

In earlier times, I had assisted a young mother whose parents had been deported. As this tragedy has unravelled over ensuing years, I have had to continue to support Sarita. She has been through three unsuccessful marriages. She missed the wisdom of parents who could have guided her and supported her, had they lived close enough to observe what was happening to her and her three children. Her older boy especially, missed the emotional support and guidance that grandparents usually provide.

Although I did not speak of this to Naldo and Maita or their bodyguards, I couldn't let this happen a second time under my watch. Minister, Chris Evans, granted Naldo and Maita permanent visas. Naldo is now retired from working as a spray painter/car detailer, Maita works part-time as a cleaner and babysits two of their seven grandchildren after

---

13. Haines op. cit., p.332.
14. Hathaway, JC & Foster, M, 2003, 'Internal protection/relocation/flight alternative as an aspect of refugee status determination', in E Feller et al, p.396.

school; and Valentina is engaged as an interpreter for the Department of Human Affairs and Department of Border Protection. She is married with three children and does voluntary work with the Scouts.

~~~~~~~~

The couple with two primary school-aged girls arrived with piles and piles of files. Belicia and Orlondo had tried all avenues to convince decision-makers that they couldn't return to their country of origin. Belicia spoke little English and Orlondo even less. Latoya, the oldest girl, interpreted. There was a lot of pain in their story. Belicia wept continuously. Latoya and Adella were hyperactive, continually invading my house. Orlondo was so withdrawn, I wondered if he might be suicidal. I had seen this before in men seeking protection. Once I was called out in the middle of the night. The father of the family was threatening to leave home and his wife was sure he intended to go somewhere and quietly kill himself. He too had been very withdrawn. I was seriously concerned.

In his home country, Orlondo had managed a club where some clients were members of parliament involved in illegal drugs and sex with underage girls. Instead of protecting them, the police alerted the perpetrators of these illegal activities that someone had reported them. One of Orlondo's employees was murdered. After reporting this death, Orlondo was identified and pursued. He received multiple threats and, eventually, he was abducted, taken to an isolated place and bashed up. One eye was seriously damaged. It was around Easter, so he signed up for a pilgrimage to Israel. There, he obtained medical attention but couldn't stay for long. He caught a plane to Australia.

In his absence, Belicia and Orlondo's mother, Herminia, tried desperately to care for the two little girls, Latoya aged seven and Adella aged five. Belicia was located and pursued. The perpetrators wanted to know Orlondo's whereabouts. Belicia fled from one family member to another, to different cities within the same country. Eventually, she was located at her unmarried sister's house. One morning, people discovered the mutilated body of her sister in a nearby vacant allotment. She had been sexually assaulted. The horrible story was splashed over the front page of the local newspaper, the brutal photos enlarged. Belicia was distraught. She and the girls arrived in Australia with their grandmother two weeks later. Her grief was still too raw to speak about at Belicia's interview for protection. She wasn't in a position to trust anyone at that time.

Latoya, her daughter, refused to continue to interpret. It was too much for her. The only comfort I could offer was to read through the documentation and see if there was anything that could be done.

Different approaches were tried. Time went by. The children arrived home from school one day to be told that their father had been taken to the detention camp at Villawood. They were shocked and scared because they had already been separated from him when Orlondo had come to Australia a year before the rest of the family. Latoya was retraumatised by this separation. She was reluctant to visit Orlondo and only went on weekends. Belicia and Adella visited every day.

Latoya enrolled at high school. She was excited to be accepted but her mother and grandma were sad. Latoya couldn't understand why. Orlondo was locked up. Then it dawned on her that they couldn't be certain she would even be in Australia at the beginning of the school year. In Year 8, Latoya would randomly burst into tears. She refused to attend a class on sex education. Latoya said it was 'too gruesome' and she was crying so much that her mother was called. The flashbacks of her mother crying 'they killed her, they killed her' about her aunt were too much to bear.

When Orlondo was taken off to Villawood, their church community was shocked. They couldn't understand how it could be a crime for a man to work and pay rent and care for his family. They rallied around to help Belicia and the girls, paid the rent and collected food, but it was embarrassing for the family.

The grounds for political persecution for this family relate to the fact that state authorities not only tolerated murder but also tolerated the ongoing attacks on the person who reported the illegal actions of politicians. The link between political persecution and the rape of a close relative was evident. That state's unwillingness to protect its citizens suggests that persecution is 'accepted and tolerated by the State'.[15] The failure of the state to prevent such harmful practices and to stop those who engage in it should be considered 'political', especially if those actions violate fundamental human rights. I had to find a way to penetrate the now familiar attitude of negativity and disbelief in those delegated to make decisions.

~~~~~~~~

It was a lovely autumn day as we sat on the patio under the sun umbrella. After some small talk, Nankunda mentioned that her mother had been tortured and murdered. What could I say?

Nankunda had arrived in Australia at the time of major sporting event. She applied for Australia's protection but could not convince decision-makers her story was true. When she was a baby, her father and two older brothers had died after their family home was bombed. Her

15. Haines op. cit., p.332.

foot was damaged and her mother, who survived, couldn't afford to take her to hospital with her injuries. As a teenager, she was seconded by pro-government agents to 'spy' on opposition supporters. She couldn't refuse, or her mother would have been punished. When her mother didn't approve the spying, her small business was damaged by a grenade. Her mother relented but Nankunda wasn't paid. Nankunda was asked to put poison in the beer of an opposition member. She refused. Before long, when responding to a knock at the door, Nankunda, who was a mere 16 years old, was dragged out to a vehicle and taken to a 'safe house' where she was raped and tortured. The perpetrators released her, and she ran away. Her trainer sought her out and persuaded her to come back to training. He cut her hair and disguised her by dressing her in boys' clothes. She remained in hiding, masquerading as a young male until her trainer put her in touch with someone who advised her about getting to Australia. Nankunda prepared for an international event with every intention of escaping the violence she had suffered.

Nankunda arrived in Australia, participated in the event and, soon after, began a very lonely journey. A man from the same continent noticed her sitting every day on a bench in Belmore Park opposite Central Station in Sydney. After a few days he invited her to his home and the family cared for her until she received legal support.

In the decision, 'implausible' was repeated again and again in response to her description as to what had happened to her. It is a shocking experience when a deeply personal story is not validated. Nankunda was admitted to the psychiatric ward of a major hospital.

Back in her home country, when she did not return, the authorities harassed Nankunda's mother at regular intervals, questioning her about the whereabouts of her daughter. 'I do not know' was her mother's constant reply. One day they came, and Nankunda's mother disappeared. Her mother's brother and other family members couldn't find her. Around six months later she was returned to the house. She died within hours. Almost unrecognisable. She had been tortured mercilessly.

Was I going to believe Nankunda or was I going to join the ranks of those who deemed her story 'implausible'? Nankunda was scrutinising me. Fortunately, we were sitting outside. If she had been indoors she would have immediately checked where the entrances and exits were located. She trusted nobody. She needed reassurance that it was possible to escape should the conversation disturb her, or should some suspicious person arrive.

There were silences, long silences.

When we parted company, Nankunda left convinced that, had she known this would happen to her mother, she would never have fled the horrible situation she had been in. A burden of guilt had been lifted from her fragile shoulders.

Years after arriving in Australia, Nankunda was granted an employer nomination permanent visa by Amanda Vanstone. Thus, her horrible experiences of rape and torture were never validated as she was not recognised as a refugee in need of protection. The grounds for protecting Nankunda, however, are based on the nexus between political activity and gender-based violence. Australia's *Guidelines on Gender Issues for Decision Makers* states that 'rape and other forms of sexual assault are acts which inflict severe pain and suffering (both mental and physical) and which have been used by many persecutors. Such treatment clearly comes within the bounds of torture as defined by the Convention Against Torture (CAT). Furthermore, sexual violence amounts to a violation of the prohibition against cruel, inhuman or degrading treatment, the right to security of person and in some instances the right to life, as contained in a variety of international instruments'.[16]

It's difficult to persuade decision-makers that experiences are real: 'the main problem facing women as asylum seekers is the failure of decision-makers to incorporate the gender-related claims of women into their interpretation of the existing enumerated grounds and their failure to recognise the political nature of seemingly private acts of harm to women'.[17] Nankunda became an Australian citizen and the first thing she did was obtain an Australian passport. She secretly crossed the border of a neighbouring country into her homeland and wept on her mother's grave.

~~~~~~~~

I received a call from a psychiatrist, Dr Michael Dudley. I had never heard of him. He explained that someone known to me had suggested I might be able to assist a family he was treating.

I climbed the rickety stairs that led to a small flat attached to the back of a house next to a church. The local minister had provided Dmytro and Polina with low cost rented accommodation. In gratitude, Polina cleaned the church regularly. I was warmly but cautiously welcomed by them. There was a baby asleep somewhere in another room and a little girl around three years old. Julia seemed very intelligent but proved to be most disruptive when we were attempting a serious conversation in broken English. Over

---

16. Department of Immigration and Multicultural Affairs (DIMA), 1996, *Refugee and Humanitarian Visa Applicants: Guidelines on Gender Issues for Decision Makers*, p.16, para 4.6. http://refugeestudies.org/UNHCR/66%20-%20Refugee%20and%20Humanitarian%20Visa%20Applicants.%20Guidelines%20on%20Gender%20Issues%20for%20Decision%20Makers.pdf. Accessed March 2022.
17. Haines op. cit., p.327.

biscuits and tea at the kitchen table, I listened to their story through constant distractions.

Dmytro had been persecuted for human rights activism. He had been especially active in relation to the abuse of ethnic minorities in his country of origin. He had exposed a financial link between government and extreme ultra-nationalist organisations. Because of this he was bashed up and brutally assaulted by the members of these organisations. This was confirmed at a medical examination. He was hounded out of his job but the police refused to take a statement about his assault, instead saying they would charge him with slander and hooliganism. He received threatening telephone calls. His daughter Olha was attacked and threatened with gang rape. He and his family then fled the country. Their travel agent suggested that they go to Australia.

In further conversations with them during regular visits, they told me about the IVF program that gave them their two babies. They were hoping to access the program again in the future. They had embryos in reserve in Australia. Dmytro and Polina own their own home. The children are now in High School and Julia is becoming an accomplished musician, playing the saxophone, violin and piano. She mends damaged musical instruments and re-sells them, works part-time in a café, and she and her sister Luciana mow lawns.

~~~~~~~~

Although they were not part of my research program, in the following chapters, I have included mention of yet other people who sought protection in the ensuing years because their experiences illustrate important, specific aspects of the determination system. I introduce them below.

Sarita's parents were deported. At the time, the only option she had to enable her to stay in Australia with her Australian citizen child and her partner was to apply for refugee status, which was refused. The minister granted a partner visa because she had an Australian citzen child. For an example of compliance procedures in a rural area (see page 53). Sarita now has a blended family, with three grown up children and two still at school. Currently, applications for partner visas can be made without having to depart Australia.

Akith and his wife were able to reapply for protection as a result of the introduction of the Complementary Protection legislation. We had difficulty convincing the decision-makers that the documents he submitted were not fraudulent (see page 90). Their son had a permanent visa and their daughter, now a qualified doctor, had a student visa at that time. Akith has worked with adults with a disability for more than ten years and his wife initially worked in a factory, but now babysits their grandchild.

Faizon prepared his application for protection unassisted. His case was clearly related to persecution as a result of blasphemy laws, but he did not mention this in his initial application. It was extremely difficult to convince decision-makers that he needed protection (see page 53). Soon after he was reunited with his family in Australia, his wife underwent heart surgery and one of his two young sons became seriously ill with an undiagnosed appendicitis.

Zafar was recognised a refugee as a result of the Complementary Protection legislation but had to wait almost a year before the department officials granted the visa (see page 112). Having bought his own house, he now lives with his wife, children and grandchild in rural NSW. One child is now in his second year at University.

Saber arrived as a student, but after an incident in his home country while on holidays, he had to flee. I assisted him with his application for protection and following an interview, he was granted protection (see page 66).

Raja was also a victim of the blasphemy laws. I attended his initial interview and the difficulties around this interview are documented on page 66. After submitting further relevant documentation he was recognised as a refugee.

After interviewing Andy and Itan, who had been living in the community without legal status, I advised them that they did not have a basis for applying for a refugee visa. However, after they elaborated on their story, I found a reason for applying to the minister for intervention (see page 140). After many years working in the field, Itan is now a Manager in a childcare centre, while Andy has a delivery business. They continue to support Amelina, Itan's sister and her two sons.

Diego and Paola's refugee claims were not recognised. The experience of their initial interview is documented on page 65. They were required to depart Australia.

Rafi came to Australia on a student visa. He submitted a claim for refugee status on the basis of persecution as a member of a minority ethnic group. It was unsuccessful, as were his appeals. He lived in the community for many years without legal status, married and had an Australian citizen child. After the marriage failed, he became involved with Sari who was a student at the time. He submitted a request for ministerial intervention and received his visa while seriously ill with cancer. He immediately signed papers for his pregnant partner. He subsequently died and, soon after, Sari received a partner visa and his child Sabrina was born. Sari's difficulties with Sabrina's birth certificate are documented on page 140.

Georgina and Regina, two unrelated single women, were both refused protection. The minister had decided not to intervene in both cases. After a successful media campaign, the decision was overturned and they both received permanent visas (see page 48).

Mateo, a single man came to me after living in the community without legal status for some years. His claims for protection were not recognised at all levels of the immigration system. He successfully applied to the Minister for intervention in his case. Some of his difficulties can be found on page 79.

~~~~~~~~

2. The 'Australian way' with visas

The preamble to the Universal Declaration of Human Rights states that:

> *the peoples of the United Nations have in the Charter reaffirmed their faith in fundamental human rights, in the dignity and worth of the human person and in the equal rights of men and women and have determined to promote social progress and better standards of life.*

At the United Nations General Assembly in 1948, Australia was an active participant in drafting the Universal Declaration of Human Rights and, as such, agreed that we have no 'right to engage in any activity or to perform any act aimed at the destruction of any of the rights and freedoms set forth herein'.

In my experience, during the first two decades of the 21st Century, Australia's Department of Immigration consistently failed to exemplify the spirit of these commitments.

~~~~~~~~

The department's Sydney compliance office is located at the end of a large courtyard, past a coffee bar. In the foyer, people were conversing with their legal representatives. On the fifth floor, the lift disgorged a crowd of nervous people anticipating their encounter with compliance officers. I reminded myself that all the families I was accompanying had fled untrustworthy systems and violent experiences. It wasn't easy for them to come face to face with often intimidating authority figures.

I usually met families at the corner of Lee Street and the tunnel which stretches from Central Station through to the University of Technology. The coffee shop there baked delicious bread and pastries and was more private than the foyer of the Department of Immigration building.

The family's documents were in order, but they were no more relaxed than on the previous evening. I would always visit this family the night before they had to renew visas. It was difficult convincing them that these requirements were merely procedural and that they were safe until decisions on their claims for protection had been made. Nobody slept the night before a compliance visit. Belicia would always arrive at the compliance office bearing a nasty, itchy red rash on her face and arms. Nothing I could say would allay her fears.

The double doors opened at 9.00am. It was important to get there early, or we could be waiting for two to three hours. The room would fill quickly. The chairs faced counters numbered 1 to 7, divided by panes of thick glass. As each person seeking protection entered, they queued to present identity documents. They were given a number and sat waiting until the officers arrived and took their seats on the other side of the counter. They observed the people ahead of them in the queue and hoped that a particular officer, who seemed to be in a reasonable mood, would call their name.

When their number came up, their file was checked, and another visa was pasted into the passport. Provided the visa did not have the dreaded words 'no work' they could then take the visa to Centrelink and request another temporary health card. They could also attend free English classes. The health card and the temporary visa expired when their first application for protection was decided, but it could be renewed until the tribunal review decision was handed down.

Only when a family had permission to earn a living could they pay for the coffee during our debrief after these visits to the compliance office, a gesture they relished. It was so important for them to retain dignity and control over their lives. Until then, I would pay.

This ritual occurred two or three times a week, each time with a different family required to front up to compliance officials, especially after their appeals had failed and they were waiting on a decision from the minister. Following an unfavourable decision at the tribunal, the words 'no work' would appear on the visa. This degrading and cruel action meant parents could no longer earn a living to support themselves and their families.

I would front up to the compliance office with each family. With me standing by, obvious with my notebook in hand, it was more than likely that the family would be treated with dignity and respect, as fellow human beings. My accompanying these families not only provided support, but also gave me the opportunity to get to know each one a little more. I would hear more stories about the past and the present, which strengthened my confidence in their protection needs. That was how it was.

An unfavourable tribunal decision could be appealed in the court. If their claims were dismissed in the court, their last resort was to request ministerial intervention. A family could submit any number of requests for ministerial intervention if they presented new information; and if they could prove the need to earn a living, compliance officers could rescind the 'no-work' condition.

In those days, interviews were not held in the small rooms at the end of the waiting room. An exception was if the person had to leave the country and did not present the plane ticket as evidence of their intention to depart Australia. Once, at the compliance office, Nankunda was taken to a room where the light was dim. There were no windows. She was terrified and retraumatised as she waited for a long time before someone came in to speak to her. Flashbacks of the room where she had been raped haunted her. Suicidal thoughts returned. She was given a bridging visa.

Others weren't so lucky. Vasyl was ushered into the small room, exited through another door, was ensconced in a padded lift and spewed out into the dark car park beneath the building. There, a van awaited to speed off to Villawood detention camp, carrying him and other unfortunate victims. There were no goodbyes to family members, who were left shaking in fear, wondering what was going to happen to them. Perhaps they would be sent home with the command to return next week with tickets to leave Australia. They were not told the whereabouts of the disappeared person, usually the father of the family, nor did anyone suggest they contact a lawyer. The family members would ask themselves how this could happen in Australia. Sure, it could happen in their country of origin. There, white vans patrolling the streets abducted people who were never seen again. These terrible memories inflamed a genuine fear of compliance officials.

~~~~~~~~

Australian political institutions have created and enforced laws and government structures that define citizens' rights, responsibilities and privileges. This process has been discriminatory because it restricts the rights and privileges of sovereign citizens of other countries. Following the original legal premise of individual sovereignty, the Universal Declaration of Human Rights states that, 'All human beings are born free and equal in dignity and rights' and are entitled to the rights and freedoms 'without distinction of any kind, such as race, colour, sex, language, religion, political or other opinion, national or social origin, property, birth or other status'. Australia was a significant contributor to formulating this declaration. It would be consistent with international human rights law if people seeking protection, once having registered for that protection, could remain in the community working and educating their children until the end of the assessment period.

Australian law has also been tough on compliance officials who are supposed to follow the orders of their supervisors and case officers, but who also are daily confronted with people with heightened levels of fear about their safety and their future. In my experience, it was even more difficult for compliance officers when overseas students faced them, wanting to extend visas when they had been reported for poor attendance at college, even if they had been ill and held a doctor's certificate. Students had paid a lot of money to enrol at a college. A family and I watched as one woman attempted to reclaim her bond money before departure. She waved her plane ticket at the compliance officer to no avail. She had to be out of Australia before the money would be released. She had difficulty trusting the officer and feared she would lose that substantial sum.

People who overstayed their visa were also at the counter begging for the officer to recognise their need to stay longer after they had actually broken Australian law. These encounters could be nasty, as neither side would give in. They sometimes developed into shouting matches. They had to leave the country but they so badly wanted to stay. We observed it all, we heard it all, as we uneasily waited and waited.

Amora and Marco had been refused protection many times. Their case was taken to the UNHCR in Canberra and Geneva, then they were referred back to Canberra. To ensure that the family wouldn't miss out again, someone kindly offered to assist with the submission pro bono.

They interviewed Amora and Marco and spent about half an hour talking into a tiny dictaphone, giving instructions to take the tape home, transcribe it and submit. The UNHCR officer was highly impressed. He suggested a copy be forwarded to Minister Amanda Vanstone. He would contact Vanstone personally. If we experienced any difficulty with the department we were to contact him immediately on his personal mobile number. At last, someone with the power to influence the minister understood.

Confidently, Amora and Marco fronted up to the compliance officer yet again. I lurked in the background, just in case. He looked at the couple, then looked at the monitor in front of him.

'Didn't you receive the letter?' he said.

I jumped to attention. 'What letter?' I said.

'Wait, I'll get you a copy,' he said, heading for the printer.

There, before our eyes, was the inevitable refusal to grant protection once again. Aghast, I asked to speak to the supervisor. She was at a meeting. Could we return in an hour? Sure.

In the comfort of our favourite coffee shop, I hastily dialled the mobile number of the person at the UNHCR office in Canberra. He was shocked. When he had contacted Minister Vanstone's office, he had received a positive outcome. He would call back. In a few minutes, the phone rang. He was asked to resend the material because what he had previously sent had been lost! We never found out what happened to my submission.

The supervisor renewed the temporary visa one more time. After a bit of an argument, the person in the Canberra immigration office agreed to notify the Sydney office to have work rights reinstated. Not too long after this inexplicable mismanagement, Minister Vanstone granted Marco, Amora and their three children permanent, skilled sponsor visas. Their claims for protection weren't validated through the grant of a refugee visa, but they were safe at last. The annual quota for refugees must have been reached, so other types of visas were drawn upon.

~~~~~~~

Since 1948, Australia has ratified seven United Nations treaties relating to various aspects of human rights, as well as the United Nations Declaration on the Rights of Indigenous Peoples. The Labor government was responsible for six of the eight ratifications (1975, 1983, 1989, 1990, 2008, 2009). The Howard Coalition Government (1996–2007) didn't ratify any of the International Human Rights treaties. Both the Covenant on the Rights of People with Disabilities (CRPD) and the Declaration on the Rights of Indigenous Peoples (DRIP) were adopted by the General Assembly during Prime Minister John Howard's time in office. In ratifying a Convention and Optional Protocol at the international level, Australia became legally bound by the treaty. Although a particular parliament did not do the ratifying, that parliament is still accountable to the treaties that have been ratified by successive governments. Because of this international responsibility, ideally, the courts should have ensured that people who arrived by plane seeking protection were not excluded in domestic law. It is regrettable that today's judges make almost no reference to the global human rights standards that Australia played such a significant role in developing, and by which it is bound under international law.

~~~~~~~

Georgina and Regina were shocked when they arrived at the compliance office expecting to have their visas renewed.

'The policy has changed,' the officer said, 'You can no longer submit a second request to the minister. Come back next week with your tickets to leave the country'. 'Over my dead body', I whispered as we rushed through the double doors towards the lift. I contacted Ngareta, who knows every reliable journalist in Sydney. She immediately returned my call. The journalist arranged to interview the young women the next day. Georgina and Regina were desperate. They didn't want to return to Africa where they would be forced to endure female genital cutting and live with the consequences for the rest of their lives. Georgina had also unwillingly been marked to marry an elderly man. We had to work quickly. What we didn't know was that there was a ban on recognising protection status for black Africans.

The following morning, large photos of the two young women confronted readers on the front pages of *The Age* and *Sydney Morning Herald*. The young women also featured in the *SBS News* that evening. Australians were getting a glimpse of something unsavoury as the electorate was preparing to vote. Timing was everything. Georgina and Regina are now energetic, healthy, productive Australian citizens. The journalist won an award for her story.

Shamefully, some people are returned to danger. In *Human Rights Overboard*, Briskman, Latham and Goddard record the deaths of seven people who failed to gain protection in Australia and were returned to their country of origin.[18] Glendenning and colleagues claim twelve deaths of returnees, along with the deaths of three children and a spouse of a returnee. One person described the attitude of the government in 2003 when he represented an Iranian: 'Fine if they are going back to certain death or torture. The government argued, successfully, that the legislation required them to return people. It's an absolute disgrace'.[19] These examples illustrate that the government has little concern for the safety of people who aren't Australian citizens.

During 2001–2003, through restricting media access to detained people seeking protection, the Australian Government was able to influence what was emphasised and omitted in media reporting. As a censor of information and as a major source of 'credible information', the Australian Government's media relations emphasised the mobilisation of consent and the marginalisation of dissent. Prime Minister Howard recognised news journalism as a significant driver of public opinion, enormously influential in determining what people knew and the policies that they were prepared to accept. One study found that the Federal Government described people seeking protection with terms like *illegal, illegitimate, bad character* or *behaviour, the other, threat, burden* and *uncontrollable*. These words were mentioned 1,152 times, whereas positive representations such as *legal, legitimate* or *sympathetic, good character* or *behaviour, like us* or *human, harmless, benefits* and *ordered* were mentioned 125 times.[20]

Some case officers presented the human face of the immigration department. They were rational, compassionate and reasonable, and responded to phone calls from anxious advocates. One encouraged me to submit further requests to the minister. The department in Sydney had approved one family's need for protection and this officer couldn't understand why this had changed when the submission reached Canberra. I knew. Several advocates, unknown to each other at the time, had submitted complaints to the Secretary of the Department about 'that woman', in the Canberra office.

18. Briskman, L, Latham, S & Goddard, C, 2008, *Human Rights Overboard: Seeking Asylum in Australia*, Scribe, Melbourne.
19. Ibid., p.97.
20. Klocker, N & Dunn, KM, 2003, 'Who's Driving the Asylum Debate? Newspaper and Government Representations of Asylum Seekers', *Media International Australia Incorporating Culture and Policy*, no. 109, November 2003. http://www.uws.edu.au/__data/assets/pdf_file/0010/26956/A17.pdf. Accessed March 2022.

When contacting the department about the status of someone seeking protection, his case officer in her frustration was actually crying over the phone. Shocked, I found myself counselling her. In this political environment it was difficult for fair-minded assessors to distance themselves from people seeking protection with realistic claims. For them to have to suffer as a result of having to act against their own moral judgements is unacceptable and also cruel. It wasn't easy for anyone with a scintilla of integrity.

The Howard Coalition Government was hostile to human rights criticisms of its purported belief that 'Australia's sovereignty on domestic issues' justified its cruel policies towards people seeking protection. The government was 'particularly affronted that critics would publicly label its policies as the causes of human rights abuses'. At the same time, the Prime Minister was redirecting 'the attention of international human rights bodies to non-democratic nations'.[21]

Domestically, the Howard government discredited human rights reports, diminished mandates and redirected funding to non-advocacy non-government organisations. Howard directed attention away from his government's poor treatment of refugees and proceeded to blame those seeking protection. Immigration Minister Phillip Ruddock called refugee advocates bleeding hearts and doctor's wives, middle class women with nothing better to do.

Howard's shrewd preoccupation with Australia's sovereignty and parliament's resistance to international and domestic criticism of immigration policies can be seen as a form of national narcissism. Advocates and academics continued to claim that 'those seeking refuge are exercising their rights according to the Refugee Convention'. As a signatory to this Convention and its 1967 Protocol, Australia arguably has the international obligation to consider their refugee claims. It also has an ethical duty to do so without causing people seeking protection any further trauma or suffering.[22]

During the Rudd government, when Kalyna's parents were granted permanent visas, the law did not allow Kalyna herself the same privilege. She was born after the parents applied for protection and so was not included in the original applications. I went with her parents Zofia and Olek to the compliance office to renew her temporary visa. We were told it was a simple matter of submitting a child application. The problem was the cost. The parents had not been allowed to earn a living for many years and $1,000 was a lot of money. Kalyna was a few months short of turning

---

21. Fleay, C, 2010, *Australia and Human Rights: Situating the Howard Government*, Cambridge Scholars Publishing, Newcastle upon Tyne, pp.195, 206, 207.
22. Ibid., p.210.

10, when citizenship would be granted automatically. At our suggestion her application was placed at the bottom of the pile and her temporary visa was extended. On her birthday, the department was notified and Kalyna's citizenship certificate was sent in the mail.

When Ladonna and Jaime first attended the compliance office, Jaime was hardly in the door before he disappeared. He was eventually found and persuaded to come back up and present his identity document. Then, as quick as lightening he was gone again. He was terrified. When it was time for the two parents to sign the temporary visas for the children, Jaime again couldn't be found. 'He's gone for a cigarette', I confidently lied when asked his whereabouts. The compliance officer kindly agreed that Ladonna's signature would be sufficient.

Ladonna, Jaime and Sergio were granted permanent visas. The two younger girls, Brigitte and Daniela, were not, because, like Kalyna, they were born after the application for protection had been submitted. The department was notified of each birth, so they were on departmental records. The parents were also told to submit child applications costing at least $2,000.

Where would they find the money? Jaime had been working, as allowed under international human rights law, but not Australian law. His employer had engaged him three months before Christmas, telling him he'd be paid at the end of the contract. Jaime worked diligently, believing the employer would honour the contract. When the Christmas break was coming up, Jaime approached his employer. The boss asked to see his visa ... As a consequence, the children had no Christmas presents and the employer was hundreds of dollars better off.

The cost of the visas for the two younger children, Brigitte and Daniela, was prohibitive and they remained without visas. Did it really matter if two little girls were running around the streets of Sydney without visas? What harm could they inflict upon Sydneysiders? I approached a few concerned members of parliament even though I didn't live in their electorates: Bruce Baird, Petro Georgio and Russell Broadbent. Russell took my predicament to the Minister, Chris Evans, with a suggestion as to how the law could be fulfilled and the children could be granted visas at no cost to the family. Ladonna was notified. The department officials asked her to bring Brigitte and Daniela into the compliance office. She was to bring something for the children to eat and drink. She rang me, terrified, not realising this was good news. At the end of a day spent isolated in one of the small rooms, the girls were released from their detention. The minister could now legally grant them visas. Broadbent took justifiable credit for this creative solution.

For the first decade of the 21st Century, concerned people with authority worked imaginatively but legally to avoid the violence of the law, but it didn't last. Not only did the seating arrangements in the compliance office change but the law became increasingly restrictive.

When the government lost a case in the review tribunal or the court, the law would become more brutal. A merry-go-round of case officers ensued. Some left, and those who remained behaved like machines of the system. With the introduction of economic rationalist KPIs – Key Performance Indicators – the focus was shifted from the security of the person seeking protection to the government official, the job security of the office clerk, the case officer, the supervisor. A culture of public service was transformed into an unhealthy, anti-social and competitive workplace. This policy pitted employees against each other, created a dog-eat-dog work environment and undermined fellow employees, the public service and the wider society. But no amount of screaming, rudeness or bullying would deter a family seeking protection. They had endured far more than this before fleeing to Australia.

The compliance office seats were bolted to the floor and turned around to face a blank wall with a television at one end. It was like waiting for a bus in an interstate bus terminal. We could no longer observe the few compliance officers as they addressed aberrant students and overstayers. People's identity was checked on arrival and a case officer allocated.

At the appointed time people were called into one of the five or so small interview rooms where the chairs were also bolted to the floor. A case officer accessed their information on the monitor and collected documentation for photocopying. I wondered about the necessity to photocopy passports at every visit. The case officer would lecture the unfortunate people trembling in front of them about the necessity to prepare to leave the country should the minister not grant a visa. Often tearfully, the people seeking protection would object, but their words fell on deaf ears. The officer would hastily announce the time of their next appointment and hand the family an A4 sheet: their visa, laying out the conditions applying to them. It would be a huge relief to note the absence of the 'no-work' condition, which meant that a person could legitimately earn a living and children could attend school without paying overseas student fees.

It wasn't long before this ritual evolved into an intelligence-gathering exercise. People seeking protection were interrogated, information was recorded and passed on to the case officer in the Ministerial Intervention Unit. One officer wanted contact details for a young man's former girlfriend! Fortunately, he didn't have the information on hand, but was instructed to fax the details by the following day. I intervened. Was there no respect for a person's privacy? I would sit behind the person being interviewed, taking copious notes. The compliance officer's boundaries needed scrutinising and sometimes restraining, and the person in the hot seat required protection from these people.

Sometimes the case officer later became the interviewer. While this might have been a practical, time-saving solution for the department, it presented a serious dilemma for the person seeking protection. Should the family reveal any 'changes in circumstances' requested at interview? If they didn't, were they being dishonest? If they did, this information would be filed and not deemed 'new information'– a necessary criterion for subsequently requesting ministerial intervention.

I travelled to Canberra to speak about several cases to an immigration officer in Chan Street, Belconnen. He dismissed three of them in one breath, with pathetic excuses. My patience was running out when he told me a negative decision for Faizon had been made, but the letter had not yet been sent. The reason? The compliance officer had not noted a change of circumstances. He had not told him his father suffered a heart attack soon after Muslim guerrillas visited his house in search of Faizon.[23] Had they found him, he would have been killed. He was accused of blasphemy, a death sentence.

In no uncertain terms, I told this man in Canberra that Faizon was in a no-win situation. He couldn't have submitted a request to Minister Chris Bowen with all the accompanying evidence if the compliance officer had already passed on this 'new' and significant information to the Ministerial Intervention Unit. If he had revealed this information, it would not be 'new' and therefore he would not have had the grounds to apply to the minister again. Never mind the critical information, which included the evidence revealing the violence visited upon Faizon's father and his family. The unfortunate immigration officer had to pick himself up off the floor when I exploded. I was too angry to decipher what he muttered as I stomped out of the building. I checked the letterbox regularly. The letter containing the negative decision never arrived.

~~~~~~~~

Compliance officers operated differently in rural areas. A rural parish priest, Sarita's advocate, described how she discovered she was not legal. At about 5am, Sarita was driving some people to work on a farm about three kilometres away. A small group of police were blocking every vehicle on the road and testing people with a breathalyzer – yes at 5am! As they performed their duties, before sunrise, another more numerous group of

---

23. I use the word 'guerrilla' to highlight the fact that they are a minority. Most Muslims in my experience are peace-loving citizens.

agents with badges emerged from the darkness. They began checking the passports of passengers, and their identity documents. Sarita explained that her passport was at home and that she was on a bridging visa. She was immediately branded an illegal immigrant and locked up in the Police Immigration vehicle, parked in a nearby street. She waited there for half an hour, her vehicle left on the roadside. With other prisoners, she was transported to the police station. The Chief Compliance Officer made the arrest and took charge at the site, and in the town's police station. Sarita begged to call her husband, who was waiting for her at home, caring for their baby daughter. She was told she was an illegal immigrant and had no rights. After a brief interview, she was locked in a cell at the police headquarters and left alone.

She told the priest that she was wondering what sort of a country this is! Eventually, at about 10.30am, the officer issued Sarita with a Bridging Visa E, obliging her to leave the country by 24thDecember – just 13 days away. She was ordered to send a photocopy of her ticket within a week. Sarita had told the officer about her husband and her child. She tried to explain her circumstances in Australia, but he showed neither interest nor sympathy: 'According to your visa, you are an illegal immigrant, and must leave the country as stated – December 24th'.

This anecdote illustrates how immigration officials co-opted police, who created an opportunity to examine people's identity documents. The police also colluded with departmental officials by providing resources such as the police van and cells at the station where Sarita was prevented from breast-feeding her baby, an Australian citizen. It demonstrates the pressure applied by departmental compliance officers to make arrangements to depart Australia, regardless of circumstances or the trauma they caused. This example also uncovers the bullish attitudes prevalent in the Department of Immigration at that time. The priest's friend made a submission to the minister and a bridging visa was granted.

~~~~~~~~

In the Sydney office, compliance officers began to pin their nametags to the hem of their shirts. The high counters made it hard to identify them if anyone wished to complain. Some departmental officers signed correspondence using a number rather than a name. This led to the preposterous situation of addressing correspondence to 'Dear 603284'.

Later, the process changed again. People wishing to update their visa status were expected to do it online. Often this meant that they needed to find a friend with an internet connection, an email address and the required standard of English to understand the form and the process, to help them.

No face-to-face conversations. No questions could be asked. No identity document photocopied. On the bright side, there were no intelligence-gathering interviews.

~~~~~~~~

3. Surviving while waiting

The discriminatory, immoral and – under international human rights law – illegal 'no-work' visa condition has many adverse effects. No longer having a regular income meant that families for whom I was advocating had to find more affordable accommodation. Ladonna described her cheaper home: 'Fibro – the home is very, very cold in winter and very, very hot, in summer, oh my goodness!'

For the most part, the dwellings were fitted out with whatever could be collected from suburban streets on council 'hard rubbish' collection days. Walking the streets at night and lugging home heavy pieces of furniture came at an emotional cost. Sabina said that if somebody had told her one day she would be picking up 'stuff' on the streets, she would have said 'no way'. They were embarrassed, crying as they dragged the furniture home.

For single women it was particularly difficult. Without an income, Nankunda was receiving some assistance from advocates but she felt her loss of dignity keenly. Telling someone she didn't have sanitary pads was very shameful. She was used to being independent and now she had to ask for and accept charity. She said, 'I'm young, I can work. This money has to be given to disabled people, pensioners, older people – not me'.

It was also difficult for single men. Mateo resented being dependent on his younger brother. He said it made him feel 'like a child'. Naldo, an able-bodied father of four, said, 'The worst moment – we had many moments – but the worst was when they said you can't work. It was very sad for me then'.

Belicia, a parent with two young children, maintained her dignity while pragmatically accepting the need for informal bartering to get by saying, 'You do something, and you receive something in return for it. You know what we mean?'

For people seeking protection, the 'no-work' visa condition can be regarded as discriminatory according to International Human Rights conventions ratified by Australia. It has a negative effect for a very long period of time. Marco stated angrily that they applied for protection but lost more than ten years waiting for residency. 'Fighting with the criminals, with the law, with everything. It's hard, it's very hard.' A lack of access to the right to self-determination through the deliberate cancellation of the right to earn a living, for some people (people seeking protection) but not others (the broader Australian community), is systemic discrimination.

Under the International Covenant on Economic, Social and Cultural Rights, state parties to the covenant recognise everyone's right to the opportunity to gain their living by work, which they freely choose or accept. Australia is obliged to safeguard every person's right to work, and yet Australia's parliament creates laws that contravene an international covenant the government has ratified. A multiplicity of international human rights abuses can occur as a result of the withdrawal of the right to work. Some had to resort to petty criminal activity or working 'illegally'.

The people in my study were willing and able to work even if it was not their preferred employment. Jaime, a former university student, painted, rendered and maintained air-conditioners. For him, changing trades was stressful. People seeking protection took the risk of being caught working to support themselves and their families. Sarita was a hard worker. She did a lot of overtime to feed her two children and pay rent. According to her, the 'big problem in Australia was permission to work. I think the government should understand. How will people survive with kids, without permission to work?'

Even after Orlondo had been confronted one night by '10 or 15 officers' who told him working was 'illegal', the pressure to support a family of three adults and two children was paramount. As far as he was concerned, 'I wasn't doing anything illegal. I was working honestly and honourably … I couldn't keep working with tax. I had to work with money. I got paid straight away'.

This tension between international human rights and illegitimate domestic law was not the exception but the norm for people arriving by plane seeking protection who had to pay rent and support themselves and other family members.

The no-work condition was hard on young people too. Ladonna was concerned about her son, Sergio, who had finished high school and spent six months at home playing on his play station. She believed that if 'you can't work it's very hard to start work' later, and in the meantime he would 'get into bad habits'. For Valentina, waiting for her parents to arrive after school was particularly stressful. If they didn't arrive as expected, she would think, 'Oh my God, they have caught them'. When he lost the right to work, eighteen-year-old Grisha continued working. 'How are you gonna survive?' he asked. 'Of course, you're gonna work or the only other choice would be to steal or rob people. You have to work.'

This enforced poverty was combined with no access to Medicare. Mateo took a desperate risk when he was in terrible pain and needed to go to hospital. He told his brother he was afraid of dying. His brother was nervous but gave him his Medicare card. Mateo 'needed to put in his head his brother's date of birth because in the hospital they can ask you any time'. He went to the hospital and his kidney problem was treated. Mateo was forced to lie at the chemist or dentist when asked for his Medicare card.

Access to education presented problems as well. Grisha did a short course as a crane operator. He just ticked the box saying he was an Australian permanent resident and that was it. Ladonna's son, Sergio, faced problems being accepted into Year 7 at high school. They asked if he was a citizen and he ticked the citizen box when they prompted him. 'Luckily everything went smoothly', Ladonna said.

By not demanding papers, were school and hospital administrative staff colluding with this so-called illegal activity? Or, by contrast, would they have been discriminating between children seeking protection and other children in their school?

~~~~~~~~

The police, breath-testing drivers on their way to work in a rural area, colluded with immigration officials when they allowed them to accompany them and request drivers' identity documents. Targeting people seeking protection on their way to work discriminates against people who work on farms versus those who work in town centres who are not required to present residential status documents when breath-tested. A driving licence is usually sufficient for identification, but not for people seeking protection.

When an over-zealous compliance officer interpreted the Migration Act's restriction on 'any work' to include voluntarily helping friends out, Grisha's brother, Aloysha found himself detained in the Villawood Immigration Detention Centre. The assessor at the tribunal overturned the decision and he was released, but government officials continue to claim that 'no work' includes voluntary work. Orlondo was detained after his employer contacted the 'dob-in' line, and if Jaime had insisted on being paid the $17,000 that was owed to him, he too would have been 'dobbed in' by his employer. Ladonna said sadly, 'That December was difficult, very difficult ... That was very stressful because every child waited for the present'.

~~~~~~~~

Systemic discrimination involved not only educational arrangements, but also discriminatory law and order officials and abusive employers. Enforced criminality arises from a combination of employer exploitation and forced recourse to Medicare and education fraud.

If an Australian citizen breaks the law, they have the opportunity to go to court and defend the charge. They might receive a fine rather than a custodial sentence. But if a person seeking protection breaks the law by volunteering or working without permission they can, upon the decision of a public servant, immediately be incarcerated. The person is jailed in a detention camp, 'detained' without any knowledge of the length of the sentence. They will not have been legally charged and there is no opportunity to attend court before incarceration. The only possibility of release from the detention imprisonment is to appeal the decision at a tribunal.

Holders of a temporary Bridging Visa E, although able to work legally, often had limited functional English and limited mainstream employment opportunities. Employers aren't interested in training people who may not stay long. Mateo, with a tertiary degree, applied unsuccessfully to the national postal service, Australia Post, and a recycling company. After responding to advertisements, Vasyl, a qualified lift mechanic, would be questioned by employers about his immigration status. Although he could work legally, a temporary bridging visa was unacceptable. His English was poor. 'The company would promise to ring him back, but never did.'

Despite the toll it took on personal dignity, the desire and necessity to gain employment won out over the discriminatory 'no-work' visa policy. The International Convention on the Elimination of all Forms of Racial Discrimination states in Article 5:

> In compliance with the fundamental obligations laid down in Article 2 of this Convention, State Parties undertake to prohibit and to eliminate racial discrimination in all its forms and to guarantee the right of everyone, without distinction as to race, colour, or national or ethnic origin, to equality before the law, notably in the enjoyment of the following rights: ...(e) (i) The rights to work, to free choice of employment, to just and favourable conditions of work, to protection against unemployment, to equal pay for equal work, to just and favourable remuneration.

A person seeking protection who is working for cash in hand has no access to superannuation, workers' compensation and tax refunds. Excluded from permanent employment, they cannot access paid annual leave, sick leave, maternity leave or special leave if a child is ill. Nor is there a guarantee of receiving the basic wage or indeed any remuneration from unscrupulous employers.

Contractors who organised farm work in rural areas were unreliable. Sarita reported that she didn't get paid for three weeks' work picking rockmelons. Later, she worked in a packing shed and the contractor 'ran away with the money. Not only my money. Too many people's money'. Being poorly paid in urban areas was a constant complaint. Marco spoke cynically of his payment for floor sanding – '$300 Monday to Saturday. I paid $200 in rent and $100 to eat'. He said his employer told him he 'would never find somebody with better pay in this country. Imagine!' Olek said that, when he went to work, his employer paid a small amount of cash 'something, sometimes'. Ladonna told of her husband receiving $50 a day and how difficult it was to receive $250 a week while paying $200 in rent.

Poor pay caused tensions in the family. Pressure from family to repay loans to relatives in their original country was compelling, especially knowing that violent threats could be realised. Amora's brother told her how 'they threatened to kill him if he didn't pay for the tickets. My family was calling, very stressed, and I had to solve the problem and it was a very bad situation'. In Australia, Sarita suffered domestic violence. She left her husband and had to support two young children without the single mother's pension or family tax benefits.

Article 10:1 of the **International Covenant on Economic, Social and Cultural Rights** states that

> the widest possible protection and assistance should be accorded to the family, which is the natural and fundamental group unit of society ... it is responsible for the care and education of dependent children.

However, in Australia, there is a lack of support systems for families in desperate circumstances, not just in need of protection but in terms of basic human rights.

To adequately care for family in a foreign country, knowledge of the language is paramount. Before the application review decision, adults could access free English classes if they submitted applications for protection within 45 days of arriving, but classes would cease after a negative decision was handed down. The provision of English classes is critical for social integration. Sabina described struggling with the language. 'I don't know how we can survive because you don't know English. And you don't know what you must do. And you live the life falling apart and you don't know how to pull it together.'

Without functional English, some parents rely on their children to interpret and guide them through the cultural challenges they face. The time taken to convince the Department of Immigration of the need for protection made it difficult for some to settle into a relationship, and stressful for others worried about the children they were unable to bring with them and with whom they could not be reunited. Mateo felt it was not appropriate to begin a relationship until his visa status was resolved. He explained how he managed the added stress over a period of 12 years. 'I put in my head I don't like to think about it, maybe later.' But fellow workers ask, 'How many kids do you have? Sometimes it's embarrassing for me. Too many questions'.

Several people seeking protection couldn't afford to remain in hospital or attend follow-up sessions at the local doctor. Sabina collapsed after visiting her husband in the Villawood camp and recalled the reception she had received when taken to a nearby hospital without a Medicare card. When told it would cost $1000 a day in the hospital, she panicked. She had just borrowed money to get her husband out of detention. She swallowed some tablets she had in her handbag and her friends took her to a local doctor who provided free medication.

The second time Grisha broke his arm, he 'had to give up the follow-up visits'. He was out of work for about two months and that 'hit my pockets'.

Following the traumatic delivery of her baby daughter and the child's subsequent death, Zofia experienced intermittent heart problems. She asked her mother (also a medical practitioner) to send medication from overseas because she had no access to Medicare and couldn't buy tablets without prescription in Australia.

Parents could not deny their children access to health services. Sabina explained, 'If kids are sick, you go and pay money – $35, up to $40, just to see the doctor. We always collected money for the black day'.

Working without permission or not working were springboards to mental ill-health. Grisha, 19 years of age at the time, struggled to comprehend why the government didn't allow people to work and study. 'Keep them occupied. Keep them stimulated', he said. 'Otherwise, they go crazy. Go bananas, and they do all kinds of stupid things'.

After discovering she wasn't supposed to work, Nankunda, aged twenty-one, stopped because she was 'too scared'. Not working had an adverse effect. She began drinking 'a bottle of scotch in two days. Lucky, I didn't have malfunction of the liver, but I was drinking heavily, because I had a lot of nightmares and actually this is the time when Mum was murdered'.

Mateo spoke of how stressful it was for him when he was working illegally in his brother's pizza shop. A man was shot nearby and dragged himself into the pizza shop to ask for help. Frantically, he called the police and the ambulance and was terrified when a large number of police arrived.

Sergio, Latoya and Valentina, children at the time, were concerned about their parents' mental state. They had been struggling in their home country but when they came to Australia, it got worse. The stress was really getting to them. Most of the time Sergio said they 'were lost and my dad sometimes would go weeks or maybe months without a job'. Latoya was retraumatised by sex education classes at school, having read a detailed account of her aunt's rape and murder. She said teachers 'showed us a pretty gloomy video on sex'. She didn't want to watch it and her mother had to be called. She was ashamed that she was crying, and she couldn't talk about it to her friends. She couldn't explain what had happened to her and she 'just started crying randomly'.

In Year 11, Valentina was depressed and stopped going to school. 'I couldn't do it. I would just get up in the morning, and I was staying in the shower and not getting out of the shower because that was my comfort place. It was where I felt okay.'

Mateo, Maita and Nankunda reported regular nightmares. Ladonna and Amora spoke of living with husbands with depression. Amora explained that Marco was upset all the time, stressed out over the simplest things. He was nervous and so stressed that he fought a lot with the children. It was yet another problem she had to handle.

Some people seeking protection experienced physical reactions to stress. Amora and Sarita, both from different countries, suffered eye problems. Sarita's right eye became inflamed and she was told her body was reacting to stress. If not controlled, she might lose sight in the eye. Without a Medicare card, she spent a lot of money on treatment.

When Naldo spoke to me he often needed prompting from his daughter, Valentina, who interpreted. He believed he had lost his memory as a result of stress. Olek described the strain he and his wife Zofia suffered when they lost their baby daughter, Natalka. He was frightened of also losing Zofia because she felt so bad after the delivery. She suffered intense psychological pressure because he had no work, they had no money, and they had lost their child.

A right to the 'highest attainable physical and mental health' was out of reach because of a discriminatory 'no-work' policy and an unfair determination system that resulted in the need to live without legal status. Enforced unemployment, lack of access to Medicare and poor health care led to deterioration of mental health and emotional burdens for children, partners and parents. This combination amounted to systemic cruelty.

~~~~~~~~

The Convention on the Elimination of All Forms of Discrimination Against Women states that State Parties shall take all appropriate measures to eliminate discrimination against women in the field of employment in order to ensure, on a basis of equality of men and women, the same rights. Art11:1e affirms the 'right to social security, particularly in cases of retirement, unemployment, sickness, invalidity and old age and other incapacity to work, as well as the right to paid leave'.

The social security system for Australian citizens and permanent residents is not available to people arriving by plane seeking protection. The vulnerable people I helped had no access to unemployment benefits, compensation for work injuries, holiday pay, superannuation funds (all adults in the cohort); maternity allowance after delivery of a baby (Ladonna, Zofia and Sarita), single mother's pension (Sarita), sickness benefits (Mateo, Zofia, Amora and Nankunda), family tax benefits and school children's bonus (Orlondo, Vasyl, Naldo, Sarita, Olek, Ladonna, Marco and their families), teenage entry to tertiary studies (Grisha and Sergio), aged pension (Herminia).

A surgeon was keen to operate on Nankunda's foot which had been damaged when she was a baby. They had never performed such a procedure on an older person in Australia. While she received first class medical care, Nankunda's protection claims remained unresolved and she was entirely dependent on a generous advocate as she had no social security. Nankunda had to learn to walk 'with a straight foot again'. The process of moving from plaster to crutch to walking independently took nine months.

Had Grisha and Inna, Orlondo and Belicia, Zofia and Olek and Ladonna and Jaime been granted humanitarian visas soon after arrival, instead of eight or more years later, they would have been entitled to Humanitarian Settlement Services and received the integration package which included 510 hours of English tuition, certain white goods, Newstart allowance (if unemployed), an aged pension (Herminia), job seekers assistance, rent assistance, Medicare, Centrelink benefits for children and non-working mothers, and they could have opened bank accounts. Those who eventually received temporary visas (Vasyl and Sabina) could access only the 510 hours of English. Those who received other types of permanent visa couldn't access Newstart allowance, job seekers assistance or white goods available to people found to be refugees. They could access Centrelink benefits only after a two-year wait. Naldo, Mateo and Nankunda were required to find people to put up bonds (assurance of support) for a two-year period ensuring they wouldn't access Centrelink over that time. Even though all of this cohort were legally working and paying tax and had integrated into the local community, these discriminatory settlement policies flowed from the choice of visa the minister bestowed.

~~~~~~~~

Under the International Covenant on Economic, Social and Cultural Rights Article 13 (1), State Parties recognise everyone's right to education. When people who arrived by plane on legitimate tourist or visitor visas applied immediately for protection, their children could attend school and the adults could attend English classes. After a negative review decision, however, adults were forbidden to study. Parents were expected to pay international student fees for public and private schools as well as for post-secondary education. Latoya, a child at the time, was mortified when her parents had to tell the school that sometimes the fees couldn't come in on time. In a country where everyone has the right to compulsory education, Australian policies made it unaffordable for these adults and children, and introduced laws that restricted study if, perchance, they could afford it at all.

Educational institutions could not accept children who lacked permission to study. This policy soon changed and, although parents could neither work nor study, the children could attend school. In public schools, fee waivers were negotiated but parents had to continually prove their legality by producing their visa every time it was renewed, usually every three months. At time of publication, this policy remains and the overseas student fees for a primary school child with a Bridging visa E in a public school remains much the same at around $5,600 per year.

Amora wrote to the Department of Education and gained a fee waiver for her youngest child. Sabina approached the Catholic Education Department and was eventually granted a fee waiver for her child to begin school in Year 3; and Zofia displayed an Australian birth certificate upon which no further questions were asked regarding her child, who was already six. Because of her illegal status, Zofia had been afraid to send Kalyna to school. She knew it was time to begin her schooling instead of 'sitting like a worm' at home, in Zofia's words. She didn't know who to talk to or whether a school would accept Kalyna.

During the period of my research, two high schools took the children, whose immigration status was almost resolved, on reduced fees; and another child creatively managed his status. Latoya and her younger sister, Adella, Sergio, and Valentina and her brother, and Amora's two older children were enrolled in school prior to their tribunal decision. But it was clear that because of enforced poverty children were isolated and deprived of extra-curricular activities like school camp.[24] It 'was always the little thing that we couldn't do', lamented Latoya.

~~~~~~~~

24. While Marco's son was able to attend school camp the following year, Marco was reticent about his daughter's camp not only because he couldn't pay but also because he worried about her. I found the money to pay and she was allowed to go with her school friends. I also found money to pay for reading glasses for two little girls who could not see the blackboard. I taught Vasyl to drive because he couldn't afford a driving instructor and the company that employed him offered him a vehicle if he obtained his licence.

4. The assessment decision

A much-dreaded brown envelope containing news of the outcome of a person's application for protection decision had to be delivered by the postal service into the hands of the person to whom it was addressed. If they weren't at home, a formal note was deposited in the letterbox.

If the recipient didn't understand English well enough, they may not realise that they had to go to the post office to sign for and collect this significant mail. They were more likely to assume it to be unsolicited advertising and to throw it out. The dreaded brown envelope always contained a negative decision.

~~~~~~~~

When a family arrives in Australia intending to seek Australia's protection, they submit a claim for protection as a result of persecution. To obtain a decision, they must fill in a detailed application form in English as soon as possible, including as much reliable evidence as they can produce in support of their claim. A fee of $30 is required. If they fail to submit the application within 45 days after their arrival, they can't access Medicare. Many could not also earn a living for the period in which the claims were being examined.

Initially, a decision was based on this information alone; and it was critical that the application include evidence, translated into English. People from other cultures, however, did not always comprehend Australia's need for documents, particularly documents that were not fraudulent.

Later, interviews were introduced, giving the decision-maker the opportunity to clarify doubts that may have emerged from the application. The person seeking protection also had the opportunity to present further evidence. No support person or lawyer was allowed to attend the interview. In some cases, there was no interview to clarify anomalies. The brevity of the decisions handed down and the unwillingness of assessors to conduct an interview suggest a lack of interest on the part of the assessor to evaluate refugee status fairly, and even a possible preference for negative outcomes.

When interviews became common practice, support people were allowed to attend as observers. Nevertheless, officer Dennis Donohue refused to allow me to support a young couple during their interview. From that moment, I knew the interview wouldn't go well. Diego and Paola emerged, shocked. They couldn't believe the rudeness of the man. They were embarrassed by the fact that Donohue laughed at them when they responded to his questions. They felt totally belittled. Disgusted.

I supported Raja who became agitated when he realised the interpreter for his interview was a Muslim because his claims were about persecution by Muslim fighters. Raja knew, he said, by 'his name. He told me his name and I knew straight away'. Raja didn't wish to discuss his claims in his presence. He felt he couldn't trust the man to keep his information confidential. I advised him to tell the assessor at the beginning of the interview that he would manage without an interpreter. The assessor launched into a tirade, screaming at Raja. This abuse lasted several minutes while Raja insisted on his ability to communicate without an interpreter. The interpreter signed the papers and departed. Raja was so stressed by the incident that, at one point during the interview, he burst into tears. I was ashamed and disgusted at the unprofessional treatment of this vulnerable person. I couldn't believe the department would engage a Muslim interpreter when they knew the case involved persecution by people of that religious background.

There were people in the department who were far more in touch with the adverse experiences of people from different cultures, but they were few and far between. While waiting for the assessor to arrive, Saber responded to a comment of an interpreter in his own language. When I asked him to tell me what he had said, he replied, 'you're lucky, this is a good one'. After explaining his situation, it was a relief to hear the decision-maker say, 'I have studied your country. I have visited your country. I clearly understand what you are saying'.

Some departmental officials concluded very quickly that a family didn't need protection. Their jobs were on the line. These officials had to improve their 'performance ratings' – according to a set of criteria that were clearly unrelated to the fairness of decisions. If assessments had been fair, the person seeking protection, although suffering disappointment, may not have been traumatised by an adverse decision, and an affirmative decision would have avoided years of trauma relating to ongoing appeals.

Over the years, I discovered that some decision-makers were devious. Decisions presented incorrect information, withheld information, or ignored information. Decision-makers manipulated the material to allow them to refuse a protection application. In his *Inquiry into the Circumstances of the Immigration Detention of Cornelia Rau*, Palmer called it 'a culture preoccupied with process and quantitative, rule-driven operational practice'.[25]

~~~~~~~~

Belicia's application for protection was possibly jeopardised when her assessor did not interview her. Officer, Bill Brown noted in his decision that 'little detail is provided (regarding the fear of injury or death)'. Belicia arrived in Australia about two weeks after her sister, who had been sheltering her, was brutally raped and murdered. Her sister's body was found in an unoccupied enclosure nearby to her house. Had Belicia been interviewed, more information might have been forthcoming.

Nankunda's protection application, according to officer, Angelina Pilon, contained 'omissions, inconsistencies and lack of detail ... [that] lead to doubt ... the applicant has not explained why .... Has provided no information about this event [which was] referred to twice ... without saying what happened'. Nankunda's fear of torture and rape, her actual experience as a teenager, would have been exposed and clarified during an interview. For Pilon to claim that the fear of persecution was not well founded was a serious breach of procedural fairness and can be seen as an example of gender bias. Did Pilon really want to know? Torturers don't hand their victims evidence that can be confidently handed to a judge. There may not be obvious physical scars.

Nankunda's first opportunity to explain the content of her application form came when she appealed the decision at the tribunal. The documents she originally submitted to support her claims were misinterpreted by the reviewer, Ros Redberry. Redberry conveniently concluded that those documents were not based on true incidents. She claimed that Nankunda 'composed her claims using ideas and terminology she found in a random assortment of articles downloaded from the internet'. Other people had experienced what Nankunda had undergone but, rather than indicating that similar incidents occurred in that country, publicly available documentation was used against Nankunda. Cultural bias may have also been a factor.

In an unpublished letter in 2002, a former departmental employee revealed explosive information to a psychiatrist. The minister had instituted an elaborate procedure for applications from people seeking protection with particular cultural backgrounds, such as black Africans. Nankunda was of African heritage.

As the Minister's Delegate assessing Nankunda's claims, Pilon would have submitted a draft of this 'sensitive case' to Canberra-based legal officers before handing down her decision. It is not clear whether it was Pilon's decision or whether her decision was altered by Canberra-based lawyers. Freedom of Information (FOI) documents blanked out up to eighteen consecutive pages. This was information the government didn't

25. Palmer, M, 2005, *Inquiry into the Circumstances of the Immigration Detention of Cornelia Rau*, Report, Commonwealth of Australia, https://www.homeaffairs.gov.au/reports-and-pubs/files/palmer-report.pdf. Accessed March 2022.

want curious people to access, and it calls into question the independence of departmental assessors and tribunal reviewers.

Later, during the period of my research, the dreaded brown envelope came to be replaced by an email sent to me. I had the choice of forwarding the decision electronically or personally handing a printed version to the unfortunate family. I chose the latter, not because I enjoy the experience of watching traumatised people fall apart but because someone needed to be present to provide a cushion to prevent further bruising. These experiences of a flawed system always led to frustration, anger and pity.

As I examined each decision forensically and developed a deeper relationship with each person challenging systemic bias, the disconnect between the decision records and the lived experience of people seeking protection became clearer. Olek, a persecuted businessman, had a right to protection under international law because he belonged to a particular social group. Delegate Ben Bodham wrongly concluded that, in Olek's protection claim, 'the particular social group of entrepreneurs and businessmen could not exist independently of the claimed extortion and threats'. This subtle distinction seriously affected Olek and his wife Zofia's futures.

It was entirely wrong to find that all businessmen and entrepreneurs were persecuted and formed a social group because of the *persecution*. This is a common form of fallacious argument. A more trustworthy finding would be that Olek was persecuted because he belonged to an independent social group of businessmen and entrepreneurs based on *talent and entrepreneurial skills*. Bodham failed to recognise that a businessman is persecuted because of his business. He applied the unrealistic argument that he could exclude Olek because all businessmen were persecuted, which of course wasn't true. In order to be able to refuse Olek, Bodham manipulated the definition of a particular social group and denied his basic human right to a fair decision.

Decision-makers have to reach a decision, but this is no reason for failing to think responsibly about such questions or by mistaking incomplete for complete evidence. They should not suppose that a case can be proved by merely selecting instances favourable to their view, while ignoring other possibilities. Whether narrowing his field of vision was policy within the Department of Immigration or Bodham's personal attitude is unclear. Whatever the case, his approach was consistent with restrictive decision-making processes that led to negative outcomes for many people arriving by plane and seeking protection.

In the refugee determination assessment regarding Olek's daughter, Kalyna, Bodham quoted Kalyna's mother's earlier statutory declaration attesting to the child's claims of fear of persecution because Zofia and Kalyna's half-sister Daryna had experienced regular threats made against them. Zofia claimed that if she and her husband and their daughter Kalyna returned, they would all face serious risk of harm or death at the hands of the men who demanded Olek's business.

Kalyna's solicitor argued that the reason Kalyna and Zofia were concerned for their safety was precisely because they were Olek's immediate family members. Kalyna was a member of a particular social group in that she was an immediate family member of the man, her father, who faced persecution. The mafia would not hesitate to kill or injure her. Bodham claimed to have difficulty with this submission. He opined that Kalyna was claiming she would be harmed if her father were harmed. Bodham argued that Kalyna was not actually being targeted. By introducing this dilemma, Bodham imposed a distinction where none existed.

While the statutory declaration claimed that Kalyna *would probably be harmed if* it were not possible to harm her father, Bodham stated that *the child is not claiming* to be targeted. Bodham overlooked the fact that if Kalyna's father was targeted or harmed, this could make his daughter vulnerable in trying to access her basic human rights, particularly if Olek were killed. Further, if Kalyna were abducted to put pressure on Olek to pay, this would target or harm Kalyna as well as her father.

Bodham, in assessing Kalyna's application, had again used the strategy of 'proof by selected instances' to argue against the possibility of Kalyna being in danger.[26] He concluded that even if Kalyna claimed that, should she return to her parent's country, she would be targeted by a criminal gang that had sought to extort money from her father, he did not accept there was a real chance that Kalyna would be targeted due to her membership of a particular social group (namely, her family).

Bodham speculated that Kalyna would be targeted primarily to pressure Olek to meet extortion demands. Membership of her family group was the only other possibility. Incredibly, Bodham suggested that *if the extortion motive were eliminated*, he did not accept that Kalyna would be targeted. Therefore, family membership was not sufficient grounds for a well-founded fear of persecution for a Convention reason.[27]

---

26. Thouless, RH, 1964, *Straight and Crooked Thinking*, (Revised Edition, 8th Print), Pan Books Ltd, London, p.29. This small book justified my discomfort and uneasiness regarding the decisions handed down, opening up a greater awareness of how information can be convincingly manipulated. A new edition was printed in 2011 authored by RH Thouless and CR Thouless.

27. However, during the period of my research, Australian law changed so that it no longer recognised 'Membership of a family group' as a persecuted group as specified in the Refugees Convention.

Bodham drew conclusions from inaccuracies, and then speculated on an improbable scenario. While the speculative method may be used to suggest what might be, it can never be used to conclude what is. If it isn't possible to eliminate the extortion motive, it is not possible to conclude that the child is not vulnerable.

Without the correct facts, speculation can only lead to error. This assumption culture within the Department of Immigration allows rigid, narrow thinking that stymies initiative and limits the ability to deal successfully with new and complex situations. A wider questioning and enabling culture are essential.[28]

To strengthen his case for refusing protection, Bodham entered the realm of the 'inconsequent argument'. He claimed that Kalyna wouldn't be vulnerable to attack because her grandparents and uncles and aunts were not of interest to extortionists. Bodham argued that if these extended family members were not harmed, the criminals were only interested in Olek.

This inconsequent claim is not a reasoning process but a device for creating conviction in those willing to be convinced. It does not follow that Olek's child is not in danger because she has extended family that have not experienced danger. Tautology offers protection to those in power and is a rhetorical device used to undermine the legitimacy of marginal voices, or outgroups such as people seeking protection.

There is no evidence that Bodham considered that the best interests of the child were of primary concern, despite Australia being a signatory to the Convention on the Rights of the Child. In the cases of the child applicants that I examined, the decision records suggested that the assessors and reviewers accessed all family files. This implies a bias against independently assessing the merits of a child refugee's claims as a person in their own right, with precise protection needs.

Bodham's two assessments regarding Olek and Zofia on the one hand, and Kalyna on the other, illustrate the powerful position of decision-makers in the refugee determination system. They demonstrate patterns of reasoning which, on the surface, seem logical and within the law. On closer examination, the reasoning becomes transparently dishonest, resulting in serious injustice. Such decisions demonstrate a culture of negativity that rewards assessors who refuse protection claims. This departmental culture relies on performance indicators weighted against positive decisions and does not allow for service quality and outcomes to be considered in any meaningful way.

28. In his report, Palmer claimed that matters were allowed to go unquestioned within the Department of Immigration's 'assumption culture'.

These arbitrary and objectively unfair decisions at this first stage of the refugee determination process adversely impacted people seeking Australia's protection emotionally, physically and economically. After receiving the dreaded brown envelope containing the refugee determination negative outcome, the person seeking protection could either make arrangements to leave the country, apply for a Review of the Decision within 28 days, or live in the community without legal status. If the family did not actually receive the decision, and subsequently did not appeal within the required time, the tribunal review was not accessible after 28 days.

If government officials allege that the claims of people seeking protection have been assessed and they have been found not to be deserving of Australia's protection, be skeptical. These two examples illustrate that the assessment of persecution claims can be seriously flawed. One consequence of an unfair decision is deportation. When returned to countries of origin, people have been further persecuted and some have died.

~~~~~~~~

5. Reviewing a negative assessment decision

The tribunal appeal was the one place where the merits of the claims could be reassessed. Parliamentary changes to the law introduced by Philip Ruddock, however, banned court reviews from considering the merits of claims. Judges were then restricted to making a judgement of an error in the law, but they no longer had the power to make a finding on humanitarian or compassionate grounds. They judged the tribunal reviewer's decision, not the person seeking protection's claims. However, the person seeking protection was required to pay the court fees if the court found in favour of the reviewer. If the government appealed a tribunal's favourable decision, and the tribunal lost, it was the person seeking protection who was required to pay the court costs, not the tribunal (or the government who finances the tribunal).

A ministerial request submitted on behalf of Olek and Zofia alerted departmental officials that Olek might appeal the initial refugee status determination decision. Although we obtained copious documentation through Freedom of Information (FOI), there was no tribunal decision on file.

To be assessed as a refugee, a person must be outside their country of nationality or their usual country of residence when seeking protection. They must also be unable or unwilling to return or to seek the protection of that country due to a well-founded fear of being persecuted for reasons of race, religion, nationality, membership of a particular social group or political opinion. If the person seeking protection is fearful of being persecuted upon return for any of these reasons, the reviewer must take this into consideration.

At the tribunal, Ros Redberry meticulously reviewed baby Kalyna's claims. Like other reviewers, Redberry entered the tiny hearing room carrying a pile of files. Zofia and Olek, Kalyna's parents, had to stand and wait to take their seats. After introductions and oaths, Redberry informed the parents who represented Kalyna that the tribunal was an independent body that was not a part of the Department of Immigration. This was despite the fact that it is the Minister for Immigration who contracts the reviewers. The minister was a member of the government where the Department of Finance at that time provided $2,400 per application finalised. The minister decided whose tenures would cease and whose would be renewed.

Decision-makers don't bite the hand that feeds them. In 2000–2001, of 5,646 decisions, only 620 were successful, a 'set-aside' rate of a mere 11 per cent. Of the 5,026 negative decisions upheld, 914 applied for judicial review and only 148 of these decisions were favourable.[29]

Redberry alerted Olek and Zofia to the fact that she had studied the departmental files on Kalyna. Since these parents were fully aware of previous negative decisions, such an opening statement is intimidatory and could have created a suspicion of preconceived bias before the interview began. Redberry would be aware of the negative conclusions in Olek and Zofia's application. Even though Kalyna's story might be revised, there would be a bias favouring the first impression. This process cultivates vulnerability. It placed Olek and Zofia in an unequal and inferior position.

Protocols at the tribunal are not unlike those in the judicial system, but reviewers were not always lawyers, and people seeking protection were not assisted by lawyers. No crimes had been committed. Olek and Zofia had arrived on legal visas and Kalyna had an Australian birth certificate. Olek and Zofia, like other people seeking Australia's protection, had fled a country where they were highly suspicious of, and feared state authorities who they believed had failed or refused to protect them, or abused or threatened them.

Fear of authorities was not unusual. In another case, tribunal reviewer Diana Dicker was informed that the people who attacked Vasyl were in collaboration with the police, as he 'was told not to approach the authorities because they would know straight away'. Orlondo had been attacked by people working for authorities; Jaime was so scared he couldn't remain in the compliance office for more than a few minutes; and Marco had other reasons for fearing the police.

For Olek and Zofia, surrounded by strict court-like protocols where prestige is used with an overbearing technique of suggestion, responding to Redberry may have been impossibly difficult. These quasi-judicial formalities don't provide the psychological space for people like Olek and Zofia to present their cases without feeling intimidated. The atmosphere made it hard to speak freely. Nankunda didn't trust Redberry enough to explain in any detail the torture and rape experienced in the 'community' house. Previously, it had been too soon after the murder of Belicia's sister for her to mention this frightful experience to Sally Bland. The Australian legal system was foreign to Olek and Zofia and it was the first time they had confronted the power of a court. The court-like atmosphere and the reviewers' access to all previous negative opinions and decisions militated against independence and created an environment favourable to Redberry and unfavourable to Kalyna.

The review tribunal claims it is mindful of the need for consistency in decision-making, and decision-makers are encouraged to have regard to outcomes in other cases. And yet the tribunal also claims that reviewers

29. Refugee Review Tribunal Annual Report 2001/2002.

are not given any directions as to how they should decide individual cases. Previous negative assessments that reviewers were encouraged to access provide clear directions!

The consistency premise undermines an independent decision on the merits of a claim. This was evident in Kalyna's case where Redberry relied heavily on Bodham's two earlier negative decisions regarding Zofia and Olek and Kalyna. Access to previous negative decisions eliminates the possibility of examining the case on its own merits and puts pressure on the reviewer not to overturn a negative decision by a colleague, departmental officer or minister. It also discourages a departure from a 'previously established view'. Again and again, officers Judith Mullhead, Sally Bland and Carmel Petitie reinforced the 'previously established view' provided in files containing negative assessments and unsuccessful reviews, in rejecting Orlando and Belicia and their daughters' ministerial requests.

Assertions of independence would be more credible if reviewers only examined the merits of the claims to protection in assessment decisions of the person before them. However, they also had access to departmental notes and memos, and previous unfavourable decisions made by case officers with a possible bias towards negative outcomes. Nor, where previous ministerial refusals were included in the files, was this conducive to independent decision-making. Under such procedures, it couldn't be said that tribunal decisions weren't influenced by the minister or the department.

The language of some review decisions manifested structural exclusion. The reviewer's access to *all* the family's Department of Immigration files raised further questions. As Freedom of Information (FOI) material showed, departmental files contained not only decision records, but all interactions departmental officers had had with people seeking protection and their advocates and lawyers, as well as interdepartmental discussions about their claims. After accessing departmental files, reviewers couldn't avoid knowing the attitudes of significant people in the department or government about people's access to protection and being influenced by what they read.

Reviewers didn't always explore significant information regarding protection claims. Cherry-picking was common. When Marco's mother-in-law sent three documents at the same time, two were rejected. Reviewer Philip Hirst was prepared to accept Marco's father's death certificate, but another of the documents was of deep significance to Marco's protection claims.

Marco had requested and been denied a bodyguard. In the letter from the justice officer, the reason given was that he was too insignificant. Marco felt it was too dangerous for him to bring the letter with him through US customs, so his mother-in-law put it away safely. Hirst noted that Marco had not mentioned this refusal to protect him in his initial claim.

Had Marco been advised by an experienced lawyer, he may have made sure he had the letter signed by a public notary. In Australia great importance is placed on documents being signed by justices of the peace. However, a notarised document may not have influenced Hirst because of the suspicion of fraudulent documentation. In my experience, overseas documents signed by public notaries or on letterhead of high-profile people, including lawyers or bishops, are not given the same respect as those witnessed in Australia.

Even so, it is surprising that Hirst would not have explored the genuine possibility that Marco had been refused protection. There was no further exploration in the decision record as to why Marco would want or need protection from the state. Some decision-makers reduce such a complicated body of knowledge to a simple formula with all the qualifications, distinctions, and uncertainties left out. Unfortunately for Marco, the community adviser who helped him lacked experience of Australian legal procedures. In any other circumstance, Marco's explanation for not carrying this document would sound reasonable.

~~~~~~~~

In Nankunda's review, Ros Redberry omitted or ignored her initial written application claim that stated she cried from time to time when she looked at herself with her disability. She pictured herself being tortured and raped for refusing to work for government intelligence. She told of the expectation, on return, to report on people here in Australia. Angelina Pilon mentioned it in her initial assessment which Redberry would have accessed. Despite these two references, Redberry did not refer to this serious claim.

Nankunda was already psychologically fragile because Pilon did not believe her in the first instance. Furthermore, Redberry's insistence that her story was 'implausible' is a clear example of 'overbearing authority' that would have made Nankunda guarded and fearful of disclosing material of such a personal and private nature. Although Redberry made no reference to Nankunda's psychological state in her review decision, other reviewers alluded to possible psychological issues in their decisions.

Redberry overlooked a significant reference to rape and torture. In a culture of avoidance and exclusion, reviewers do not want to find reasons for an outcome that would affirm the need for Australia's protection. Not exploring the link between not being fit for the interview and references to possible rape and torture is a curious omission that disadvantages the person seeking protection and is discriminatory. Reviewers can be reticent about asking appropriate questions. Even though the law doesn't require it, the failure to adequately scrutinise protection claims is a further example of the cruelty of the law. It also shows a disrespect for the Australian taxpayer whose money is wasted.

In another of Redberry's reviews, she argued that Grisha's mother, Inna, would be safe to return to the country where she experienced racial harassment and had been raped by two different men. She concluded that she was not satisfied that harm amounting to persecution had befallen Inna 'for a Convention reason in the past (with the exception of the rape)'. To make rape an exception or an appendage displays a clear failure to understand the long-term effects of being raped, not by one but by two men, and the possibility of being retraumatised if sent back to where this occurred. Australia's non-refoulement (non-return) obligations or the United Nations Convention against Torture were not considered in this merits review.

Reviewers also included personal opinions that would support an unfavourable decision. Bland implied that if Jaime fled political persecution, his claim was not Convention-based because specific 'independent country information' suggested he would not be in danger if he returned 'now'. She did not find evidence that paramilitaries retained an interest in Jaime. She dismissed a possible Convention-related claim because Jaime just might be safe 'now'.

It's difficult to know if the outcome of Jaime's initial claim of political persecution was affected by Pilon's desire to refuse protection through, consciously or unconsciously, engaging techniques of dishonest thinking. She could also have speculated that the level of violence in his country might deteriorate further, as it clearly did, but that would have been to her disadvantage. Although produced soon after this decision, UN documents in 2002 (and 2004, 2005) and Amnesty International reports indicated this country was not at all safe.

~~~~~~~~

The use of language was a factor in the way reviewers could (re)formulate a person's story in order to construct the basis for their unfavourable review. An example is the suggestion that if 'no threats' or 'no harm was carried out', then the person must have been safe. In Mateo's case, Terry Thousend noted that the threats weren't carried out. He also noted that Mateo found employment and did not suffer any actual harm despite remaining for more than a year after the threats began. Redberry found that Nankunda experienced no serious harm when she declined to poison someone, repeating that no actions were taken against her. This statement fails to explore the submission about 'rape' and the 'community house', and it ignores the psychologist's note indicating she was too ill to attend her tribunal hearing.

In twelve specific decisions, I found the two most common words were derivatives of 'harm' and 'threat'. Six reviewers mentioned 'threat' between 20 and 46 times in their decisions. The same six mentioned 'harm' between 28 and 51 times. Terry Thousend did not appreciate that Mateo might have tried to escape the threats, and Ros Redberry did not indicate that she explored the steps Nankunda took to avoid being harmed or, more seriously, the harm she did experience. A systemic culture of avoidance indicates a priority for making negative decisions about people seeking protection.

Redberry could always fall back on the theme that 'no serious harm befell her'. Though Nankunda's mother's business was trashed and there was reference to fear of rape and torture in community housing in Nankunda's documentation, Redberry chose to ignore this. Redberry dismissed the damage to Nankunda's mother's business because no serious harm befell *her*. Throwing doubt on what Nankunda believed to be true made serious argument impossible. A statement expressed in predigested form has the great practical advantage that it can be easily remembered and easily passed from one person to another. No kind of suggestion is stronger than the repetitive conviction that everybody says 'no serious harm' was experienced.

In making a distinction between Nankunda's mother's harm and Nankunda's fear of harm, Redberry strengthened her argument that her protection claims were implausible. Strangely, though, Redberry found the claims relating to Nankunda's mother believable. She could accept that in Nankunda's culture people can intimidate and extort in an environment where corrupt police are active but could not comprehend that a young woman might be forced to spy on anti-government activity. This conclusion could be cross-cultural ignorance or intrapersonal exclusion. Redberry rejected as implausible Nankunda's claim that she was asked to form a relationship with an unknown man and then kill him. Nankunda declined to poison the man, and Redberry concluded that *no serious harm befell her* – but she, Redberry, did not investigate Nankunda's fear of rape and murder.

Another repetitive theme in the negative decisions was 'individual' or 'separate and individual incidents'. Redberry accepted claims relating to Nankunda's mother and grandmother but disconnected the mother's persecution from her daughter's. Redberry accepted that Nankunda's mother's shop was broken into and goods stolen and damaged. She accepted that Nankunda's mother had an unsatisfactory response from the police. She also accepted that the mud wall of Nankunda's grandmother's house was knocked in. She regarded these *as separate and individual incidents*, not part of a series of events designed to harm Nankunda or for a Convention reason.

Philip Hirst found that the attack on Marco was directed at him as an individual rather than as a former member of a government security organisation. In Orlondo and Belicia's case, Sally Bland claimed that Orlondo was targeted as an individual because of what he knew, what he had exposed and might expose, and not because of his actual or imputed political opinions about parliamentarians' criminality.

The phrase 'separate and individual incidents' was used to support an argument that a person was not a member of a particular social group. Although social groups consist of a number of individuals, if the individual can somehow be distinguished from the social group, reviewers could argue that the person was not persecuted for a Convention reason.

A further theme is that of 'credibility' and 'minor matters'. This is illustrated by documenting low-level mistakes (discussed in the following chapter). In Jaime's review, Sally Bland claimed that she had concerns about Jaime's credibility, apart from minor matters like his writing on the protection application form that he lived at a certain address for an unspecified time. The significance of Bland's mentioning 'minor matters' serves only to reinforce her assessment of Jaime's credibility. Why would 'minor matters' be included in a decision, if not to discredit a person? Bland takes no account of the fact that Jaime might have been traumatised and confused about details written on a form in a foreign language soon after arriving in a foreign country. Including 'minor matters' in a decision is a rhetorical device to undermine the legitimacy of claims submitted.

Redberry makes the contradictory statement in Nankunda's decision that 'the claims put forward by Nankunda in her written testimony, and re-stated (more or less) with a number of additional aspects in her oral testimony, are mere assertions'. The 'additional aspects' included the attack on the shop and grandmother's house, which she conditionally accepted. However, she didn't link these harmful consequences to the request that Nankunda refused, namely, to form a relationship with the intent to kill a man. This request Redberry deemed implausible, so that she could then avoid a Convention-related protection claim.

In Marco's review, Hirst contradicted himself when he found that Marco disclosed *without prior notice* that he feared persecution on the grounds of his political opinion. Like the refusal to protect notification, this fear of persecution wasn't included in the initial written application. Hirst devoted 22 lines in the decision to proving that Marco was not a member of a political party. Yet despite the seriousness of not being protected by the state, this point was scarcely explored. These are examples of systemic exclusion where the desire is to present negative decisions in the best possible light.

A social category of race can also be a basis for judging individuals and for predicting behaviour. Despite her qualifications in Public Management, Redberry had no overseas work experience. She claimed that recruiting young women to spy was not what a government does. She concluded that the claim was 'just too implausible'. Nankunda replied through her interpreter, 'It is not like here. The things which they are saying they do is totally different to the things that they are doing. The things which is written according to the law, that is not what they are doing'. Redberry, with her book knowledge, argued with Nankunda about her lived experience. Nankunda insisted that what is written is not what actually happens. As an example, she noted that police in uniform can be found drunk in a bar whereas according to the law police are not allowed to drink. The transcript of the interview indicates Nankunda's frustration about cultural misunderstanding. While Redberry found it difficult to believe that security organisations in Nankunda's country engaged untrained girls, her difficulty may be due to her own limitations of thought and experience. Whether or not Redberry was aware of race as a factor in excluding black Africans is unknown.

Redberry's review did not disclose that a doctor had reported that Nankunda would be too unwell to attend a hearing for months and that despite that, the hearing went ahead. Without regard to Nankunda's poor health, Redberry told her that her claims were 'completely implausible', some points 'strained credulity', that details had been 'embellished' and were 'simply not believable'.

Bland rejected 'as implausible' Jaime's suggestion that the paramilitaries would check the national database, find that he had returned and have him arrested and killed because of past party membership and activity. Bland's opinions on implausibility showed that, for her, practices in her own cultural sphere are culturally normative. On eight occasions in two decisions, Bland relied on the 'implausible' factor.

Another reason for not finding a person in need of protection is the 'relocation' option. After Mateo completed years of study in a neighbouring country (Country B), this country and his birth country (Country A) were no longer friendly neighbours. Country B would not employ him because he came from Country A. When returning to Country A, Mateo claimed discrimination on the grounds of having qualifications from Country

B, which was not a signatory to the Refugees Convention and Protocols. Despite this, Terry Thousand concluded it was safe for Mateo to live there. Thousand noted that, although the government had no formal mechanism to offer protection to foreign nationals, it honours the principle of first asylum and has provided it to a small number of persons. Thousand also acknowledged that about 43 foreign nationals living in the country were seeking asylum elsewhere. He argued that there were no reports of the forced return of people to countries where they feared persecution.

While this information might be true, it was a pointless gesture to return Mateo to Country B where, as a foreign national, he would need to 'seek protection elsewhere'. Thousand failed to consider Mateo's basic human right to work and support himself in Country B while 'seeking protection elsewhere'. There is no evidence to suggest that in deciding relocation options, access to basic human rights was considered.

Sally Bland had many years' experience working with Department of Foreign Affairs and Trade (DFAT) in Canberra and overseas but was not familiar with socio-political problems in Jaime's country that were publicised the year of the hearing. In Jaime's review, Bland quoted independent country information which testified that between 2,500 and 4,000 party members and supporters had been killed and attempts had been made on the lives of many others. Bland quoted DFAT reports that the party no longer recruited activists; had no registers or lists of members; was in financial difficulty; and that party members continued to be threatened and assassinated. She concluded that if Jaime had a subjective fear of harm in his home area, she considered it reasonable in Jaime's circumstances to relocate elsewhere within the country. Australia's non-refoulement responsibilities as a signatory to the UN *Convention Against Torture* did not feature in these decisions.

~~~~~~~~

Once one family member had been refused protection it was difficult to convince the department to override that initial decision when examining the case of a second family member. Orlondo and Belicia won an extension of time and challenged Bland's tribunal decision at the Full Federal Court. The judge found that their claims did not 'demonstrate jurisdictional error on the part of the Tribunal'. The Department of Immigration as well as Federal law and policy had locked Orlondo and Belicia out of the 1951 International Refugee Convention. Still in search of protection and on the edge of despair, Orlondo and Belicia submitted a complaint to the Assistant Secretary of the Department of Immigration in Canberra. This man advised Orlondo and Belicia to submit a separate application for protection on behalf of the children and their grandmother, and provided legal assistance for this. They were once again refused protection on the basis of their father's rejected claims, however. Likewise, with Olek and Zofia and Jaime and Ladonna, their children were refused protection on the basis of the earlier decisions regarding their parents.

By the time the application for the children was submitted, parliament had introduced a law that excluded people from making claims about persecuted family members: A partner or child could no longer claim fear of being targeted and persecuted by criminals who targeted the husband or father. In separate tribunal decisions, Judith Mullhead and Diana Dicker concluded that Orlondo and Belicia, as well as Vasyl and Sabina, did not have Convention-based claims. In almost identical paragraphs, they agreed that their submissions 'raised for the Tribunal the matter of consideration of their application on humanitarian grounds'. They then claimed that the tribunal's role was limited to determining whether the people seeking protection satisfy the criteria to grant protection visas. Consideration of their circumstances on other grounds was solely within the minister's discretion. The two tribunal reviewers suggested their claims be referred to the minister, but it was up to departmental officers to follow up with a ministerial request. There is no evidence that this occurred, a case of departmental officers undermining the authority of tribunal reviewers.

Carmel Petitie didn't recommend that Latoya, Adella and their grandmother be referred to the minister for humanitarian consideration despite being aware of the possible reasons for the request she received. Petitie recognised that Latoya and Adella had lived most of their lives in Australia, their genuine fear of being harmed in their parents' country, and their distress arising from the murder of their aunt. She also noted that their parents had become psychologically unwell.

Petitie mentioned 'advice from UNHCR' about people from their country who were not recognised as refugees but may be in need of international protection. She agreed that these included people whose lives, safety or liberty had been threatened by generalised violence, internal conflicts, massive violation of human rights or other circumstances which had seriously disturbed public order. UNHCR's view is that nationals unable to return for these reasons need international protection. Petitie agreed that UNHCR had observed that internal armed conflict continued, generating sustained and continuous levels of violence and that the human rights situation continued to be critical. She concluded that levels of violence, including homicides, kidnappings, extortion and other violent crimes affecting civilians, remained high.

However, Petitie concluded that she 'is not satisfied that the applicants have a wellfounded fear of Conventionrelated persecution'. While Petitie claimed that she did not have jurisdiction to consider the issues, it was within her jurisdiction to recommend that the minister give Latoya, Adella and their grandmother consideration. Possible reasons for not considering this option include:

- Reticence about using her authority in this area when she could pass the matter back to assessors in the department;
- Fear of being perceived as favourable towards the children's protection needs when the minister's position regarding the family was well known;
- Fear that a favourable decision might jeopardise her future at the tribunal.

The renewal of contracts by the minister could provide a serious impediment to independent decision-making by officials. When reviewers know the attitudes of departmental officers, tribunal colleagues and the minister toward a particular family's claims, they are unlikely to challenge ministerial request refusals when dependent on that minister for renewal of their own contracts. For example, Petitie knew of Ian Inglet's initial decision not to adhere to Judith Mullhead's recommendation to refer the case to the minister and that ministers Ruddock and Vanstone had already refused requests for consideration on compassionate grounds. Despite the lawyer's request, Petitie did not recommend the children's claims be referred to the minister. Two of Redberry's unfavourable decisions occurred within 12 months of her renewal of tenure. Mark Sporton was an exception. He made an 'inconsistent' decision when he found Olek and Zofia to be refugees after Redberry's negative finding and Ruddock's refusal to intervene.

~~~~~~~~

People seeking protection were in a no-win situation when they weren't satisfied with the information migration agents submitted. Inna and Grisha complained to the department 'that her first agent had not conveyed fully the information which she wanted to present' and, in her decision, Redberry reported that there was a falling out between Inna and her adviser, with the latter advising the department that he had reason to believe that Inna had made false claims'. The agent, not Inna, was assumed to be honest.

Information submitted from overseas lawyers is not necessarily respected. Redberry undermined a well-known lawyer retained by Inna. The information was later vindicated when a highly classified document from that country was submitted in a ministerial request. Redberry, not herself a lawyer, had the temerity to suggest that she was not satisfied with the veracity of the lawyer's statements or that Inna's life, along with Grisha's and Aloysha's, was in danger in either country. She claimed to be satisfied that the lawyer had undertaken actions designed to assist Inna in her claim for protection. According to Redberry, the lawyer 'specifically attempted to address the question as to why Inna would be in danger in her country of citizenship in consequence of incidents occurring in the other country'.

One would have thought that it was the duty of the lawyer to present the case for protection. Inna had asked that this lawyer participate at the tribunal through a telephone hook-up but 'it was decided that the logistics of time difference and interpreting made this too difficult'. Redberry found the case to be 'long and complicated', involving a series of events occurring in Country A and Country B. Further complications were caused by Inna being formerly an ethnic minority citizen of Country A before becoming a Country B citizen who had, nevertheless, been residing in recent years in Country A. Redberry's skepticism regarding the overseas lawyer's submission, and resistance to hearing from the local solicitor significantly disadvantaged Inna and Grisha.

Inconsistencies in evidence can be related to post-traumatic stress disorder (PTSD).[30] At the time of the tribunal hearing, Nankunda was judged not fit to attend. To expect Nankunda to adequately respond in her fragile psychological condition and, further, to claim 'inconsistencies' to support an adverse 'credibility' finding was an abuse of power. Tribunal *Credibility Guidelines* (2008) were not available when Redberry reviewed Nankunda's decision. However, 'minimum standards of fairness, that is, the need to accord natural justice' did exist and should have prevailed. The tribunal's *Guidance on the Assessment of Credibility* claims that reviewers 'take into account the factors that may affect an applicant's ability to give evidence', but they seem to be followed on an ad hoc basis at the discretion of individual Members and remain unenforceable.[31]

Admittedly, reviewers have a difficult task sifting truth from fabrication. However, skilled reviewers rely on indicators such as the person's demeanour to substantiate claims. Sally Bland seemed frustrated with Jaime's inability to be coherent. This could be interpreted as being 'vague' or evasive. It could also be a result of post-traumatic stress disorder (PTSD). A reference to 'dire psychological pressure and persecution' in his claims supports the latter supposition.

---

30. Coffey, G, 2003, 'The Credibility of Credibility Evidence at the Refugee Review Tribunal', *International Journal of Refugee Law*, vol. 15, no. 3, pp.337–417.
31. Migration Review Tribunal-Refugee Review Tribunal, 2006: *Guidance on the Assessment of Credibility*, paragraphs 4.1 and 4.3.

The transcript of Nankunda's hearing illustrates the dismissive attitude towards traumatised people seeking protection:

> **Nankunda's Interpreter:** She's asking if she can have a break
> **Redberry:** I think that we might have finished now, [Nankunda] I think that I've asked all the questions that I want to ask. And unless there's something particular that you want to tell me ... I think I have enough information.
> **Nankunda** [through interpreter]: ... the way she holds the book here and swear that she is going to tell the truth, she is telling you the truth. She goes back to her country she knows she is not in a good hand, and that person they were asking her to be involved with, that man is he still alive too, so that is another thing that if he will see her, it'll be the same situation as she was in before she ... came here. She's begging you to listen to what she is talking about and help her.
> **Redberry:** Ok ... Well, I might close the hearing now... Would you like to close up in room seven please ... Now what happens now is that I have to consider all this information very carefully ... and think about it within the terms of the Convention. Then I have to write the decision which takes a little time.[32]

The tribunal was warned of Nankunda's psychological fragility. After receiving Redberry's decision, she collapsed and was admitted to a psychiatric ward in a public hospital.

The reviewer's questioning provoked the emergence of information that had not been previously discussed. This can result in 'new information' which opens the gate for adverse credibility claims on the part of the reviewer. An illustration of spontaneous 'new information' is demonstrated in an excerpt from the transcript of Redberry's interview with Nankunda:

> **Redberry:** Now ... you say you did this until February or March? Why did you stop?
> **Nankunda** [through interpreter]: [The man] came to ask her mother if she can do another job for him. It was someone there spying on this guy this man ... he likes women so they wanted to use her to go to be with that man so they could catch him, and she asked him ... How can I go to be with him ... if or how can he approach me? What happened was they wanted her to be involved with that man so after they got involved she can poison him ... they wanted her to get him to the point that he trusted her so she can poison him.

To a further question as to whether or not Nankunda did this job, she replied through the interpreter:

> She refused because she told [this man] she had never been involved with any man – how could she do that kind of job ... how if he's sick ... she can get sick ... she never been involved with anybody ... she can't do it.

When asked if he accepted her refusal Nankunda replied:

> After 4 days when she refused ... after 4 days the mother went to work as usual the whole shop was vandalized, they broke in and vandalized everything (indecipherable) ... some of the things were stolen.[32]

Redberry in her review decision pointed out that there were a number of discrepancies between Nankunda's testimony as she had originally written it and as she had told it at the hearing, including the addition of the stories about the second job which [the man] wanted her to undertake, the attack on her mother's shop, and the threatening letters.

Although Nankunda responded honestly to the questions put to her, Redberry found her not to be a credible witness and concluded that 'her story was inconsistent at different stages of the refugee determination process, inconsistent even within the hearing, utterly implausible.'

By categorising her as 'not a credible witness' Redberry blamed and accused Nankunda while justifying herself. 'Implausibility' became Nankunda's fault rather than Redberry's inability to comprehend experiences beyond her cultural boundaries.

~~~~~~~~

32. All quotes are excerpts from Nankunda's recorded tribunal hearing obtained at the conclusion of the hearing.

6. Consequential errors

In the earlier days of my witnessing the tribunal system, reviewers were critical of minor errors in personal claims. This questioning of people's credibility led to unfavourable decisions rather than an understanding of the effects of PTSD on memory, for example, or the ignorance of reviewers. The consequences of *departmental* errors were significant for people arriving by plane seeking protection, yet departmental errors rarely even warranted an apology.

Files went missing or, more precisely, could not be found because they were wrongly labelled. Departmental personnel searched for files for Orlando and Belicia and their daughters when their country of birth was incorrectly recorded as 'Indonesian'. Emails went back and forth for a month in search of incorrectly labelled or non-existent files. A seven-page submission was stamped as received more than a year later. The note attached said:

> (To) [Departmental Officer 1]
> This request was given to our section very recently. It appears that it got lost somewhere in the Dept. I have closed the min rep on PCMS as the correspondent ~~received~~ was sent a departmental response ...
> (Signed:) [Departmental Officer 2]

On another occasion, a UNHCR officer assured Marco and Amora that the UNHCR office in Canberra supported their ministerial request. A copy of the submission was sent to Minister Vanstone's office and a letter of acknowledgement received. A departmental senior adviser wrote to Petro Georgiou, an MP who had supported Marco's request: 'This case was previously brought to the former Minister's attention and he decided not to consider it. Senator Vanstone has directed that, if a case has previously been brought to the former Minister's attention seeking intervention, she does not wish to consider whether to exercise her power unless additional information ... The additional information provided ... does not bring the case within the Minister's Guidelines. Therefore, no further action will be taken in respect of this request'. The UNHCR Canberra officer recognised the 'new information' as meeting international refugee guidelines but the departmental officer could not manage to fit the claims into the minister's guidelines. Later, the UNHCR officer reassured Marco and Amora that he had received a reply from the department about his letter. The department stated that, 'the information provided by UNHCR has been noted and referred to the relevant state office for consideration and, if appropriate, the preparation of advice to the Minister on the issue whether the new information raises a public interest reason'.

The UNHCR's submission sent to Vanstone's office had either been mislaid or dismissed on the grounds that it was a 'repeat' request. Likewise, my identical submission had been dismissed by public servants.

Similarly, Nankunda's psychiatrist wrote to the department and this letter was 'lost' again and again. An internal email records that a departmental officer called her doctor's office about his letter of June of that particular year. The departmental officer spoke to his receptionist and advised that the doctor's letter had not been received by the department and did not appear on the parliamentary database. The receptionist faxed copies freshly signed by the doctor the following day. A second letter was sent in early July.

Soon after, the Refugee Advice and Casework Service (RACS) sent a copy of the doctor's letter which began, 'As outlined in my previous letter...' and stated that his concern was

> that this woman's predicament is being aggravated by the process of her appeal. Her psychological conditions appear genuine and she is clearly suffering greatly. Her expressions of suicidal thoughts reflect this suffering and a sense of helplessness and despair about her predicament.

His strong view was that Nankunda was at great risk of suicide if she were to fail in her attempts to achieve protection. In September, the psychiatrist once more responded to a further request from the same departmental officer to send his letters of June and August yet again. It is difficult to understand how crucial documents can be treated so negligently, and the authors of these documents afforded such disrespect. Some mistakes are more serious than others but all impacted adversely on Nankunda and her advocates.

There are two sets of standards. In the initial application assessments and at the tribunal reviews, there was zero tolerance for the slightest mistake made by a person seeking protection, while departmental gaffes occurred regularly. Reviewers questioned people's credibility if, for example, they confused dates. These early adverse judgements were relied upon over and over again, through further stages of the protection process. While departmental officers clearly made blunders, mistakes made by people seeking protection were unacceptable. Departmental officers didn't have the excuse of memory impairment as a result of PTSD. There were no apologies.

Some advocates questioned the ability of departmental officers to undertake the required tasks. For example, an officer, Penny Pasory, claimed that the 'applicant attended a Protection visa (PV) interview on 01/09/20–', however her decision was made six weeks earlier (13.7.20–).

While she recognised and named the person, she then referred to him as 'they'. She also made incorrect statements regarding his nationality, stating that evidence produced was satisfactory. However, she later contradicted this by stating different (correct) identity information.

Pasory was confused as to whether she was assessing one person's claims or a number of people's claims. She repeatedly stated: 'evidence of their identity'; 'in support of their claimed identity'; 'evidence of their identity which is consistent with their narrative'. For the most part, Pasory indicated that she was assessing a male's application. However, she claimed he was a female when she stated: 'For the purposes of this assessment [country] is her receiving country'.[33]

The deputy director of a right wing think tank questioned how Ros Redberry could have found Nankunda's claims implausible. She mentioned the 'new evidence' about Nankunda's mother's death certificate. Nankunda was now also willing to allow her doctor to submit evidence and explicit details of her 'training' which included 'brutalization, humiliation, beatings and much worse'. The deputy director continued, noting that Nankunda had collapsed under the strain and had been scheduled into the psychiatric unit of a Sydney hospital. Redberry expressed doubt, without evidence, 'that a seventeen-year-old woman would be used as a spy'. The deputy director pointed out that, with only the background experience of a middle-class Australian, Redberry had claimed, 'This is simply implausible'. The deputy director argued that 'as anyone, with a small amount of information on developing countries knows, this is not implausible', and the department 'has made unreasonable, if not ignorant, suggestions regarding this case, including checking with Nankunda's destitute sister (whom Nankunda was helping by sending money) could support Nankunda if she were returned. And expecting Nankunda's supporters to make enquiries of records kept in her country of origin "safe" houses of the torture there – what a thought!!!'[34]

In Nankunda's submission a former judge stated:

> I submit with little doubt that, had the earlier tribunals been cognizant of the additional evidence, the applicant would have been successful at first instance.

If officer Pilon had initially allowed an interview and asked questions about the information on the form, she might not have been ignorant of the core claims. Had the reviewer, Redberry, not overlooked significant

---

33. A Protection Visa Assessment made in 2016.
34. An Advocate's letter to the Secretary to the Department of Immigration obtained through Freedom Of Information (FOI).

information, she would have been cognizant of much of the evidence. These are procedural errors of omission which resulted in a drawn-out, painful and cruel process for Nankunda.

Orlondo and Belicia's lawyer wrote to Minister Ruddock, pointing out a precedent in law supporting Orlondo and Belicia's claims. In a similar case, Mr X was recently granted his permanent onshore visa by the department for fundamentally the same reasons and claims. Given this precedent, Orlondo's and Belicia's lawyer submitted that the acceptance of Mr X's claims as an informer in regard to illicit drugs and payments should warrant a reconsideration of Orlondo, Belicia and family's case.

It is unclear whether the departmental officer understood the significance of 'precedents in law' or indeed, forwarded this information to Ruddock in a schedule (case summary) to assist the minister in making an informed decision. Regardless, this information had no impact on the decision.

Schedules were often selective in the information put forward. In the case of Orlondo and Belicia the schedule noted that 'the case does not meet the guidelines and the circumstances are neither exceptional nor unique'. Although the schedule cited refused requests, it failed to note that, in one instance, 'the Tribunal [Judith Mullhead] affirmed the primary decision *but* recommended the case be referred to the Minister and the departmental officer, Ian Inglet, decided it did not meet the guidelines'.

The court agreed with Mullhead's opinion when the judge remitted the case to the tribunal. The author of the schedule did not discuss the inconsistencies between the two tribunal decisions. Mullhead found that, in the light of the violence perpetrated on those close to Belicia and Orlondo and the power of the agents to harm in such a country, this case raised compelling humanitarian grounds.

In the ensuing years, this point was never raised in the many submissions put to the minister by departmental officers. Rather than admit there were reviewers in favour and reviewers against, departmental submissions regarding Orlondo and Belicia focused on Bland's negative decision, citing 'inconsistencies'. Minister Ruddock had received submissions that omitted facts that might favour the couple.

~~~~~~~~

When I found people gaming the system, I immediately withdrew from their cases. I insisted they tell the truth in as much as they could remember. Not only was that in their best interest, but my reputation was at stake.

I am not so naive as to believe people don't lie from time to time, but I also know ways of discovering more truthful versions of a story. As a member of an international congregation of Catholic nuns, I had recourse to sisters and sometimes priests in different countries to whom I could turn to check certain facts. It is easy, and was a common practice, for assessors to declare documents obtained from overseas fraudulent, despite being signed by notaries. When it transpired that Akith's documents were wrongly declared fraudulent it happened that the priest author of one document which was on official letterhead was in Australia. Akith's friend, a photographer, video-taped a conversation with the priest, prominently displaying his letter. This was forwarded to the department.

The examples I have given indicate a negative bias within the department. The bias of ministers' personal assistants sometimes blocked favourable submissions. The Migration Matters Senate Committee expressed concern at the preparation of submissions or schedules for the minister.[35] The Senate Legal and Constitutions Committee found that submission preparation 'was critical to the success or otherwise of individual cases' and recommended that people requesting ministerial intervention view and comment on a draft of the submission before it is sent to the minister.[36]

We all make mistakes. My concern, though, is that assessors and reviewers who sometimes themselves make significant mistakes do not tolerate the insignificant mistakes of people seeking protection.

~~~~~~~~

35. Senate Committee on Ministerial Discretion in Migration Matters (2005), https://www.aph.gov.au/Parliamentary_Business/Committees/Senate/Former_Committees/minmig/report/index p62. Accessed March 2022.
36. Senate Legal and Constitutional References Committee (2006), 'Administration and operation of the *Migration Act 1958*', https://apo.org.au/sites/default/files/resource-files/2006-03/apo-nid2950.pdf pp.129, 149. Accessed March 2022.

7. Consequences of discriminatory policies

Because I met families at the end of the application process, hope was scarce. I had to walk a delicate line between imparting some hope, but not false hope. I accompanied everyone to the compliance office because these people were fragile. Many felt they were not respected; their personal dignity was undermined. Whether because of the questions asked or the way they were put to them, many left feeling diminished. My presence ensured that they would be treated respectfully by the compliance officer, and it gave me an opportunity to check on their psychological and emotional wellbeing.

During home visits I would too often hear the words, 'I'm tired', followed by a long pause. People weren't talking about physical fatigue so much as psychological and emotional despair. Behind the pause were the unspoken words, 'I'm tired of living'. This worried me. At this point, no amount of talking could convince a person to trust outsiders or persuade them to visit a psychologist. Fortunately, I've completed some training in counselling and I'm sensitive to stress levels.

Discriminatory policies meant lengthy periods of assessment and review. While waiting, vulnerable people suffered shame, embarrassment, anxiety and psychological stress as well as health problems and poverty as they attempted to protect themselves and their families. At such times, telephone calls to, and home visits by, me became more frequent. I stayed through long silences. The important thing wasn't time, but restoration of a sense of self. Until I was reassured on this score, I couldn't leave. Sometimes I stayed for five hours.

We often prepared ministerial submissions together. This engaged everyone in the process and began to build self-worth and dignity. It was always helpful to include a psychological report with the documentation. Hesitantly, someone would agree. Generally, they trusted people I recommended. Psychologist, Paula, was a marvel. She interviewed and wrote comprehensive reports, pro bono. Although it was time-consuming, she did this quite often.

~~~~~~~~

Over twenty years of my engaging with people seeking Australia's protection, there was one common thread. Almost everyone had some knowledge of international human rights law. People seeking protection knew their rights. They knew their rights were being abused.

There are effective laws and deficient laws. Faced with deficient law, there is a choice to collude with lawmakers and enforcers or do what is right according to international law and personal conscience – the ethical principle of *epikeia* or reasonableness. The concept of *epikeia* holds that laws are, of their very nature, universal. On the whole, lawmakers legislate for the general run of cases, and not for a concrete instance. But as particular details and circumstances are almost limitless in number and nature, no legislator in framing a law can foresee all circumstances which may arise. They enact laws according to what usually and ordinarily happens. They are not, however, ignorant of the possibility that their laws, though just and good in general, may be deficient in particular. In response to my complaint about fairness in a particular situation, the business manager, Multicultural Affairs and Settlement, wrote in 2005, 'it is the law not fairness that determined the primary decision'.

Epikeia is a virtue because it recognises that it's sometimes necessary to set aside the law to protect justice and the common good. In an age with an increasing number of laws and regulations, and a decreased emphasis on prudence, *epikeia* reminds us that laws are made for human beings, not human beings for laws. However, in Anglo-Saxon law when we invoke *epikeia*, our action may not be morally wrong, but it could still be punishable. Hence my dilemma. Do I act immorally in order to avoid punishment, or do I invoke moral principles and accept the inconvenient consequences?

~~~~~~~~

Ladonna understood that human rights doors included the right to non-discrimination, rights to life, physical and moral integrity, effective remedy, physical and mental health, privacy and procedural guarantees. She pushed all the doors, but they were closed.

According to the **International Covenant on Civil and Political Rights** (ICCPR), Article 26:

> All persons are equal before the law and are entitled without any discrimination to the equal protection of the law, in this respect, the law shall prohibit any discrimination and guarantee to all persons equal and effective protection against discrimination on any ground such as race, colour, sex, language, religion, political or other opinion, national or social origin, property, birth or other status.

All participants in my study suffered from discrimination regarding equal protection under the law. People who arrived by plane and sought protection expected that their experiences of persecution would be understood.

Vasyl was bitterly disappointed when this was not the case. He said they came to Australia hoping for a better future because this country protects people, not like in his country 'where everyone is a criminal and there are no laws'.

In some cases, on the basis of their nationality and social group, discrimination occurred because assessors and reviewers couldn't accept or comprehend particular types of persecution. Belicia and Zofia suffered discrimination because of gender, and Sergio, Latoya and Adella because of age. Inna, Belicia and Nankunda suffered discrimination in the refusal or inability to recognise sexual and gender-based violence. Nankunda suffered discrimination because of disability. As well as having a physical disability, she suffered from serious PTSD, a psychological disability.

Sometimes people compared the frustration of receiving unfavourable outcomes to their applications and appeals with earlier stressful experiences. Latoya's grandma Herminia said after they received the minister's letter requesting that they leave Australia, she didn't think it would be as bad as 'it would have been in our country'.

It's difficult to assess the level of discrimination with ministerial refusals because there is no transparency about the basis for ministerial decisions. The International Covenant on Civil and Political Rights Article 2(3a) states that each State Party undertakes:

> (a) to ensure that any person whose rights or freedoms as herein recognised are violated shall have an effective remedy, notwithstanding that the violation has been committed by persons acting in any official capacity'.

What could the motive of a ministerial decision to challenge a tribunal's favourable decision possibly be?

There's no doubt that in Australia, for people seeking protection, the 'rights or freedoms as herein recognised are violated'. The review process at the tribunal is definitely not an 'effective remedy'. The lack of expertise about international law and the varying levels of cross-cultural experience of assessors and tribunal reviewers indicates that some people are inadequately equipped for assessment and review work. The courts struggle to be an 'effective remedy' given parliament's interference through the ongoing introduction of laws avoiding Australia's international obligations.

The International Covenant on Civil and Political Rights, Article 17 states that: 'No-one shall be subjected to arbitrary or unlawful interference with his privacy, family, home or correspondence nor to unlawful attacks on his honor and his reputation'. The tribunal can access all government files on a person's relatives, not just the application at hand. This is a breach of privacy, especially in the case of child applications. The means by which assessors and reviewers rely on 'credibility' and 'implausibility' claims are attacks on the honour and reputation of the person seeking protection. Further attacks occur when reviewers give weight to anonymous derogatory letters, which happened to Vasyl, Olek and Zofia.

All persons shall be equal before the courts and tribunals according to ICCPR Article 14:3(d). A person is 'to be informed if he does not have legal assistance, of his right; and to have legal assistance assigned to him, in any case where the interests of justice so require, and without payment by him in any such case if he does not have sufficient means to pay for it'. Demonstration of respect for this unequivocal statement of the right to free legal representation was not forthcoming. For a time, a barrister could request a fee waiver in the court, but this was later withdrawn for people arriving by plane. Clearly, insisting upon fees and not providing free legal assistance to people who are not allowed to earn a living is discriminatory, as is a court hearing without appropriate representation in an adversarial process. Providing inappropriate and inefficient interpreters is another form of discrimination. Following the tribunal hearing, Nankunda explained feeling judged by the interpreter. She said that once when she said something, the look on the interpreter's face was like, 'No, I don't think so'. Sometimes he would 'give a different answer'.

Nowadays, before citizenship is granted, any outstanding debts to the government must be paid. These debts usually result from court and tribunal fees. They are not waived when the immigration minister acknowledges that a person is eligible for Australia's protection.[37]

~~~~~~~~

Article 1 of the Convention Against Torture was the basis for supporting the claims of most of this cohort of people. ICCPR Article 7 also states: 'No-one shall be subjected to torture or to cruel, inhuman or degrading treatment or punishment'. Article 33(1) of the 1951 Refugees Convention, which was believed to be an added protection, clearly states:

> No Contracting State shall expel or return (*refouler*) a refugee in any manner whatsoever to the frontiers of territories where his [or her] life or freedom would be threatened on account of his [or her] race, religion, nationality, membership of a particular social group or political opinion.

Not assessing claims appropriately is abuse of power. It is also inhumane and degrading. The moral integrity of a minister who shows little respect for tribunal decisions in favour of people seeking protection must be questioned. Rather than accept the 'independent' umpire's decision, the minister sometimes challenged them in the courts. A successful challenge is an opportunity for the minister to further tighten refugee law and to intimidate reviewers, who might hesitate in the future to find a person in need of protection.

Assessors' integrity can be questioned when, while admitting they had questions about information on application forms, they reached a negative outcome without interviewing the appropriate people. Tribunal reviewers' integrity can be questioned when they do not allow women their own review of their application assessment decision. The migration agent encouraged Zofia to wait until her husband arrived before submitting an application, which then focused on his claims. In other cases, they did not assess child applications in accordance with child refugee needs, nor did they access documents pertaining to the review of one person's application and decision but accessed the files of other family members who had been previously refused protection (children of Orlondo and Belicia, Jaime and Ladonna and Olek and Zofia).

This cohort of people arriving by plane seeking protection arrived at a particularly difficult time. Because Prime Minister Howard's defensive approach to sovereignty would not countenance international or domestic criticism, he denied Australians and people seeking protection recourse to Australia's international obligations. Immigration policies and practices, especially the prohibition of the right to earn a living, had wide-ranging effects. Multiple human rights breaches experienced consecutively exacerbated the adverse effects of lengthy prejudiced assessments. Lack of access to social services while awaiting decisions on protection claims compounded these problems. The adverse experiences of people who arrive by plane seeking protection illustrate the consequences of exclusionary policies and practices of a government that bestowed upon itself the power to forgo its international obligations.

Under international law there are no privileged or marginalised people. All people are equal without exception or discrimination.

~~~~~~~~

37. Orlondo and Belicia's application for a loan to buy a house was refused because their name had been put on a bad debt register. When they alerted the department about others at that time receiving waivers when they were granted refugee visas, their name was not removed from the register. Years later, when they went for a short holiday, on their return, customs officers at the airport took Belicia into a room and reminded her that she had an outstanding debt with the government.

8. The impact of a successful court challenge

Olek and Zofia got lucky. They didn't receive the dreaded brown envelope. During the nine-year gap between the negative assessment of their claims and their opportunity for appeal, a successful court challenge by Mr Chan Ta Srey turned around the policy disallowing appeal if not submitted within the limited timeframe.[38] Anyone who had been affected by this restrictive practice could subsequently take their case to the tribunal to appeal their initial assessment. Redberry was no longer working at the tribunal. Mark Sporton was nearing the end of his tenure, and a KPI-driven decision was no longer an imperative. Why worry about quotas if you had one foot out the door? John Howard was no longer Prime Minister and Philip Ruddock no longer responsible for the immigration portfolio. The stars were aligned. Such is the arbitrary nature of the review process.

Olek and Zofia hadn't received their refugee determination assessment decision – the brown envelope – during the prescribed time for submitting an application for review. According to an internal memo, the address to which their initial negative decision was sent was correct, but the certified mail was returned. This suggests that the note left in the letter box providing instructions to collect the registered letter wasn't understood by the intended recipients whose English was very poor. Eventually, the couple retrieved their papers from the migration agent who hadn't notified or contacted them about a review. They then contacted the tribunal but were advised that their application wasn't valid because it was outside the mandatory time limit.

Zofia and Olek's protection application and Kalyna's were both assessed by Ben Bodham. Predictably, both had negative outcomes, allowing for the possibility of a conflict of interest on Bodham's part. It was highly unlikely that Bodham would contradict his previous decision. The parents hadn't been granted an interview after submitting their protection application, or the child's application. Such an interview would have exposed a very obvious facial scar from Olek's left ear to the corner of his mouth that may have verified a claim of persecution.

Two successful High Court challenges took place after Olek and Zofia's assessments, but before their tribunal hearing. The outcome of one of these challenges gave some people the right to a review. The second was relevant to this family.[39] Reviewer Mark Sporton's tribunal decision accepted that

---

38. *Chan Ta Srey v Minister for Immigration & Multicultural & Indigenous Affairs* [2003] FCA 1292 (12 November 2003), commonly known as 'Srey affected' applications.
39. *Dranichnikov v Minister for Immigration and Multicultural Affairs* [2003] HCA 26.

'there were certain similarities between his case and another one'. A short interview did take place, but Sporton stated that he was inclined to approve Olek and Zofia's protection visa application on the papers submitted.

In the nine years between Kalyna's tribunal decision and Olek and Zofia's, Australia's political environment had changed. A change of government took place in December 2007. Although not as high as Minister Vanstone's figures, significantly more decisions were 'set aside' – in other words, favourable to those seeking protection – in 2009 than in 2000 (see table below). Chris Evans was appointed Minister for Immigration in the Rudd Labor government at the time of Olek and Zofia's decision, while Philip Ruddock had been Minister for Immigration in the previous Howard government at the time of the two refugee assessments and Kalyna's tribunal review.

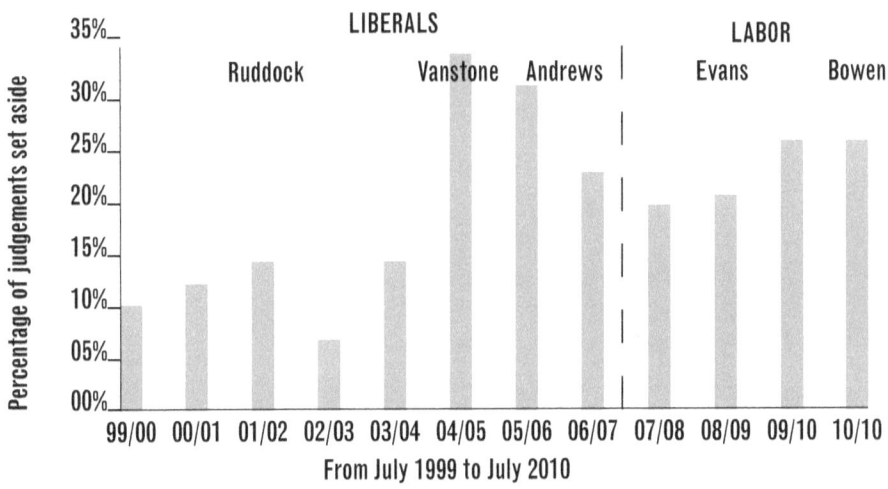

Favourable review tribunal decisions by minister (percentage), 1999–2010.
Source: Refugee/Migration Review Tribunal Annual Reports 2002/2003-2009/2010.

It was the custom in the department for the same assessor to examine multiple applications for protection from the same family. Bodham examined Olek and Zofia's initial application and also Kalyna's. Inglet assessed two of Orlondo and Belicia's. Assessors sometimes did a cut-and-paste job from a previous decision, occasionally neglecting to update names and other relevant details. However, a different tribunal reviewer heard Olek and Zofia's appeal, but still accessed all files relating to the family's previous negative assessments and reviews.

An analysis of the decision process, as well as the low but consistent rate of favourable decisions, may suggest that reviewers knew that there was an unspoken expectation that an unfavourable decision rate was more acceptable. More broadly, this pattern indicates a structural problem of systemic exclusion of a vulnerable group within Australian society, namely, people arriving by plane seeking protection. It may also suggest that a quota had been imposed for the few positive outcomes for people seeking protection, implying possible ministerial interference.

In my estimation, in any independent system, a person is a refugee regardless of a cut-off point. A friend and former tribunal member did not reapply to renew her tenure because she would not operate under a quota system. Talk of a quota system was rife but, curiously, there was no evidence confirming this. According to a former diplomat, the quota was 20% in favour and 80% unfavourable at the time he was at the tribunal. He did not observe the quota for making unfavourable decisions, and for this he paid the price. Although he was recommended by three people, the minister didn't renew his five-year contract.

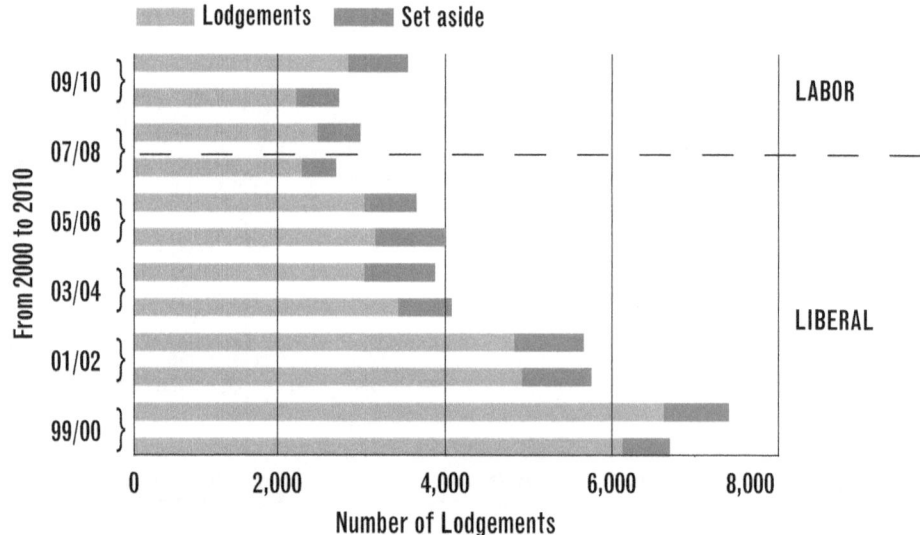

Favourable review tribunal decisions and applications for reviews lodged (no.) 1999–2010.
Source: Refugee/Migration Review Tribunal Annual Reports 2002/2003-2009/2010

In 2000, there was a high rate of lodgments of decisions for review and fewer favourable decisions, whereas in 2009 there were fewer lodgments and a slight proportional increase in favourable decisions. There was a possible increase in favourable assessments at the refugee determination stage, which might account for the lower review lodgment figures. There were fewer people seeking protection in Australia during the latter years, a high proportion of unsuccessful assessments, and a low rate of favourable tribunal reviews across the years.

~~~~~~~~

Olek and Zofia felt that both baby Kalyna's and their own negative assessments were unjust. They were too afraid to return to their country of origin. Despite the difficulties and for their own safety, they opted to live in the community without legal status for many years rather than return to a dangerous situation. Following negative tribunal reviews, Mateo and Jaime and his wife Ladonna did likewise.

The United Nations Convention on the Rights of the Child (CROC) which emphasizes that which is 'in the child's best interest' is an important document seemingly overlooked by Redberry when deciding Kalyna's future. In 2012, the Principal Member (CEO) at the tribunal provided an insight as to why. He claimed that there was no policy requiring decision-makers to take into account these guidelines. He said the UNHCR guidelines can provide guidance, but are not themselves binding, adding that, 'it would be an error of law to regard them as such'.[40]

While there was uniform recognition of the family's core claims, Redberry found Kalyna was not a refugee and yet Sporton found Olek and Zofia *were* refugees. After having presented background information regarding the family's claims, both reviews recorded the same material regarding the relevant law, although Sporton's review included extra court references. Both reviews documented in full the lengthy statutory declaration submitted by Zofia in Redberry's review. This illustrated the arbitrary nature of decision-making, where a successful outcome can be the 'luck of the draw' when it comes to a reviewer's decision to validate protection claims or not. Sporton's decision indicated that Redberry's decision about Kalyna was incorrect. Whether the decision was subject to personal or political bias is unclear. Nevertheless, it indicates that some opinions were more 'correct' than others.

Sporton stated openly that what Olek and Zofia asserted had, from the outset, been attested to and at no stage had been disputed in nearly 11 years. In the earlier review, Redberry claimed that, as Kalyna was two months old, her claims were presented on her behalf by her parents, *whose previous application for a protection visa had failed*. A stark difference in interpretations.

Having accessed the family files, Redberry knew that Kalyna's parents had not had the opportunity to test the failure of the previous application at a tribunal. An impartial statement wouldn't have changed the fact that Kalyna's parents represented her. However, including the phrase *whose*

---

40. A further set of guidelines was produced by UNHCR in 2009, 'Child Asylum Claims Under Articles 1(A)2 and 1(F) of the 1951 Convention and/or 1967 Protocol Relating to the Status of Refugees', https://www.unhcr.org/en-au/publications/legal/50ae46309/guidelines-international-protection-8-child-asylum-claims-under-articles.html. Accessed March 2022.

previous application for a protection visa had failed might add weight to an argument for a negative review at the same time, and it indicates a preconceived bias towards such a decision. Redberry would have known that the determination assessment had not been reviewed at a tribunal hearing. Nevertheless, what we cannot doubt may simply be based on a very deeply rooted habit of thought and may well be false.

There is a serious need for intellectual honesty and the awareness that the power of suggestion predisposes people to accept something independently of reasonable grounds. Redberry's erroneous thinking may not have been because she lacked knowledge of logic but because there were obstacles in her own mind or prejudices on certain subjects. While Redberry could have had a fixed adverse viewpoint, there may have been other obstacles, including performance ratings, governed by quotas for preferencing negative decisions and the political environment.

~~~~~~~~

At Kalyna's tribunal hearing, her parents had their first opportunity to discuss their claims face-to-face. Previous decisions had been made without an interview. Redberry claimed that Kalyna's case was not a de facto review of the merits of her parents' previous case. However, she could still have been guided by considering what happened to members of Olek's family.

It is unclear whether Redberry understood that the 'particular social group' referred to Kalyna's family rather than Kalyna's father's family. In not focusing on Kalyna's family, Redberry is consistent with, and possibly influenced by Bodham's interpretation in Kalyna's refugee determination assessment, which Redberry was 'independently' reviewing. Bodham's original assessment found that the criminal elements' interests did not include her grandparents but were limited to Kalyna's biological father, implying a lack of interest not only in extended family but also in Kalyna, Olek's daughter.

Evasive strategies matter most when they have serious practical consequences. For this family, the consequences were either withdrawal from the immigration process soon after having received such a misconceived and unfair review or the likelihood of persecution if they returned to their former country.

Kalyna's mother Zofia described what it was like for her after she and her daughter Daryna (Kalyna's half-sister) moved in with Olek. There were years of extortion threats and payments and Zofia was anxious when Olek could no longer pay. Feeling she and her daughter were vulnerable, they sent Daryna to relatives in the countryside. She feared being killed or attacked. Her husband's face was slashed and another assault resulted in a broken leg. She received threatening calls as did the wives and children of the other four partners in the business. Olek reported the attacks to no avail and was disappointed and angry at having to leave the country because their lives had been 'ruined by criminals'. Olek's parents were threatened and had to move. Zofia strongly believed that they would all be at risk if they had to return.

Zofia said it was well known that the mafia wouldn't hesitate to persecute members of the family of a person who refused to comply with their demands. If they didn't achieve what they wanted, they would harm family members out of anger and revenge, and to teach others a lesson. This is why they sent Daryna away. Obviously, she and Kalyna, her baby, would be at risk of being harmed directly or indirectly had they been returned. It may sound extreme to a person who does not live in that country, but the mafia would kill or harm a baby if they thought it was in their interests.

When she heard that their business partners had all left the country, Redberry noted that nothing had happened to Daryna or 'the applicant's brother' (she probably meant the applicant's uncle, as Kalyna had no brothers). Redberry went on to refer to 'the applicant's husband's parents' receiving phone calls and threats related to 'the applicant's husband' inaccurate statements, since the applicant was a baby at the time. This confusion about the identity of the person whose case was under review was further blurred by Redberry's statement at the outset of the hearing that, 'only the applicant child is the subject of the primary decision for which review is sought'. Redberry's use of the word 'applicant' in the case of Kalyna's father or mother is technical jargon used with an overbearing technique of suggestion. It gave Redberry scope to overlook the case of the 'principal applicant', Kalyna, and cloud the issue as to whose case was being examined.

Redberry required Zofia to set out her experiences, then indicated that she would be guided by what happened to members of Kalyna's father's family. By choosing this path, Redberry deliberately discounted the persecution experienced by Kalyna's father. These strategies are poignant because if Redberry had directed her attention to Kalyna's family and her father's persecution, the outcome of this review might have been significantly different.

Including extended family may not have been enough to change Redberry's conclusion, but it may have created doubt about her ability to establish a fair review. It may also have raised suspicions that Redberry had decided on an unfavourable decision before the interview began.

In her affidavit, Zofia pointed out that the solicitor described the particular social group she belonged to as comprising her husband and *his* 'immediate family members'. The mistake of using 'his' rather than 'our' or 'the child's' left it open for Bodham (in his initial protection assessment) and, later, Redberry to broaden the definition of family to include Kalyna's extended family, as opposed to her immediate family. The similarity of thought could not be coincidental given the access Redberry had to departmental files and was consistent with not departing from 'a previously established view' – a clear example of 'consistency' jeopardising fairness and impartiality, and the independence of reviewers at the tribunal.

Kalyna's mother claimed it was precisely their membership of the group of immediate family members that meant they would 'face a very high risk of serious harm which would amount to persecution' if returned. She said that it was public knowledge that mafia had infiltrated the government and police. Even if they lived in another region, they would always be looking over their shoulders, wondering when they would be discovered. Zofia concluded that they would be in a very vulnerable position if they returned, and the risk of serious harm was high.

At the time of Bodham's two assessments and Kalyna's review by Redberry, the immediate family could have been recognised legitimately as 'a particular social group'. This means Kalyna could have claimed fear of persecution as a member of a family whose father had been persecuted. By broadening the definition of family to include extended family, Bodham and Redberry failed to focus on Kalyna's best interests by recognising the vulnerability of her immediate family. Kalyna's legitimate fear of persecution is demonstrated by the fact that one significant member was persecuted because he refused to comply with extortionist demands and the state would not protect him. Redberry's collusion with Bodham maintained 'consistency in decision-making' but demonstrated a lack of independence regarding the merits of the review.

In his review, Sporton could also have been tempted to deviate from Olek's 'core initial claims' and speculate on the danger to the broader family social group but, instead, he bypassed Bodham and Redberry's conclusions and made an independent decision that was not consistent with the previous assessments.

Redberry argued that 'no member of the particular social group *in question* has suffered harm that could be called persecution for reason of their membership of that group'. The argument was that neither the extended family nor Kalyna's mother and half-sister had been physically harmed.

Conveniently for Redberry but, unfortunately, for Olek, Zofia and Kalyna, the merits of the particular social group *claimed by the applicants* were not reviewed. These were the very claims on which Sporton based his decision when he found Olek and Zofia to be refugees.

Redberry speculated that Daryna was sent to the countryside not because of a fear of persecution but for better educational opportunities and to be voluntarily reunited with Zofia's estranged husband. Zofia denied this, claiming it was because of the threatening phone calls. Reviewers can be tempted to make their judgements without the necessary basis of fact, but speculation should not replace observation and interpretation of facts. Redberry had before her a five-page statutory declaration detailing Olek's, Zofia's and Daryna's traumas. Why would Redberry turn legitimate facts into an argument based on false premises? There is no factual basis for concluding that the move 'may have been voluntary, perhaps based on a desire to be with her father and/or superior educational opportunities'.

Redberry questioned Zofia at length on numerous details about her threatening experiences and how she managed during these unpredictable times. She discussed with Zofia Olek's business partners; the assault on Olek; the process of reporting the incident to police; the decision of the business partners to close down; and their decision to leave the country. Difficulties obtaining visas and arriving in Australia were recorded. Redberry concluded that despite all that had been discussed about Olek's experiences of persecution by extortionists, she did not ask Zofia to 'repeat orally' the events that overtook Olek. Redberry concluded that Zofia had not personally been party to these events and did not invite Zofia to comment on the *impact* of these events on her and her child.

By not discussing the impact of Olek's persecution on Zofia, it appears that Olek's persecution was of little interest to Redberry. Although Redberry noted Olek's business in some detail in Zofia's affidavit, Zofia was not employed in the business. Redberry, rather conveniently, did not discuss with Zofia 'the events that overtook' her husband because of a lack of personal involvement. Redberry avoided discussion around 'the core claims' about Kalyna's father, the very point that Mark Sporton relied upon when finding Olek to be a refugee nine years later.

Similarly, in the review of Grisha and Inna, Redberry reported that the core claim in country A (Claim 1) revolved around the murder of Inna's husband who was Grisha's father. The claim was concisely outlined by the adviser who emphasised the manipulation of the justice system. State authorities were involved in the cover-up, using state organisations. Therefore, the case was a political Convention-related claim. In her review, Redberry derided the adviser and introduced a fake dilemma. She complained that it was 'immensely difficult' because Inna had introduced new issues 'during her lengthy oral testimony that conflated many events so that one seems to be dependent on another, or the cause of some particular consequence'. Redberry concluded that 'when examined dispassionately, a number of incidents of unrelated (sic); or their history has been re-written or re-interpreted'. In raising this dilemma, Redberry created a distinction. Despite her 'dispassionate' review, Redberry worried about whether the incidences of persecution are related or historically correct, rather than examining the nexus between incidences and the Refugees Convention. Redberry appears overwhelmed by the amount of information. She repeats the words 'long and complicated' and 'complex'. Her persistent claims of vagueness may relate either to her own inability to understand the culture, or an unwillingness to delve into the specifics of the claims.

In a third review, that of Nankunda's case, Redberry avoids discussion of significant claims. Nankunda's review document has no mention of Redberry discussing significant aspects of the young woman's initial claim that, if returned, she could 'picture herself being tortured and raped'. Redberry noted that Nankunda's initial application included an article requesting an inquiry into an attack on a journalist who had done an investigative report on whether torture was used in 'safe houses' run by the security agencies. However, there was no evidence that Redberry explored the significance for Nankunda of 'safe houses', a term mentioned three times in her original application. A 'safe house' in Australia would mean a place of refuge. In this context an exploration of the nexus between 'torture in safe houses' and her 'picture' of torture and rape, may have provided the psychological and emotional space for Nankunda to clarify what was revealed, much later in her immigration process, as her key claim. She had in fact been raped more than once and tortured while detained in a 'safe house'.

A reviewer who omits investigation of aspects of core claims, including references to possible experiences of persecution, is scarcely credible. Ben Bodham in his assessment and Ros Redberry in her review did not recognise Kalyna's immediate family as a 'particular social group'; Angelina Pilon in her assessment and Redberry in her review did not recognise the significance of the reference to 'torture in safe houses' in Nankunda's initial application for protection; and Redberry in her review derided Inna's advisers regarding government collusion in the murder of her husband.

This emerging pattern of avoidance suggests that some reviewers did not want to identify claims that might mean that people seeking protection would be found to be refugees.

~~~~~~~~

9. An inquisitorial process

When reviewers interview people seeking protection, they have had a disincentive to find them to be refugees because of pressure to meet targets. Reviewers may come to their decisions quite quickly, without exploring with the person or family in more depth or detail the nature of their protection claims. Conversely, they may question a person in order to build a case for the implausibility of their claims: in other words, refusing to believe them.

When Olek and Zofia were invited to focus on Kalyna's future, and the possibility she would be vulnerable to persecution, Redberry redirected the focus to them. A judgement based on substitution, however, will inevitably be biased in predictable ways.

According to Redberry, she sought to move from a general appraisal of the situation to a more specific one. She suggested 'that the "gangsters" (if such they were) who harassed the applicant's husband previously would no longer be interested in him as he no longer has a business'. Kalyna, a two-months-old baby, was the applicant, and too young to have a husband! Only two years earlier, Kalyna's father had had his leg broken because he was unwilling to pay extortionists. Understandably, he retained his fear of 'the gangsters'. Redberry's speculation that they had lost interest in him, that the danger had evaporated so soon, was without evidence.

The bracketed phrase, 'if such they were', suggests Redberry's disbelief or even cynicism. Redberry's unwillingness to imagine or consider more broadly amounts to drawing conclusions from her limited experience rather than accepting the observed facts. Redberry tended to judge problems from her own experience. She seemed unwilling, or unable, to consider information outside her world, or contrary to her values and beliefs.

Redberry found Nankunda's claims 'implausible' six times, 'unbelievable' or 'incredible' once, and twice said they 'lacked credibility'. Redberry came to the bizarre and damaging conclusion:

> ... that the claims put forward by the applicant in her written testimony, and re-stated (more or less) with a number of additional aspects in her oral testimony, are mere assertions. They are not based on true incidents involving the applicant, but rather, were composed using ideas and terminology the applicant found in the fairly random assortment of articles downloaded from the internet prior to her writing her protection visa application.

> The Tribunal has considered the applicant's oblique and unpursued references to harm occurring in [the year she was born]; harm which killed her father and brothers.

Here we have a failed strategy, a complex contradiction. Similarly, in Nankunda's case, Redberry quotes various sources of country information which testify to the fact that the organisation which Nankunda claimed to be working for remained under the direct authority of the president. She discovered that although the organisation was primarily an intelligence-gathering body, its operatives had the power to arrest and detain civilians. Redberry quoted a document confirming that 'the police Human Rights Desk ... received 620 new complaints, including allegations of excessive force, torture, assault, rape, and murder'. Another article that Redberry read stated that: 'A Judicial Commission of Inquiry Report into corruption in the police force ... was set up to investigate incidents of mismanagement and abuse of office, brutality, killings, theft, and robbery by police forces'. Despite this information, Redberry asserted that Nankunda was not telling the truth.

~~~~~~~~

Redberry was not alone in her inability to comprehend violence in a foreign country. Sally Bland mentioned the word 'implausible' four times in Jaime and Ladonna's review and found that the political party Jaime belonged to was in financial difficulty and party members were threatened and assassinated. At least two deaths occurred in the previous few years. Bland accepted that Jaime was a party member for about seven years and agreed with Inglet that Jaime was 'one of some hundred active members'. She did not accept that Jaime received threats and speculated that it was *extremely odd* that Jaime was threatened 'out of the blue and after years of being publicly active in the party without incident, over a 5-day period', and that they resumed again for a few days nearly a year later. She found the time periods *suspicious*, as the first set just predated the time he got a passport and the latter just predated his departure.

Bland suggested that Jaime could relocate elsewhere and remarked that 'his response was confused'. She 'had great difficulty getting a coherent oral account', an indication that Jaime could have been traumatised. For Bland to find intermittent threats 'extremely odd' and 'suspicious' is on the one hand, understandable given that Jaime's adviser was found to have embellished some people's claims. However, Bland had had many years' experience in government positions in DFAT in Canberra and overseas, and several years' experience at the tribunal. It is surprising that she could have been unaware of the crisis emerging in Jaime's country which led to UNHCR producing a document regarding 'international protection considerations' for this country.

The practice of saying over and over again something which is to be believed is known as 'repeated affirmation', a process that makes use of 'human suggestibility'. It has been known to be practised by those wishing to influence opinion. People who repeat themselves using similar but slightly different words do this partly to avoid monotony, and partly to conceal the method. This technique was evident in a large number of decisions that I read. It caused me to become suspicious of the truthfulness and authenticity of the review or assessment.

In attempting to engage Zofia to focus specifically on the dangers Kalyna would encounter, Redberry shifted to a discussion on possible relocation. Redberry then made a tenuous connection between Zofia's earlier claim of the need to change names in order to facilitate visas because they were 'already thinking of going somewhere'. While it is unclear in her decision whether this meant to another country or another town within the same country, Redberry speculated that the change of names meant that if they moved to a different part of the country, Olek would have a new name and could thus begin afresh. Redberry's conjecture was confirmed as mere speculation later in her review when she found that Zofia and Olek 'said no goodbyes, they just disappeared. People probably think they are dead'. Redberry claimed that she put it to Zofia that the latter point would be to their advantage: they should be able to start again elsewhere with no ties to the past. Zofia informed Redberry that in that country, when people move from one city to another, they must register their presence using their official identity card. Therefore, new names would not be useful.

Rather than recognising a previous error of judgement, Redberry referred back to her speculation to confirm her belief that taking on new names allowed relocation within the country. Clearly, for Redberry, 'relocate' had a specific meaning, however, for Zofia 'thinking of going somewhere' did not mean local relocation. A sound argument based on false premises does not prove the conclusion.[41] When information is scarce, which is common, there can be a tendency to jump to conclusions. If a satisfactory answer to a hard question is not found quickly, a person will find a related question that is easier and answer it.[42]

Diversion is another common device. This is the defense of a proposition by another proposition which does not prove the first one, but which diverts the discussion to another question, generally one about which the person who makes the diversion feels more certain.

As Redberry noted, Olek disagreed with her view that the extortionists would lose interest if they relocated. He claimed Kalyna would suffer 'because mafia do not forgive', and because 'he has caused the mafia a lot of trouble and if they cannot get him, they could get his wife or child'. Redberry found that one threat made to Kalyna's mother was to

---

41. Thouless, op. cit., p.50.
42. Kahneman, D, 2011, *Thinking, Fast and Slow*, Farrar, Straus and Giroux, New York, p.97.

the effect that if she didn't bring Olek to his senses, Zofia would *bear the responsibility*. Redberry then created a diversion by responding to an earlier suggestion by Olek that Kalyna would be denied an education. She pointed out that Kalyna would not be denied the usual state services. The adviser explained further the infiltration of mafia in departments such as education. Zofia, in returning to the point, claimed that 'the wife and daughter are the most vulnerable part of the family. Threats, blackmail and other harassment were made by way of wives and children'.

Redberry then turned her attention to the claims of threats made toward Zofia, namely, that she would 'bear the responsibility' and that she and Kalyna would 'pay the price'. Redberry interpreted this in a way whereby 'bearing the responsibility' did not mean a threat of attack on Zofia but rather, that Zofia would be made responsible for an attack on Olek, because she could not persuade him and his company to pay extortionists. This suggestion that Zofia would be responsible for an attack on her husband allowed Redberry to conclude that Zofia was not the target of harm. Redberry further claimed that 'no harm befell them'. She didn't discriminate between physical and psychological harm resulting from intimidation. Because Zofia did not change her address or workplace, Redberry again surmised that extortionists had no interest in her. Redberry doesn't indicate whether or not she discussed with Zofia extra precautions she may have taken to avoid extortionists fulfilling their threats. Redberry could properly use the speculative method to suggest what might be, but not to conclude what is.

Olek and Zofia did not remain in the country to pursue the cases of assault lodged with the police, 'and indeed were not available to assist with further enquiries'. Redberry concluded from this that she was 'not satisfied on the evidence before her that the state had been unwilling or unable to offer its protection to Olek'. The further attack resulting in a broken leg that precipitated Olek's departure was not considered. In contrast, at the later tribunal hearing, Mark Sporton stated that the core claim included the fact that 'his request for assistance had been declined' and he was satisfied with the summary of claims presented by Redberry regarding the decision on Kalyna's application.

Redberry referred to a document reporting that 'journalists who write on organised crime and corruption, are at risk', 'as are "businessmen, tax inspectors and politicians who refuse to co-operate with organised crime figures"'. Redberry argued that the article makes no mention of family members *being the first to be targeted*. After mentioning that 'a number of killings are enumerated', she noted a wife's involvement in a robbery. Redberry then concluded that she 'found no evidence that family members were at risk when organised crime targeted businessmen or other figures'. The report that businessmen are at risk is consistent with the original claim. However, effectively targeting wives and children does not translate to 'family members being the first to be targeted', which was Redberry's interpretation of 'will always' in her conclusion that Olek was harmed in an assault. Redberry concluded that this negated Kalyna's parents' 'claims that gangs *will always target the wife and children* as the most effective means of getting at the intended victim. This was a claim which the applicant mother repeated several times'. Redberry stressed the word 'always'. Such an argument does not negate the fact that wives and children are targeted and remain vulnerable.

There was no evidence to suggest that Redberry's unfavourable review was challenged in court. A request for consideration on humanitarian grounds citing a similar case with a successful review was submitted to Mr Ruddock but he declined to intervene in Kalyna's case.

It seems that, following the negative and adverse review of Bodham's negative assessment for Kalyna, Olek and Zofia opted to remain in the community without legal status because of their fear of further persecution if they returned to their country of origin.

It was at this point of their journey towards residency in Australia that I first met Olek and Zofia. There seemed no hope of gaining protection in Australia. They were very vulnerable. This was the moment they were about to give up the quest, ten long years after submitting their first application for protection. They had tragically lost a child, Natalka. Their surviving daughter Kalyna, born and bred in Australia, was now nine years old.

Reluctantly, they were packing for the trip back to the country where they had suffered so much. They were saying their goodbyes to friends they had nurtured here in Australia when I was asked to speak to them. How could I refuse the beekeeper who generously gave me unadulterated honey? After I read their documents, I was confident they deserved a better deal.

The first hurdle was to obtain a visa that would grant them legal status. A request couldn't be submitted to the minister if Olek and Zofia were not legally in Australia. It was a gamble. I persuaded them that they would have to come out of the shadows. They weren't enthusiastic. We hatched a plan.

After spending a few days forensically examining the material provided by the Freedom of Information Office, I put together a detailed account of Olek and Zofia's efforts to gain Australia's protection. This included mention of an earlier case where a man in similar circumstances successfully engaged the court in his pursuit of a safe place to live and raise his family. I was mystified that there was no evidence of Olek and Zofia's appealing their decision at the review tribunal.

With this proposed request to the minister in hand, Olek, Zofia and I tentatively fronted the compliance officer. We convinced the officer that the request could be sent to the minister as soon as Olek and Zofia received a temporary visa allowing them to be legally in Australia. He obliged and granted a two-week temporary visa. We met for the mandatory coffee and debrief at the coffee shop across the courtyard. The aroma of freshly baked pastries was inviting. We celebrated this promising step and soaked in the temporary relief from the anxiety and tensions Olek and Zofia had endured for many years.

Ten years after arriving in Australia, on Olek and Zofia's behalf I submitted a nineteen-page document in support of a ministerial request to intervene in their case. When their case was in the system, Olek and Zofia were then granted three-monthly visas until the minister made a decision.

The department requested further information, and Olek and Zofia were advised that their initial protection application assessment was 'Srey affected', a reference to a successful 2003 High Court challenge by Chan Ta Srey to the minister that entitled them to have their assessment reviewed at the tribunal. The earlier nineteen-page document was submitted to the tribunal in support of their case. In keeping with well tested tradition, we met about fifteen minutes before the tribunal hearing to discuss the process and go over the court-like routine. The need to look the reviewer in the eye when speaking rather than turning to the interpreter was important. Interestingly, in traditional communities, Aboriginal Australians are uncomfortable looking elders and figures of authority directly in the eye. In court, this has led to false assumptions of evasiveness and even guilt when it is actually respect that is being signalled. Stay calm, answer questions truthfully. One could never predict the outcome. Whatever will be, will be.

Whenever I walked into the hearing room, my heart slightly lifted or my hopes plummeted as soon as I cast my eyes towards the name on the desk. With some reviewers, I wanted to leave immediately. I already knew the outcome and that the hearing would be farcical, a stressful waste of time. I would stay because I didn't want to alarm the people enduring what promised to be a ludicrous process. A couple of memories remain imprinted on my mind.

On one occasion, I was sitting quietly in the back of the tiny room taking notes, as was my practice. This must have disturbed one reviewer. He knew I wasn't a lawyer. I declared that I was a support person. He was not satisfied and suggested that I might be acting illegally. I took this serious intimidatory accusation to a barrister who simply replied, 'Bring it on'!

My second recollection is of a hearing about a claim of female genital cutting where a male was appointed to review this sensitive material. When

I heard his name, my blood boiled. I complained to the person in charge of the tribunal, pointing out the insensitivity of appointing a male reviewer in these delicate circumstances. Fortunately for the young woman, he was taken off the case and she received a favourable outcome.

On the day I walked into the tiny room with Olek and Zofia, I immediately read the name on the desk. I had never heard of Mark Sporton, even though he was in his ninth year at the tribunal. Notebook in hand, I remained cautious as the hearing began. Sporton pointed out that he was making a decision on Olek and Zofia, not Kalyna. Her case had been reviewed years earlier.

In his assessment of the claims, Sporton did not accept 'many of the propositions put forward over the years'. However, he stated that, based on the nineteen-page ministerial intervention request, he found that Olek 'had already established his claims for refugee status to his satisfaction'. Sporton recognised Olek and Zofia's core initial claims as presented in the protection application that they had a well-founded fear of being persecuted or murdered by corrupt state officials and/or criminals if returned: Olek's request for assistance and protection had been declined by state authorities; he had been repeatedly assaulted and attacked by racketeers. Sporton had checked on the danger the family might face given that eleven years had passed since the couple had fled. He identified the central issue as being that whether Olek 'received effective State protection' at the time and, more particularly, would do so in the future if he returned, not whether Olek had a well-founded fear of serious harm amounting to persecution 'because of these attacks by gangsters'. Sporton's review contained thirteen paragraphs of country information supporting Olek's claims and also found the previously submitted reference to the High Court's decision of 2003 to be 'directly relevant'.

Importantly, he found that Olek was 'consistent and honest' and 'has not at any stage sought to embellish' his claims. He concluded that he was 'a credible witness'. In other words, nothing was 'implausible'. Sporton also considered the Convention link: 'his particular social group as an independent businessman who reported attacks to the authorities' and whether or not there would be 'effective state protection from the criminal elements who are continuing to operate'.

Sporton concluded that Olek's 'fear of again experiencing serious harm amounting to persecution because of his particular social group is in this case sufficient to be a well-founded fear, notwithstanding the passage of time'. He wasn't satisfied that Olek would 'be able to receive effective State protection from the authorities given all his circumstances'. Sporton found Olek and Zofia to be refugees.

Even though I had warned Olek and Zofia that the hearing could take at least two hours, it was all over in about twenty minutes. Stunned, we quietly piled into the lift, rushed towards a quiet spot at a nearby cafe and breathed a heavy sigh of relief. Eleven years of anxiety almost visibly lifted from the shoulders of the couple. We needed to sit and let it sink in. Their future was assured. So too was Kalyna's. She would turn ten in a few months. The review decision was in my office by the time I arrived back. It had been faxed through.

What happened next? Olek bought a house, renovated and sold it. Olek and Zofia bought a second house. Olek had a career change. He now has a thriving house painting and maintenance business; Kalyna is a third-year student and tutor at the nearby university; and baby Natalka is now buried here in Australia. Zofia's daughter Daryna is married. She and her husband arrived in Australia on skilled migration visas. They are all Australian citizens. So too is Olek and Zofia's delightful granddaughter Daniela. Mark Sporton can sleep satisfied that his favourable review has allowed a diligent family to make a positive contribution to Australian society.

I couldn't help wondering whether all of this would have happened had Olek and Zofia received the dreaded brown envelope and their tribunal hearing had taken place ten years earlier. Given the political atmosphere then, I doubt they would have received a positive outcome. Definitely not if Redberry had reviewed their earlier negative assessment.

~~~~~~~~

Sporton wasn't the only reviewer who abided by international standards regarding the refugee status of people seeking protection. In a more recent case, I arranged for Zafar to be picked up from the psychiatric ward of a rural hospital to attend his tribunal hearing. His psychologist agreed to be a witness if interviewed by phone. Zafar was clearly vulnerable. The reviewer, Robert Roundaboot, noticed his delicate state and offered to adjourn the hearing. Zafar began sobbing, pleading to go ahead with the hearing as he could not bear the thought of coming back again. He had faced Australian authorities too many times and had reached the stage where he couldn't take any more.

With the assistance of a lawyer, the hearing proceeded. Robert Roundaboot contacted the psychologist and, shortly after, made his decision to remit the matter for reconsideration, with the direction that Zafar satisfied Section 36(2)(aa) of the Migration Act. I was so anxious that I couldn't handle a compassionate response from a reviewer. As soon as we left the room, knowing Zafar would no longer suffer, I burst into tears of relief. Zafar's case is an example of the best and the worst of authority figures assessing and reviewing the claims of vulnerable people seeking protection.

Before his visa was finalised, Zafar had to submit police checks and undergo health checks. These procedural requirements usually take a couple of months but the department demanded a police check from a country where Zafar had never lived. There was no record of him ever entering the country, so it was an implausible and impossible request. We argued back and forth with the officer in Onshore Protection, Department of Immigration and Border Protection.

Zafar was notified that he was issued his visa eleven months and two weeks after he had been recognised as a refugee at the tribunal.

~~~~~~~~

Why did Sporton find Olek and Zofia to be refugees when the minister, a tribunal review officer and a department official on two occasions had found them not to be in need of Australia's protection? Was it Sporton's life experience before working at the tribunal or his nine years' experience there? Was it the change of government, a well-prepared submission, the influence of the successful court case, the difference between fair-minded and tricky thinking, or a more disciplined approach to the core and consistent claim? A similar case that was successful at the tribunal was submitted in support of a ministerial request but did not result in a positive outcome from Mr Ruddock in the previous Howard government. However, a previous successful similar case in the court may have influenced Sporton.

It could be concluded that 'tricky thinking' has been an influential link between the proportionally large numbers of unsuccessful claims compared to lodgements. A focus on negative outcomes supported by the practice of exclusionary decision-making was systemic and this procedure is clearly structural.

If the tribunal, supposedly an independent body, was interested in producing fair and trustworthy reviews, they would heed RH Thouless, author of *Straight and Crooked Thinking*, when he warns that,

> One obvious condition that must be fulfilled before a real discussion can take place is that both parties must have a sufficiently lowly opinion of the finality of their own judgements to be willing to have their opinions changed by what the other person tells them. That is a condition which most people find rather difficult to attain unless it is in talking to someone for whom they feel a considerable respect, but it

is a necessary condition for the discussion to be of any real value. If we are in that state of mind, discussion with another person may result in changes in our opinions not only because the other person may tell us facts that we did not know before, but because he may point out to us inconsistencies in the opinions which we already hold.[43]

If this condition were not merely a dream but a reality, there would be fewer tribunal review, court appeals and requests to the minister. With less psychological and emotional pressure on reviewers and assessors, the preposterous KPIs might become insignificant. The Department of Immigration might become less toxic without pressure to fill quotas, and if assessors were allowed to make moral and ethical judgements in accordance with international law when assessing the claims of people seeking protection. It would make sense economically, socially and perhaps, with inspirational leadership, politically.

~~~~~~~~

43. Thouless, op. cit., p.162.
44. Gageler, S, 2010, 'Impact of migration law on the development of Australian administrative law', *Journal of Administrative Law*, 17, pp.92-105.

10. The court examines tribunal reviewers' decisions

Australia has established procedures whereby people who seek protection can be excluded and expelled simply because it is within the law and the system allows it. The Australian legal system countenances serious breaches of the inalienable rights of people who arrive by plane seeking protection. People have a limited time to appeal to the Federal Court. After that period has expired, it is possible to appeal to the High Court whose only authority is to allow a hearing in the Federal Court, an expensive and round-about way of achieving justice for these outcasts of Australian democratic society. Nevertheless, in the instances discussed in this book, the Australian government vigorously defended unfavourable tribunal reviews when they were appealed against, and occasionally defended a favourable review.

In 2010, Justice Gageler, Solicitor General at the time, wrote of his concern about the high volume of migration litigation as a result of the introduction of laws limiting the power of decision-makers. He stated that: 'The most ambitious of the amendments that have been made since 2001 have been the continuations of attempts, ongoing for some time, to spell out expressly and with precision just what the procedural limitations on decision-makers are intended to be'. He continued that 'the experience has been that rigidity brings the risk not only of unfairness but occasionally of absurdity; flexibility brings the risk of uncertainty and administrative inconvenience; and getting the appropriate balance is not particularly easy'.[44] Not getting the appropriate balance can have devastating effects on ordinary people needing a safe and secure place to live their lives.

While a pending court appeal was an expensive means of remaining legally in Australia, people who arrived by plane and sought protection, if they did appeal to the courts, did not have to face the immediate prospect of being deported to the country they had fled. Some made numerous appeals, and suffered the anxiety of having to remain always within the law. They feared returning to danger in their country of origin, and worried about legal costs to defend their stay because they weren't allowed to work. Unreliable or inexperienced migration agents accentuated these tensions.

Vasyl's appeal to the Federal Court for an extension of time to enable him to make an application to the High Court for a judicial review of his tribunal decision was unsuccessful. The judge didn't appreciate 'the unsatisfactory explanation offered for the delay in making the application to the High Court and the fact that a favourable grant of relief would be unlikely'. Vasyl's solicitor submitted the application to appeal after Vasyl had made several unsuccessful ministerial requests. The Australian Government Solicitor would have been well familiar with the mind of the minister in this particular case. The judge speculated that, 'an approach to the Minister to exercise powers under s417 indicates an acceptance of the decision of the Tribunal and is not an explanation which will ordinarily justify the grant of an extension of time'.

The belief that one can discover something about real things by speculation alone is one of the most long-lived delusions in human thought. Such suppositions lead people away from the facts to the 'spinning of fanciful theories'.[45] The speculative method can suggest what might be, but conclusions should be based on facts.

It could have been contested that applying to the minister was not an acceptance of a tribunal review decision but, rather, a matter of financial disadvantage, given that Vasyl was not allowed to earn a living and could not afford to engage a lawyer at an earlier stage. While it costs nothing to submit a ministerial request, as a temporary visa-holder, Vasyl couldn't open a bank account or take out a loan. It is surprising that a lawyer would suggest instigating a court appeal if the ministerial requests would have jeopardised a court decision. The time delay was clearly not a problem for the High Court, which suggested the appeal to the Federal Court did not transgress the law. The fact that Vasyl was already 'out of time' was made out to be a matter of concern. Furthermore, the judge stated that she was strengthened in her view in that 'the only ground of review sought to be pursued if an extension of time were granted relies upon an issue not relied upon before the Tribunal'.

For the tribunal, Vasyl was assisted by a migration agent and the judge speculated that he 'may be assumed to have been familiar with the terms of the Refugees Convention and the authorities which touch upon its proper construction'.

Between 1997 and 2006 at the Refugee Review Tribunal, any migration agent with a non-English speaking background would have been hard pressed to keep abreast of the complexities of the ever-changing immigration policies. The judge's speculation and assumptions reveal reluctance to consider issues relating to the inalienable rights of Vasyl to seek Australia's protection.

The issue not relied upon by Diana Dicker at the tribunal was membership of a particular social group, comprised of people who are seen to be wealthy or potentially wealthy, but who are less powerful than other wealthy people. The judge claimed that 'it is far from self-evident that such a group would be recognised in that society as a group identifiable within the society'. Before this appeal was made, the UNHCR had produced guidelines for assessing the well-founded fear of being persecuted for reasons of a person's membership of a particular social group. The guidelines state that: 'While persecutory conduct cannot define the social group, the actions of the persecutors may serve to identify or even cause the creation of a particular social group in society' and also that 'members of a particular group need not know each other or associate with each other as a group'.[46] These guidelines include the fact that there is no requirement for group cohesiveness. The judge took a narrow approach to membership of a particular social group despite the UNHCR's 2002 guidelines. If Diana Dicker had been objective, she could have considered Vasyl's membership of a particular social group without being compelled to do so.

While the judge could not make a decision on the merits of the case (see over and Chapter 16), unlike the judge who remitted Orlondo and Belicia's case back to the tribunal for further consideration, this judge dismissed Vasyl's appeal. She deprived Vasyl of the opportunity to test his claim of membership of a particular social group. Why did she do this? Because she could.

When procedures take precedence over the content of the appeal, it is the person seeking protection, not the solicitor, who loses out. Marco's solicitor was a day late in submitting the application to appeal. The judge in this case didn't allow the appeal and claimed that not applying on time was 'incompetent'. He did not consider the consequences of incompetency for Marco and Amora, whose opportunity to challenge serious tribunal errors was lost.

I was gobsmacked each time I sat in the pews at the back of the small courtrooms. I knew nothing about the difference between 'black letter law' and the 'merits' of the case. I discovered that 'justice' was not about 'fairness' but whether the procedure in assessing a claim was 'illegal' or legal, jurisdictional or non-jurisdictional. Black letter law.

For Marco and Amora, this system was mysterious and debilitating. They were familiar with human rights law and couldn't reconcile Australian immigration law with United Nations human rights law. The Australian legal system meant that Marco and Amora were reliant on the cleverness of their legal representative to find mistakes in the previous decisions that were not accepted in law as jurisdictional errors.

45. Thouless op. cit., p.70.
46. UNHCR, 2002, *Guidelines on International Protection: 'Membership of a particular social group' within the context of Article 1A(2) of the 1951 Convention and/or its 1967 Protocol relating to the Status of Refugees*, http://www.unhcr.org/3d58de2da.html. Accessed March 2022.

Migration law was frequently changing, and community lawyers were hard pressed to keep up, but the government lawyers were highly proficient. Judges could rely on their arguments if they wanted to make an unfavourable decision. Equity and fairness were out the door especially when Amora sat alongside top government lawyers, attempting to defend herself.

When Minister Ruddock took away the possibility for a judge to decide on the merits of the case, it put judges in an invidious position where decision was constrained, even if they may have known the claims warranted recognition in law. While, in Marco's case, one judge explained that he agreed with the decisions of two other judges, he drew upon other cases in support of his decision. At the same time, he strongly recommended that Marco make a request to Minister Vanstone, where he thought Marco might receive a favourable decision. In other words, Marco's claims had merit but the judge himself could not decide on the merits of the case.

Marco's case could also have been remitted to the tribunal for further consideration. People arriving by plane seeking protection found themselves in the predicament where they trusted reviewers to be fair and open. Returning to their country of origin was too frightening to contemplate. Just as some migration agents were not up to the mark, some 'incompetent' solicitors and reluctant judges also let them down.

Although the timing of the lodgements of the appeals in two cases was the apparent fault of the lawyers, the applicants, none of whom could work to support their families, were left with the burden of paying court fees, plus the fees of the barrister (who did not appear at Marco's court hearing) and the solicitor. People seeking protection are vulnerable, reliant on legal advisers to do the right thing by them and trusting them to follow due process regarding court requirements. In not keeping up with the appeal system, some lawyers caused their clients unnecessary anxiety and difficulties. Despite the delays and difficulties in making an appeal on time, there was no redress when it came to paying the bills.

~~~~~~~~

In immigration law, an action or decision is either one that falls within decision-makers' lawful authority or it is not. 'If it falls within a decision-maker's lawful authority, then any error is made "within jurisdiction". If it does not fall within the decision-maker's lawful authority, then the error is a "jurisdictional error" and as such it cannot be a valid action or decision.'[47] Thus, if errors are made 'within jurisdiction' it follows that immigration law protects, encourages or allows reviewers to make wrongful decisions which arise from legal bias and systemic exclusion.

Two serious aspects of Nankunda's original claims were not tested in the court but they illustrate the problem with non-jurisdictional errors. The first was that Ros Redberry omitted to explore the rape and 'community house' fears at the tribunal. The second was Redberry's unfortunate undervaluing of supporting documents. Redberry knew of Nankunda's psychological state at the time of the hearing. Her psychologist had notified the tribunal that Nankunda wasn't fit to attend. The hearing went ahead. She had to be present or the appeal would be decided on the papers alone.

Regarding the second point, Redberry made the dubious assertion that Nankunda had concocted her claims using supporting documentation downloaded from the internet. Nankunda had included the documents to indicate that what happened to her was happening elsewhere in the country. Not an unreasonable claim. Redberry could make these unfair and unjust conclusions because of the 'violence of the law', to use Agamben's term, which allows Federal Parliament to create laws that are discriminatory and harmful.[48] A law that allows reviewers to make errors of judgement by claiming it is within their jurisdiction indicates a greater need for due diligence regarding the separation of powers.

In Nankunda's appeal at the Federal Magistrates Court of Australia (as it then was), the judge on this occasion found that it was 'open to the Tribunal':

1. to not make the connection regarding the nexus between Nankunda's work for a security agent and the attack on her grandmother's house;
2. to conclude that this attack was unrelated;
3. to make an adverse credibility finding;
4. to conclude that Nankunda's claims were implausible;
5. to conclude that the intimidation and extortion suffered by the mother was not part of a series of events designed to harm Nankunda;
6. to reject the claim of involvement with the security agent.

Claims 1–4 were judged to be seeking 'merits review' which was not available in The Magistrates' Court. This judge found that claims to membership of a particular social group only arose if Redberry accepted the claim that Nankunda had been a spy, that she was recruited, but refused to poison someone. The claim that, as a woman, she would not be protected by the state also depended upon the claim of her being a spy. The judge could not find jurisdictional error in the above claims because of restrictive,

---

47. Justices Hill, Branson and Stone, the Full Federal Court in *SDAV v Minister for Immigration & Multicultural & Indigenous Affairs* (2003) quoted in Gageler op. cit., p.104.
48. Agamben, G, 1998, *Homo Sacer: Sovereign Power and Bare Life*. Translated by Daniel Hedler-Roazen. Stanford University Press. USA.

discriminatory legislation such as the privative clause.[49] Immigration Minister Philip Ruddock, the doyen of unjust tightening of the screws in immigration law, has explained the 'privative clause' as a clause that 'operates to give decision-makers wider lawful operation for their decisions that reduces the grounds on which the courts can set aside such decisions as being unlawful'.[50]

Mr Ruddock's explanation indicates the Australian Parliament's willingness at that time to breach Article 2(3a) in the International Covenant on Civil and Political Rights (ICCPR). This article states that: 'Each State party to the present Covenant undertakes:

> (a) to ensure that: any person whose rights or freedoms as herein recognised are violated shall have an effective remedy, notwithstanding that the violation has been committed by persons acting in any official capacity'.

The Magistrates' Court handed down Nankunda's judgement on Christmas Eve. She didn't find out about it until mid-January. She appeared unrepresented in the Federal Court appealing for an extension of time. Despite the Government Solicitor and lawyer's claim that the appeal was 'misconceived', this particular Judge allowed the extension.

Nankunda's case is a clear example of the need for Australia to introduce human rights legislation. The unjust decision regarding Nankunda was made possible by Federal Parliament's categorisation of people arriving by plane seeking protection as non-citizens. Regardless of the constituted powers of the court, parliament had discriminated against sovereign citizens of other countries with inalienable rights.

Agamben argues it is the responsibility of the courts to challenge laws passed in the parliament that restrict the inalienable rights of all human beings. However, this isn't easy when parliament regularly attempts to introduce restrictive legislation which, in 2014, again included an act to curtail peoples' access to protection. 'Complementary protection' had been introduced in 2012 to ensure Australia's compliance with international treaty obligations, but Prime Minister Tony Abbott wanted this repealed.[51]

A court could overturn a decision if the reviewer was 'not acting in good faith' in making the decision. Notwithstanding the privative clause, in an inquisitorial process at the tribunal, one could legitimately wonder why Redberry did not ask questions that might establish issues of 'implausibility' and matters of 'credibility', in order to satisfy the criteria of 'acting in good faith'. Unlike other migration tribunals, the authority to seek information only meant that the Refugee Tribunal reviewer must respond to the claims of the person seeking protection, not explore what might be 'implausible'. This systemic bias meant that the tribunal reviewer had no obligation to seek out further information.

When the reviewer finds something to be 'implausible' but doesn't explore the claim, this doesn't meet the 'acting in good faith' test. 'Implausibility' need not be accepted as a 'within jurisdiction' error. This administrative exception is discriminatory because people seeking Australia's protection don't have equal opportunities to access the same rights as other Australians at different tribunals.

In the subsequent Federal Court hearing, Nankunda's counsel raised two concerns regarding the right to respond to issues of credibility. One of the Government's most experienced counsels objected, arguing that the government would be disadvantaged. He argued that if certain issues had been raised, the government would have run the case in The Magistrates' Court differently by seeking to cross-examine Nankunda. He concluded that to allow Nankunda to raise them now would prejudice the government.

Despite pointing out that it was possible in law to allow the inclusion of the extra matters, the judge at this time sided with a top government lawyer in concluding that the government would be prejudiced if these issues were to be raised now and, in his view, 'the interests of justice do not require it'. In his decision, this judge leant on adverse credibility questions regardless of the fact that Nankunda was not psychologically fit to appear at the tribunal hearing. Because the credibility of Ros Redberry remained unchallenged, Nankunda was the one disadvantaged by the disallowance. Without merits review in the courts, there was no hope of righting 'non-jurisdictional' errors.

This is consistent with the problem of parliament's attempts to control the courts through introducing discriminatory laws; and certain judges' ignorance of the courts' constituted powers or lack of independence regarding a separation of powers. Rather than dismiss a case, some judges would remit it to a lower court. Generally, the lower court would dismiss it, (except in the case of Orlondo and Belicia, where the court remitted their case to the tribunal, which avoided the court finding). Although Australia is supposed to be a modern democracy, the reach of the Australian Parliament extends beyond government's legitimate authority and undermines the authority of the courts and the authority of the tribunals and, most importantly, threatens individuals' human rights.

49. 'A privative clause is a provision in a statute that seeks to deny or limit review of administrative action in a designated type of case. By this means it affords some 'protection' against challenge by such means as judicial review'. Enright, C, 2012, *Anatomy of a Privative Clause*. Maitland Press, Newcastle NSW, p. xiv.
50. Ruddock, P, 2002, 'Immigration Policy and the Separation of Powers'. *Upholding the Australian Constitution*, vol. 14, The Samuel Griffith Society.
51. Migration Amendment (Regaining Control Over Australia's Protection Obligations) Bill, 2013.

It is not difficult to avoid scrutiny of significant claims. Inna and Grisha appealed Redberry's decision in the Federal Court. While they were unrepresented, the government once again provided a most experienced counsel, and another lawyer, in support of Redberry's tribunal appeal. The so-called independent body, the tribunal, is under challenge, not the government. The judge found no jurisdictional error and stated that 'the Tribunal was not obliged to take evidence by phone' and 'its explanation for not doing so was reasonable'. However, had he been contacted, the overseas lawyer might have shed light on the complicated case.

The appeal was dismissed. In Inna's and Grisha's appeal before the Full Federal Court, the three judges, in dismissing the claim, stated that the 'proceedings before the Tribunal are vitiated by her fear or duress'. Inna and Grisha's claim that 'the Tribunal viewed country and other information incorrectly' was also dismissed because 'Courts must necessarily be sceptical of claims made so late and which are not capable of being properly tested'.

Inna and Grisha's counsel, Eric Emporer, pointed out that 'the Court had power to remedy the situation on principles of justice'. However, one of the judges argued that the submission assumed that the court must accept Inna's story, which the government had not had the opportunity to test. He said the only possible ground to which such facts might be relevant is procedural fairness.

Overriding the possibility of granting Inna and Grisha an opportunity to test Inna's story, the appeal was dismissed. If the merits of Inna and Grisha's claims had been examined there may have been cause to understand why Redberry focused on a secondary issue rather than the claim of politically motivated persecution and murder of a significant family member. This omission could possibly have been considered under the 'acting in good faith' requirement. The legitimacy of considering a particular social group of family members who feared persecution according to the UNHCR Guidelines was not possible by this time. It was possible at the time of the initial determination and the tribunal review before the restrictions introduced by Mr Ruddock and the parliament. It seems strange to equate lack of 'procedural fairness' only with the government's perceived lack of opportunity to test claims, whereas being unrepresented in the unfamiliar adversarial Federal Court system, might have also been in breach of procedural fairness.

In Nankunda's case, the judge found that Redberry was 'under no obligation to put conclusions on credibility to an appellant' and that 'the jurisdiction of this Court does not extend to reviewing the Tribunal's decision', on the issue of the nexus between Nankunda's harm suffered and systematic harassment of the grandmother and mother. Given the acceptance of the claims regarding Nankunda's grandmother and mother, it was open to Redberry to dispense with the need for material to meet strict criteria for admissibility. She could have accepted the spy claim based on the nexus between the refusal to spy and kill, and the intimidation of family and extended family with whom Nankunda was living. Compounded by Nankunda's difficulties understanding Australian culture, Redberry failed to understand the facts of the case being put. This illustrates how errors of fact leading to a critical adverse finding are not open to judicial review, despite the absence of fair processes and consistent decision-making.

This judge reiterated that it was open to the tribunal to find that it did not believe Nankunda's claim. When Nankunda objected to the conclusion that the motive behind the attack was business-related, he justified Redberry's transparently wrong assumption. Section 424A does not require Redberry to invite Nankunda to comment on her conclusions. Redberry emphatically rejected these claims, not only because they were 'inherently implausible' but also because of inconsistencies in Nankunda's account.

Redberry's view that Nankunda's claims were inherently implausible was an assumption, not a fact. The judge further rejected the ground of appeal because he concluded it was an invitation to reconsider the merits of the appellant's claim. The 'evidence' of questionable 'inconsistencies' unfortunately was not substantiated by Nankunda's counsel, Mr Betts, who could have argued that documents obtained through FOI revealed Nankunda's psychological state at the time of the hearing. The judge, rather than dismissing the case on the grounds that the court could not examine the merits of the case, could have remitted the case to the tribunal for a fairer hearing.

Nankunda suffered as a result of inexperienced legal advice and rapidly changing migration policies during this period. Nankunda, Orlondo and Belicia and their daughters Latoya and Adella, as well as Ladonna and Jaime suffered from systemic discrimination because of questionable decisions of inept (or fearful) reviewers who were protected by law. Judgements made in accordance with the narrow cultural experiences of the reviewers are protected in court because of the prohibition on 'merits' reviews and allowance of errors that are 'non-jurisdictional'. The possibility of some judges being intimidated by very experienced government counsel is difficult to determine. However, the fact that some continued adversarial hearings when some people seeking protection were unrepresented indicates some degree of bias in favour of the government.

~~~~~~~~

Ros Redberry and Sally Bland completed their tribunal reviews of Nankunda, Orlondo, Belicia, Latoya and Adella and Ladonna and Jaime during the period following the peak of Minister Ruddock's court challenges to cases where tribunal reviewers had decided in favour of people seeking protection. It's not surprising that Redberry and Bland resorted to reasons such as 'implausibility' to make unfavourable decisions about refugee claims. Their knowing that Ruddock challenged favourable decisions could have intimidated them.

Court precedents are arbitrary in that they are selectively chosen or avoided to support a decision depending on the cleverness and experience of solicitors, rather than providing justice. In Nankunda's case, the judge affirmed the government's submission that leave to raise certain issues should be refused on the basis that the case differed from two previous cases. He pointed out that a party who is unrepresented, speaks little English and is unfamiliar with the Australian culture and legal system, as is the case with many people seeking protection visas, might succeed in putting a case on appeal that was not put at the trial.[52]

The judge argued that Nankunda had been represented, and dismissed the request. But in the case of Marco and Amora, in their first court appearance in Australia their judge did not refer to the judgements of 1978 and 1988, even though he recognised that Marco was unrepresented. Marco spoke little English and was 'unfamiliar with the Australian culture and legal system' which could have met the requirement of 'exceptional circumstances'.

Marco was assisted by an unqualified advocate of whom the judge remarked, 'it regrettably became quite apparent that he had no concept of the limited basis upon which this Court might intervene in judicial review proceedings under Part 8 of the Act'. This judge viewed Marco as unrepresented and in accepting the submission 'made ultimately on behalf of the respondent', dismissed the case. While he realised that he had an 'invidious task' to make a judgement when Marco was unrepresented, the fact that he did not grant an extension of time in order that Marco be adequately represented is of concern. If legal restrictions or time constraints and potential costs were the motivating factors in this decision, the fact that Marco's claims were not adequately aired borders on systemic abuse. In not giving Marco the opportunity to engage a lawyer (and counsel), the judge would have failed the 'acting in good faith' test applied to tribunal reviewers. Inexperienced though she was, Amora went to the High Court which remitted the case back to the Federal Court.

In attempting to address the need for a fair hearing, Marco's lawyer appealed again to the Federal Court. The judge this time concluded that, because Amora and Marco did not appeal the previous judgement, it was an 'abuse of the process' of the court. The judge's finding that Marco did not appeal the earlier decision merely highlights again the fact that foreigners

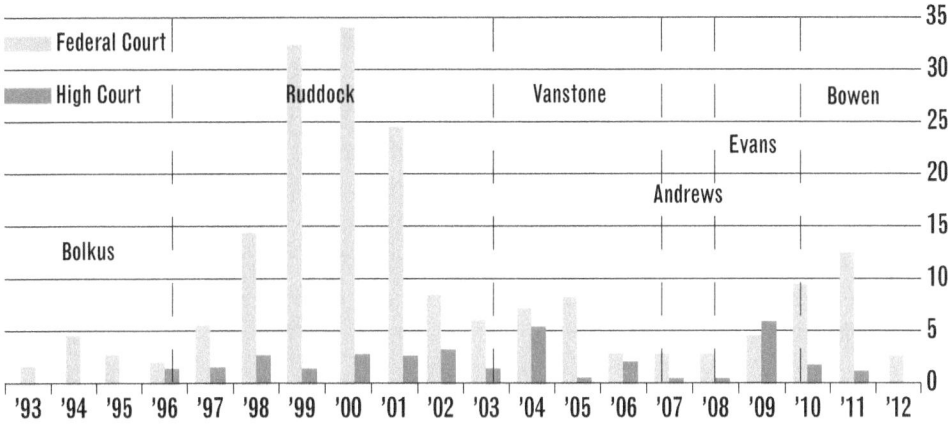

Favourable review tribunal decisions by minister (percentage) 1999–2010.
Source: Refugee/Migration Review Tribunal Annual Reports 2002/2003–2009/2010.

who are unrepresented are ignorant of their legal rights and unfamiliar with the adversarial nature of Australia's legal system. When they became aware of such rights, they were inaccessible. Again, the problem of merits versus jurisdictional review was pointed out by the judge who also found that, what was in fact sought before this court was review on the merits of Philip Hirst's tribunal review, which was not available to Marco.

The inability to accommodate Marco in either of the earlier courts could be regarded as systemic discrimination. Try as they may, Marco and Amora could not obtain a fair hearing of their legitimate claims. Marco's solicitor went back to the Federal Court again seeking an extension of time, but because she did not file and serve a Notice of Appeal within the required 21 days, there were added problems. The judge declared that the earlier decision must be seen as 'finally disposing of the subject of litigation' and that an appeal of the most recent decision was 'barred by the doctrine of *res judicata*'.[53]

The fact that this judge took the unusual step of recommending the appropriateness of ministerial intervention indicated that this family had legitimate claims to defend. For the government respondent to claim 'abuse of process' when previous court documents indicated that Marco and Amora's claims were not adequately aired or addressed illustrates

52. In *Maloney v Commissioner for Railways (NSW)* (1978) 52 ALJR 292; and *Water Board v Moustakas* (1988) 180 CLR 491 at 498 it was established that a case on appeal that was not put at a trial would be permitted in exceptional circumstances. Those that might succeed are those unrepresented, speak little English and are unfamiliar with the Australian culture and legal system.
53. *Res judicata* is a Latin term meaning 'a thing decided'. It is a common law doctrine meant to prevent relitigation of cases between the same parties regarding the same issues, and preserves the binding nature of the court's decision. Once a final judgment has been reached in a lawsuit, ... /

not only arrogance but also the government's vested interest in defending the decisions of the 'independent body', the tribunal, at any cost. Gageler astutely observed that 'the judicial review of administrative action has come to be seen to be anchored not in the developing common law but in the fairly rigid Australian constitutional structure: its existence mandated, and its scope constrained by the separation of judicial power'. He went on to say that 'within jurisdiction is power, outside jurisdiction is error and invalidity ... To the judges the law; to the others the merits'.[54]

'Outside jurisdiction' is a further example of the cruelty of the law. The consequences are illustrated through the inaccessibility of human rights for people arriving by plane seeking protection. While the role of the court is to administer justice to all, regardless of citizenship status, Federal Parliament has confined itself to protecting Australian citizens, with scant regard for those outside this narrow criterion. In so doing, parliament has restricted access to the law by creating exceptions for people seeking protection who arrive by plane. This is a dynamic whereby parliament increases its power to control non-Australian citizens and undermines the authority of the courts to administer justice to this section of Australian society. In 2015, the parliament further reduced the courts' authority when the International legal definition of a refugee was replaced by a ministerial interpretation.

Injustice is costly. Marco and Amora, without the right to earn a living, found themselves with a $9,618.97 debt for the government's legal costs and $3,355 to be paid to the barrister who didn't even appear in the court. The costs would have been even higher if he had!

~~~~~~~~

from p.125 ... subsequent judges who are presented with a suit that is identical to or substantially the same as the earlier one will apply the doctrine of *res judicata* to uphold the effect of the first judgment (USLegal.com http://definitions.uslegal.com/r/res-judicata/). Accessed March 2022.
54. Gageler op. cit., p.104.
55. Sackville, R, 2004, 'Refugee law: the shifting balance', Judicial Conference of Australia, Darwin, Federal Court of Australia, http://classic.austlii.edu.au/au/journals/SydLawRw/2004/3.html Accessed March 2022.
56. Ruddock op. cit.

11. Politics and power

During the period of my research, the courts struggled to hold their power to administer justice to sovereign citizens of other countries seeking protection. Philip Ruddock, the immigration minister at the time, and a bipartisan parliament continually tried to undermine the inalienable rights of people seeking protection who arrived by plane. Constrained by the boundaries of Australian legislation, one family moved beyond the Australian legal processes for the administration of justice and sought legitimacy at the UNHRC in Geneva.

Through parliament's exceptions or legal restrictions, tribunal reviewers made decisions contrary to the Refugees Convention and these conclusions were prevented from being challenged in the courts. Protection for vulnerable people arriving by plane in Australia is politically motivated. If there had been the political will, many people seeking Australia's protection could have had their claims resolved in the first stage of the determination assessment system. If tribunal reviewers were not permitted 'non-jurisdictional' errors, people seeking protection may have avoided the courts. Others would not have needed to approach the minister for humanitarian consideration if the courts had been permitted to continue to examine the merits of their claims. The minister would not have been put in the position of 'playing God' as Minister Chris Evans described his role.

Refugee law in Australia 'has developed extremely rapidly, over a short period of time'.[55] It has been challenging for lawyers, migration agents and advocates attempting to keep abreast with not only the changes but also the systemic discrimination that occurred with increasing legal restrictions. This happened at the same time that Minister Ruddock (2002) was complaining about applicants abusing the appeals system,[56] which in itself made it possible for reviewers to 'abuse', sidestep or not comply with UNHCR protection guidelines.

If people arriving by plane seeking protection believed they were unfairly assessed, they relied upon lawyers and the legal system to right the wrongs meted out to them in an impossible exclusionary situation where errors of fact were beyond scrutiny. The government and immigration law were discriminatory. They introduced laws and regulations that:

1. favoured the tribunal reviewers to the detriment of people arriving by plane seeking protection;
2. disallowed claims in the courts that did not emerge in the inquisitorial tribunal process;
3. allowed non-jurisdictional errors, that is, reviewers could make mistakes, but not people seeking protection;

4. did not always respect the independent body's review;
5. intimidated reviewers by challenging decisions favourable to people arriving by plane seeking protection;
6. represented the independent body when people arriving by plane seeking protection challenged the decisions of the independent tribunal (not the government); and
7. placed applicants at a severe disadvantage when appearing self-represented.

When parliaments introduce exceptions to the law they appropriate the power of the courts to establish the truth. Parliamentarians are thus absolved of guilt regarding unfair and cruel decisions, policies and practices that result in discrimination against vulnerable groups.

The boundaries between the government and the tribunal are blurred and the government's defence of the tribunal in the courts further indicates their disquiet about successful outcomes for people arriving by plane seeking protection. The government's pattern of appealing some favourable decisions made by tribunal reviewers may be seen as looking for opportunities to create more legal restrictions for people arriving by plane seeking protection and to intimidate reviewers. Such appeals remind reviewers that not all positive outcomes for people arriving by plane seeking protection are acceptable. It might even be concluded that these court appearances were a display of the government's power in its ability to dominate and or subdue the court. Minister Ruddock's 2002 admission that the law 'reduces the grounds on which the courts can set aside such decisions as being unlawful' is an example of the importance of the 2012 Parliamentary Committee on Human Rights to safeguard the rights of all sovereign citizens, not just Australian citizens.[57] Then again, a powerful parliament need not comply with the committee's findings just as parliament ignored the findings of the 2004 Senate Select Committee on Migration Matters.[58]

Of particular concern is what Humphreys calls the 'encroachment of rule by exception' in relation to non-nationals and the danger of 'profiling' whether it be race, ethnicity, religion or nationality.[59] According to Agamben, the exception is 'something that is included solely through an exclusion'.[60] In Australia, an early example is that of the British excluding Indigenous Australians' sovereign rights from the law. Proclaiming *terra nullius* meant British 'settlers' were included, and Indigenous Australians were excluded.

Western political structures only consider certain forms of human life sacred. Excluding other forms of life was consolidated in Australia with the introduction of the Australian Constitution in 1901.

By categorising Indigenous Australians in the same class as flora and fauna, the Constitution legitimated the violence perpetrated upon them over the previous hundred years, and in the years that followed. Similarly, contemporary categorising of people seeking protection who have legitimate persecution claims as 'non-citizens' or 'illegals' (people that sit outside the law) exempts politicians and decision-makers from guilt, justifying the perpetration of violence upon these people.

In Australia at present, the courts are fighting to preserve as much independence from parliamentary power as possible. Courts, however, can be ineffective and succumb to parliament's usurpation of their power. If the court extricates itself from parliamentary power, however, there is a greater chance of limiting cruelty perpetrated by the state. Parliament (sovereign power) depends on the courts to maintain order within the state and yet the responsibilities of the courts extend beyond the state. Courts are obligated to protect all human beings, not just citizens of the state.

Constituted power exists only in the government, and is inseparable from a pre-established constitutional order, whereas constituting power (the court) is situated outside of or without the state. This relationship is termed the 'paradox of sovereignty'. Agamben maintains that in 'an era where everything tends to be regulated by rules, few are willing to claim that the constituting power of the court is original and irreducible. It cannot be conditioned and constrained in any way by a determinate legal system and it maintains itself outside the parliament's constituted power'.[61]

When the court submits to discriminatory laws introduced by parliament, it becomes ineffectual, parliament becomes unaccountable and vulnerable groups within society suffer. A zone of indistinguishability between law and life emerges and the law loses meaning or significance. A result of law without meaning arising from *terra nullius* was that early Australian 'settlers' in most jurisdictions could kill Indigenous Australians with impunity. Under the contemporary politics of people arriving by boat seeking protection, and held in offshore detention camps, politicians and guards can do whatever it takes to expel or subdue these vulnerable people. Denationalisation is the first step to stripping people of rights: 'the rightless, stateless, and homeless, with neither national nor legal rights,

---

57. The role of the committee is: a) to to examine Bills for Acts, and legislative instruments that come before either House of the Parliament for compatibility with human rights and b) to examine Acts for compatibility with human rights.
58. Legal and Constitutional References Committee 2006.
59. Humphreys, S, 2006, 'Legalizing Lawlessness: On Giorgio Agamben's State of Exception', *The European Journal of International Law,* vol. 17, no. 10, pp.677-687.
60. Agamben op. cit., p.13.
61. Ibid, pp.28–29.

can be (and are) excluded from the basic conditions of life'. They 'become subject to a condition of exception and exclusion and are thus driven away, interned and, at worst, exterminated'.[62]

When power is enmeshed in law-making, Agamben asserts, 'the function of violence specifically establishes as law not an end immune and independent from violence' but rather, an end necessarily and intimately bound up with violence.[63] The parliament, in suspending access to the court, protects the powers of the court and, in making legal exceptions, assumes the truth of the court's power. When parliamentary exception becomes law, the power of the parliament is beyond the power of the court, and people and sovereign citizens are abandoned. Agamben argues that it follows that the violence of parliamentary law is constituted in the affirmation of the decision of a forbidden act, for example, settlers could kill Indigenous people and people seeking protection can be abandoned in offshore camps. The life of the exile, the person seeking Australia's protection, is affected by tensions within the state between the power of human beings (court protection) and the power of the state (parliamentary power).

The tie between the rights of human beings and the new biopolitical determination of sovereignty makes it possible to understand that, at the end of the eighteenth century 'at the moment in which native rights were declared to be inalienable and indefeasible, the rights of human beings in general were divided into active rights (political rights, rights *by* which society is formed) and passive rights (natural and civil rights *for* whose preservation society is formed)'. At that time, children, those with a mental disability, minors, women and those condemned to punishment were not considered citizens.[64]

Sovereign citizens are inclusive of state citizens. However, the invisible power or the 'secrets of the empire' emerge when state citizens exclude sovereign citizens whose origins are in other states, such as people coming from elsewhere to Australia seeking protection.

When parliament institutes laws that harm some people and privilege others, this is not democracy. Parliamentarians are not acting in the best interest of all people living in Australia. Our democratic system is fractured and in danger of being so undermined that it will no longer be recognised as democratic. When some parliamentarians claim that 'this is democracy',

---

62. Holt, M, 2003, 'Biopolitics and the "Problem" of the Refugee'. *Critical Perspectives on Refugee Policy in Australia*, 89–101, p.97, https://citeseerx.ist.psu.edu/viewdoc/download?doi= 10.1.1.207.2803&rep=rep1&type=pdf. Accessed March 2022.
63. Agamben op.cit., p.42.
64. Agamben op. cit., p.77.

that they govern for 'all Australians', it is fraudulent because they are not governing in a way that equally respects all people living in Australia. Parliament is also undermining the separation of powers in obliging the courts to cause harm to some people in the society and privilege others. The role of the courts is to administer justice fearlessly, regardless of the cleverness or otherwise of smart barristers who play the government's game, perhaps in the hope that, one day, they too will sit in judgement of others.

Our damaged democratic system will be transformed when parliamentarians are committed to the best interests of all people living in Australia, not merely their own. We will know this when parliamentarians cross the floor when laws that harm some people and privilege others require their vote. Until such time, we need an independent body that can maintain the distinction between parliamentary lawmakers and judiciary law guardians to ensure that democratic institutions protect each person living in Australia from being harmed or diminished, and to uphold a democracy that is in danger of being further fractured.

Notwithstanding all that is argued above, it is in the power of the people, not that of parliamentarians, for the possibility of a democracy where all people are protected under the law can flourish. We, the people, can effect change. We vote. We elect and re-elect people who continue to introduce and allow cruel policies and practices to be made law people such as former Immigration Ministers, Philip Ruddock, Scott Morrison, Peter Dutton and former Prime Ministers, Kevin Rudd and Julia Gilliard. Not re-electing parliamentarians with cruel tendencies is achievable: the second longest sitting Prime Minister, John Howard, was not re-elected in 2007. Neither was former Prime Minister Tony Abbot re-elected in 2019. A more fair and inclusive society is a possibility.

Just as the people seeking Australia's protection were courageous, we too can be more responsible human beings. They embarked on a second journey of adversity when they arrived at Australian airports. With resilience, they grappled with the devils let loose from Parliament House, which is surrounded by a fence to protect parliamentarians from society's outcasts. We can elect people to parliament who have the integrity to recognise that we have no human rights law to contain the cruelty of the law and protect Australian society from parliament's deviants.

The perseverance of people seeking protection was rewarded when, soaked in sheer relief, they held their citizenship certificates tightly. However, we the voters, have little of which to be proud.

~~~~~~~~

12. **Playing God: the minister's non-reviewable powers**

The final step in the Australian legal process for a person seeking Australia's protection involves applying to the minister to have the case considered on humanitarian grounds. This is known as a ministerial request. If, for whatever reason, the minister refuses the request for humanitarian consideration, the person is expected to make arrangements to depart Australia regardless of their fear of persecution on return to their home country.

~~~~~~~~

Complexity can serve the purposes of government, limiting criticism and access to protection. The less legislation and regulations are understood and the less they are open to people seeking protection, the greater the possibility for manipulation by government and the bureaucracy.[65] Gillian Triggs, former President of the Australian Human Rights Commission, contends that refugee law has been constantly amended over many years, even retrospectively, to respond to political priorities.[66] While ministerial discretionary power provides an avenue for determinations in favour of individuals, it adds a layer of potential confusion, capriciousness and inconsistency.

Mr Ruddock had made it clear that he, the minister, did not have a duty to consider whether to exercise the power under Section 417(7) of the Migration Act 1958 in respect of any decision, whether requested to do so by the person seeking protection or by any other person, or in any other circumstances. The minister has the discretionary power to make a decision that is more favourable to the applicant if they think it is 'in the public interest to do so' but is not obliged, nor can they be forced, to engage these powers. This power is 'non-compellable, non-reviewable, and non-delegable in domestic law'. Twice a year the minister must table a statement in each House of the Australian Parliament (Representatives and Senate) regarding the decisions to grant visas. Without identifying the person seeking protection, the submission must include the tribunal review decision, the minister's decision and the reasons the decision is in the public interest.

However, the Legal and Constitutional References Committee (2006) concluded that the discretionary rights are also found to be inappropriate in a 'system based on the rule of law'. [67] It is curious that the parliament would introduce laws into the Migration Act with no obligation to adhere to them. Why create the law in the first place? A law to 'not act' could be perceived to benefit one party over another and therefore have the potential to be seriously biased and misleading. It is concerning that lawyers within the department would draft laws that seem to ignore international law principles. For Minister Ruddock to create 'guidelines' that he does not have to act upon is tokenistic, creating a false impression that the requests of those seeking protection are taken seriously, and frustrating honest public servants who formulate ministerial submissions.

Between July 1999 and June 2005, the percentage of ministerial interventions was very low. No reasons were provided as to why some people received humanitarian visas and others did not.

	1999/2000	2000/01	2001/02	2002/03	2003/04	2004/05
Requests	4,597	4,220	5,650	5,969	5,435	3,797
Interventions	265	398	362	483	932	239
Percent	5.8	9.4	6.4	8.1	17.2	6.3

Use of ministerial discretion 1999–2005
Source: Legal and Constitutional References Committee 2006:125

People seeking Australia's protection can only request the minister to consider humanitarian needs if their initial decision assessment has been reviewed at the tribunal. Minister Kevin Andrews used his discretionary powers in Orlondo and Belicia's favour, albeit grudgingly. Their health checks were clear. Two police checks arrived within the prescribed time of around three months, but Orlondo's was missing. He waited and waited. Weeks went by. This was very unusual.

I made enquiries at the Australian Federal Police (AFP) office and, yes, it was still 'in process'. I was mystified. Once again, I visited the tiny two-bedroom unit where grandmother, Herminia, slept on the couch in the living room. Was there any possibility that Orlondo had done something to upset the police? Orlondo appeared to be a man who wouldn't hurt a fly. Belicia and Orlondo thought for a while before something dawned on them.

Around this time, Orlondo had received employment security clearances that reported two 'disclosable outcomes'. During the year that

65. Markus, A & Taylor, J, 2006, 'No work, no income, no Medicare: the bridging visa E regime'. *People and Place,* vol. 14, no.1, pp.43-52, p.43. https://tapri.org.au/wp-content/uploads/2016/02/v14n1_4marcus.pdf. Accessed March 2022.
66. Triggs, G, 2020, *Speaking Up*, Melbourne University Press, p.177.
67. The Senate Legal and Constitutional References Committee: Administration and Operation of the Migration Act 1958, Mar 2006, p.149.

Orlondo was here in Australia alone, he stumbled across a telephone box where someone had crossed the wires and he was able to make free telephone calls to Belicia to check on the family's safety. He couldn't afford regular telephone cards, so he made the journey across town to this telephone booth about once a week. He was shocked to be confronted by police one evening when he left the telephone booth. Because of past experiences, police terrified him. He declared that he was not the one who had crossed the wires, but he did take advantage of the free calls. He was charged. He believed he was told by the court to pay $10,000 for tampering with public telephones and making free international calls. Belicia, who had worked in a finance office in her home country, meticulously kept all the receipts she received from the postal notes at the Post Office. The family paid $100 per month for more than two years to Telstra without ever receiving a receipt. Copies of the Australia Post receipts for money orders to the amount of $2,900 were submitted to the department with a letter that concluded: 'Given that this was a very minor offence that occurred almost ten years ago and the family fulfilled their obligations regarding remuneration, I am wondering why it is taking the AFP so long to process the request. It is now more than three months since the application for the police check was made'.

Three days later the police clearance arrived. Case closed. Permanent visas were issued to Belicia, Orlondo, Herminia and the two children, Latoya and Adella. Ten years in the making. Safe at last.

~~~~~~~~

Applying for an AFP check isn't always straightforward. A simple departmental data entry mistake meant Amora, who was on a low income, had to pay for three Federal police checks. The health checks were clear, but Amora had to have a second police check because, unknown to her, her date of birth was entered incorrectly on one of the departmental records: the entry was 22.10 whereas her true date was 12.10. Although Amora couldn't apply with the wrong date in place because it wasn't true, the immigration department insisted on a further check that was rejected because of the way the application was made. After the third attempt, where the two dates were written on the same form (even though there was no space for the incorrect date), Amora received the report. Amora paid three times—around $36 each time—a total of more than $100 because a departmental officer made a data entry mistake and no-one had the common sense, humility or authority to apologise for it.

~~~~~~~~

When the minister receives a sympathetic advisory memo from department officials, they will decide if they intend to respond favourably and whether to require health and character assessments. If someone must undergo a health check with doctors specified by the department, the results are sealed and sent to the department. The cost is around $300 per person. During the time I was undertaking my research, when a case was being actively considered by the minister, the person or family in question could seek a variation of their Bridging visa E and obtain legitimate employment.

Polina and Dmytro endured the full gamut of decisions that I came to believe were mostly spurious. Their initial application was refused, as were those of their daughters, Julia and Luciana. All three tribunal reviews were unfavourable. A Magistrates Court appeal was unsuccessful, as was a Full Federal Court appeal. Polina and Dmytro had the misfortune to engage a bogus migration agent, paying $11,500 without receiving a single receipt. She led them to believe she had renewed their visas and they had no idea that they were not legal. Polina suffered a miscarriage during this time.

During Luciana's tribunal hearing, Dmytro became so distressed that he was crying, confused and stuttering. I'd never known him to stutter. The reviewer, Brian Billboy, very possibly searching for reasons to make an unfavourable decision, quibbled about inconsequent details such as whether the older child, Olha, was fourteen or fifteen when she was attacked more than ten years earlier. Despite consistent support from John Murphy, the family's then member of parliament, requests for the minister's consideration were refused by Philip Ruddock, Chris Evans, Chris Bowen and Brendan O'Connor.

In utter desperation, I wrote to O'Connor, outlining a serious miscarriage of justice. After confirming that Dmytro and Polina lived in his electorate, I asked my local member, Anthony Albanese, to personally hand deliver it. I presented the government's perspective, and mine as a pastoral carer who had researched the family's background from different viewpoints and in different environments, also making observations including with regard to their extreme psychological vulnerability. I pointed out the 'acknowledged facts' and the 'contested facts' regarding Dmytro and Polina's consistent submissions, including my belief that Dmytro had been brutally assaulted by authorities and was terrified to return to his country of origin.

Anthony Albanese's office staff contacted me with the news that the ministerial request had been unsuccessful. I was on his doorstep within minutes. I wanted to know if Albanese had personally handed the submission to the minister. He had not. An election was imminent, and he was busy. In no uncertain terms, I explained why I didn't want that to happen and why I had turned up at Albanese's office to personally deliver the submission in the first place. I didn't hold back. I told the unfortunate staff member I had had a gutful of bureaucracies. I needed the minister to read the submission regardless of his other commitments.

The submission was reclaimed and handed to the minister. Soon after Tony Burke replaced Brendan O'Connor, Dmytro and Polina were requested to undertake the mandatory health and security checks. Burke signed off on this horrific mismanagement of justice by granting Dmytro, Polina and their two children permanent visas the day before parliament shut down prior to the election. The last I heard, Julia was doing extremely well in high school. Luciana had finished primary school. Polina had found employment in a nearby hospital and Dmytro was employed as a security guard.

~~~~~~~~

Following tribunal decisions, the 'no-work' condition imposed on people's visas continued until the minister was considering granting a visa. Without regular income, families couldn't meet the debts owed to the government resulting from court appeals. Debts of people in my study ranged from around $7,550 to $26,000.

With work rights reinstated, the debt had to be paid, as the Legal Services Section warned in boldface:

> Please be aware that an outstanding debt to the Commonwealth under Criterion 4004 of the Migration Regulations 1994 may affect any future visa application or your ability to enter Australia.

The minister might also require an 'assurance of support', an agreement from someone to financially assist a family to 'ensure that cost to the Australian taxpayer is minimised', should the family claim social security payments. Some had to organise this assurance of support with Centrelink. With certain visas, an assurance of support was discretionary – Centrelink personnel could decide whether to impose the bond. The assurer, a family member or friend, paid around $5000 into a bank account which Centrelink could access if the person, now an Australian resident, claimed social security payments such as Special Benefit, Newstart Allowance, Parenting Payment and Austudy. After two years, the remaining money was returned to the assurer and, if required, social security payments became accessible to the Australian resident. Orlondo and Belicia were required to provide bond money. Mateo paid his own.

If the minister chooses to consider the request, a visa can be granted 'even when the person doesn't meet the legal requirements for the grant of that visa'. Some of the families I worked with weren't recognised as refugees and didn't legally qualify for their visas. While holding a bridging visa, another type of visa couldn't usually be granted unless the person departed Australia and applied offshore. In later years, partner visas became accessible without leaving Australia. Some people with qualifications didn't qualify for skilled visas because they held a temporary bridging visa. They couldn't leave Australia to apply for a skilled visa because of fear of persecution or lack of money. The minister could have granted permanent visas as he did for Marco and Nankunda (employer nomination visa) and Mateo (former resident visa), but for Vasyl he granted a temporary business (long stay) visa.

When Vasyl received his work rights again, he applied for a job in lift maintenance. The employer was delighted as he had no other qualified applicants and he was preparing to advertise overseas. He went on to sponsor Vasyl for a permanent skilled migration visa. Fifteen years later, Vasyl remains at the same company.

~~~~~~~~

Lawyers and advocates submit ministerial requests outlining 'unique and exceptional circumstances', according to guidelines. It's unclear how departmental assessors decide whether the guidelines are met, or whether guidelines need to be met, before a favourable submission is sent to the minister. The person seeking protection or advisers are given no indication why the family did or did not meet the guidelines. A typical notification for a minister's decision not to grant a visa provides no reasons, merely stating that under Section 417 of the *Migration Act 1958*:

> The Minister may substitute for a decision of the Refugee Review Tribunal, a decision which is more favourable to the applicant where he considers it is in the public interest to do so.
> [The person] was referred to the Minister. However, on [date] he decided not to consider exercising his power in this case …

The Select Committee on Migration Matters recommended that a consultative process be established between the then Department of Immigration and Multicultural and Indigenous Affairs (DIMIA) and people seeking ministerial intervention where they are shown, and can comment upon, information central to the outcome of their case. A draft ministerial submission was provided as an example. It also recommended that the minister provide a statement of reasons for an unfavourable decision.

~~~~~~~~

On the train one day, Ladonna overheard a conversation. In her own language she asked the women for the name and contact number of the Catholic nun they had been speaking about. They obliged. With a friend interpreting, she rang me and we arranged to meet in a shopping mall close to her home. She arrived weighed down by a huge bundle of papers. I listened and observed. Ladonna was afraid. She and her family didn't have a legal visa. Her husband Jaime didn't want her to tell anyone about their situation, fearing trouble.

I read her papers and we met again at her home, her friend again interpreting. Jaime was at work and the older children at school. The house was an unkempt weatherboard home next to a service station. It was dark inside. Jaime was so frightened about being caught without a visa that he had blackened the windows. The children weren't allowed to play outside. It was freezing cold in winter and extremely hot in summer. They couldn't afford electricity. Jaime worked in the construction industry. From time-to-time Ladonna got work cleaning in the early hours of the morning. She'd arrive home in time to wake the children for school.

Ian Inglet had refused Jaime and Ladonna's application for protection, and Sally Bland made an unfavourable review at the tribunal. Minister Ruddock turned down Jaime's request for intervention. Jaime then went to the High Court without legal representation. The judge remitted his case back to the Federal Court. A lawyer represented Jaime and Ladonna at the Federal Court. The Federal Court judge dismissed the case with costs. After a number of unsuccessful requests for Mr Ruddock's ministerial intervention, Jaime and Ladonna lived in the community without legal status and with a $12,339.57 debt to the government hanging over their heads.

I needed to speak with Jaime. If they were to make another request to the minister, he had to be involved because they first needed to get temporary visas. He was very nervous, very suspicious. It took time to persuade him this was the only means to gain a permanent visa. He agreed to come along to the compliance office. It was difficult to keep him inside long enough to present the necessary identity documents, let alone get him to return and sign the children's visa papers.

A wonderful psychiatrist prepared a thorough psychological assessment, pro bono. This was the basis for the necessary 'new information' that allowed for another ministerial request for humanitarian consideration under unique and exceptional circumstances. We wrote to Minister Andrews for all five people in the family. I say 'we' because each family member was closely involved in the preparation of the letter. They needed to feel part of the process, helping themselves to get through this terrible situation. They told their story. I took notes and researched their files.

While the request was being considered, there was a change of government. Kevin Rudd became Prime Minister and Chris Evans Immigration Minister. Jaime, Ladonna and their first child, Sergio, received permanent humanitarian visas ten years after first applying for protection. The two younger children, Brigitte and Daniela, weren't included in the application. God was on their side when Chris Evans found a way of legally granting them protection.

Normally, following an unsuccessful outcome, if a person submitted another request to the minister, it was labelled a repeat request. If department officials decided it did not meet the guidelines applicants were told:

> [The person] has been found not to be owed Australia's protection. Their request for Ministerial Intervention was personally considered by the former Minister for Immigration and Multicultural Affairs, the Minister [name], who declined to intervene under section 417 on [date]. … subsequent requests for intervention should be referred only if additional information is provided …

In the absence of relevant new information, applicants were expected to begin arrangements to depart Australia.

With Naldo and Maito, the grandparents whose four children had permanent visas, we submitted new information pointing out the difficulties their daughter Valentina, an Australian permanent resident, would suffer if her parents received a negative decision, resulting in their departure from Australia. Naldo and Maita were eventually granted a 'more favourable decision', a Subclass 835 Remaining Relative Visa (a/g NSW Deputy State Director).

~~~~~~~~

After nine years living in the community without legal status, Mateo was notified that, 'the Minister has decided to exercise his public interest power … by granting a Subclass 151 Former Resident visa'. The covering letter to Mateo's request to the minister may have influenced this decision. It pointed out that 'at the lower levels of the department single men don't manage to meet the Ministerial Guidelines and, in my experience, are not being recommended for further consideration'. An inference of systemic bias against single men may have caused the claims to be favourably considered.

In Nankunda's case, a frustrated but experienced advocate wrote to the minister on Nankunda's behalf stating that an 'appeal to you rests on the provision of new evidence which could prevent a miscarriage of justice in her case and hence could prevent a breach of Australia's international undertakings'. She also mentioned it was in the 'public interest' to consider granting her a permanent visa.

Requests were sometimes submitted after a negative tribunal outcome or after a court appeal. People seeking protection, their lawyers and advocates argued that the guidelines were met in substantial ways. However, the requests for humanitarian consideration were almost always turned down. On rare occasions they were successful.

~~~~~~~~

Itan and Andy asked me to help them with a request to the minister. I listened carefully to their story but there was no 'hook' on which I could justify supporting them. Reluctantly, they understood. As they were going out the door Itan said, 'Sister will you please pray for my sister Amelia?' I invited them back to ask why she might need my prayers. In the course of the afternoon, I heard that Itan was Amelia's only family member in Australia. Her marriage had fallen apart, her husband was a drug addict and she had taken out an Apprehended Violence Order (AVO) to protect her two little boys. Andy was the only stable male, or father figure, for the boys. Itan and Andy were in regular contact with the boys and their mother.

Itan and Andy returned with supporting documentation and we submitted a request to Minister Evans, arguing that an Australian family would be seriously compromised should they have to depart Australia:

> Because Itan and Andy have no children of their own, they have a particularly close relationship with and emotional ties to Amelia's two sons. Should they have to leave Australia, her sister and nephews would be deprived of emotional and practical support as they endeavour to rebuild their lives following a divorce. Amelia would be left without any family support during this difficult time in her life and the lives of her two sons. The two young lads would be deprived of Andy's close male relationship as he could also be a model for them as they negotiate their teenage years.

Two years later, having completed mandatory health and security checks they were granted permanent resident return visas by Chris Evans.

Minister Evans granted the same visa in Rafi's complicated case. Unfortunately, by the time Rafi received his visa, his cancer had progressed. His partner, Sari, was pregnant. Her student visa would expire soon after her course was completed. Rafi submitted papers to sponsor Sari for a permanent spouse visa. Rafi's family believed he would get better care in his home country. The hospital discharged him, and he and Sari went back to his family. He died about four weeks later. Soon after Sari returned to Australia, Sabrina was born. Sari wanted Rafi's name on Sabrina's birth certificate. She needed Rafi's death certificate but the family would not release it because they blamed her for his death. Sari wouldn't give up. She remembered that the hospital had frozen Rafi's sperm in the event that he survived, and they wanted another child. Sari approached the hospital and they agreed to DNA testing on the sperm and baby Sabrina. Thanks to the dogged persistence of her mother, Sabrina has her father's name on her birth certificate.

These two stories show that sometimes ministers hear their cries, but they also illustrate the complex lives of those who seek Australia's protection.

It was difficult to convince a minister to overturn a former minister's decision as the table below indicates:

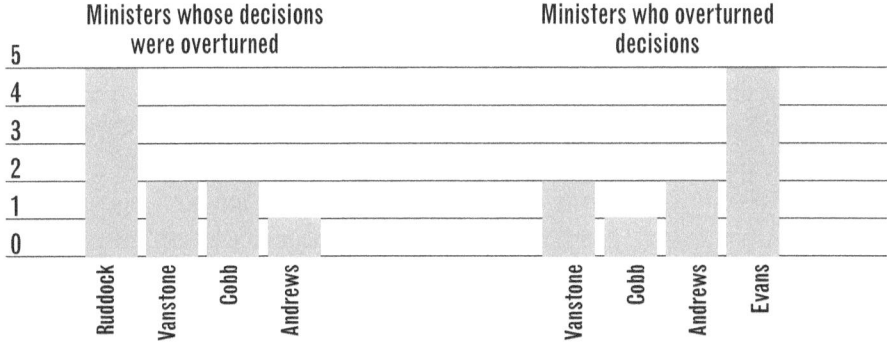

Overturning decisions. *Source: Decisions of participants in my study 2014.*

Of the main families in my study, five of Minister Ruddock's decisions were overturned, two of Minister Vanstone's, two of Minister Cobb's and one by Minister Andrews. Minister Evans overturned five decisions, all of which were made by a minister in the previous government. There were also occasions when ministers overturned decisions of previous ministers in their own government.

In examining what persuaded four ministers to overturn ten of the decisions of previous ministers, various factors emerged. For Orlando, Belicia and their family, it was the examination of the case by the UNHRC after a favourable tribunal referral carried no weight for them. A different political climate may have influenced the tribunal review in Olek and Zofia's decision. For Amora and Marco, it was the intervention and insistence of UNHCR Canberra as a result of an advocate's persuasive argument. These results highlight the strategic role of advocates interacting with cooperative departmental officers, in holding the Australian Government accountable to the Migration Act. They also illustrate the powerlessness of people seeking Australia's protection to gain traction in their legitimate quest for protection.

Ruddock's Guideline 6.6(2) explicitly stated that a repeat request cannot include claims that had already been mentioned in a previous request. 'New information' would only be considered if it fell within the 'ambit' of the guidelines. An internal email revealed that in one set of claims, 'the Minister declined to consider *all the cases*'. Minister Cobb's comprehensive dismissal could have cancelled significant claims for further requests because from then on, those claims would be regarded by departmental officers as having already been decided. It is not known whether Mr Cobb even considered whether the claims were within the guidelines before rejecting them. Whatever the case, such decisions jeopardise repeat submissions.

Emails indicate that some departmental officers were frustrated in attempting to apply the Act by what can only be assumed to be ministerial attitudes. These very ministerial standpoints could have made objective departmental officers, who put considerable effort into preparing submissions, feel dejected. If the minister rejects favourable submissions that fall within the guidelines, it calls into question the purpose of the guidelines and renders their statement of purpose farcical.

Guideline 6.6(2) discounting new information in repeat requests was relentlessly observed by certain departmental officers. Orlondo's further request was accompanied by 33 letters and 1,300 signatures of people supporting their case but the Manager of the Ministerial Intervention Unit reported that:

> the submission from [Advocate] provides UNHCR information on the general situation in [country], but in my view, did not provide information regarding the inconsistencies and credibility issues identified by the Tribunal, sufficient to result in a finding of "guidelines met" for submission to the Minister.

Advocates need to be diplomatic. Criticising the tribunal reviewer's credibility could jeopardise a claim. The attachments to this submission included:

- a UNHCR report on human rights in the country;
- international concern about returning asylum seekers and refugees to that country;
- a copy of questions put to a former security officer from that country that challenged an assumption made at the tribunal;
- an authoritative article on PTSD providing reasons why there might be inconsistencies in a person's account.

In the eyes of public servants, local community support, UN documents of 'new information' and the professional report regarding PTSD were insufficient. Orlondo and Belicia were assessed as not presenting enough information to warrant a favourable decision 'in the public interest'. A later internal email stated that: 'The Minister has been contacted by Sr Aileen Crowe who has made claims that "we" have ignored new information put forward on their behalf'.

The same month, Orlando received the now familiar but still shocking news from the Manager, Ministerial Interventions Unit, stating that his case had been reassessed: 'The additional information provided, in combination with the information provided previously, does not bring the case within the Minister's Guidelines. Therefore, no further action will be taken …'

In desperation, I contacted the Secretary to the Department of Immigration:

> Whilst I realise the minister has a "non-compellable" power to make decisions, given the above cases, one would have to ask is such authority protected from abuse? If not, why is a power that is so easily open to abuse allowed to be continued as policy? I have tried my best to obtain fair and appropriate outcomes … From the community support they have received, it is clear that the broader community would be in no danger of excluding them. Hence, as a result of years of unsuccessful attempts to prove this to Immigration I am now appealing to you in so far as you are saying you are working to develop a more acceptable DIMIA culture, and I hope a fairer system. I hope you will eventually refute the statement that came from the Minister's office declaring that "it is the law not fairness that determined the primary decision"!

The Senate Select Committee on Migration Matters was concerned about a lack of adequate accountability mechanisms regarding the minister's discretionary power resulting in the 'possibility and perception of corruption'. An internal email from the Director International Obligations and Intervention Section stated that Orlando: 'has asked for an urgent s417 to be done. He has also asked Protection Client Support to look at special payments under ASAS' (Asylum Seeker Assistance Scheme).

Mr Ruddock's guidelines seemed to have become law in the eyes of some departmental reviewers. For advocates, they are not *laws* but guidelines to *assist* in making claims that will meet legal requirements. For example, 6.6(2) states that the Minister not wishing to contemplate a further request unless certain conditions are met, *is not a law*. If the submission meets the conditions related to international and/or domestic refugee law, claims should not be dismissed 'as not meeting the Minister's guidelines' simply because they have been previously submitted.

Fear of persecution does not diminish regardless of the number of times claims are rejected by inept departmental officers or ministers who can decide whatever they like.

These conflicting values make a charade of the Migration Act because they allow the minister of the day to create guidelines, some of which allow departmental staff to act outside the boundaries of the law without redress. Despite past, poor-quality assessments, a person continuously claiming fear of persecution for a Convention reason should legally have had recourse to Australia's protection, and not have been dismissed simply because the claim was a 'repeat' request. This inconvenient truth can easily be addressed by accepting that departmental officers made inappropriate decisions in the past. If one minister can overturn decisions of previous ministers whose judgements were questioned, surely departmental officers can scrutinise previous assessments and at least amend mistakes.

Lawyers and advocates submitted persuasive arguments for people arriving by plane seeking protection, believing the guidelines were met. There was no evidence to suggest any of these people who arrived by plane and sought Australia's protection would pose a serious threat to security, or that their not returning to the country of origin would adversely affect Australia's international relations. However, if people seeking protection had to return, some would have been persecuted or killed.

The UNHCR produced three reports on one country between 2002 and 2006 pointing out the need to protect people arriving from this country and the dangers of 'relocation'. In another country, returnees would be easily located and targeted because of the high levels of corruption within the government and security agencies, and extreme poverty. In these two countries, advocates and applicants knew of people who had been returned, and who had been killed soon after arrival. Inna and Grisha, Olek and Zofia, Amora and Marco, and Nankunda had already suffered from the violent deaths of close family members or work colleagues.

Mateo would have continued to suffer discrimination and human rights abuse whether he returned to his country of origin or the neighbouring country. This was because of one government's attitudes towards his foreign education and the other government's attitude towards foreigners in general. Because of the violence experienced in both Inna's country of origin and Grisha's original country, they had legitimate fears about returning to either country.

~~~~~~~~

Gaining the minister's approval was not straightforward. There were many hurdles to overcome to convince departmental officials that people deserved Australia's protection. Even then, there could be obstacles. One departmental officer couldn't understand why applications approved in the Sydney office were not being approved by the minister. I had a shrewd idea.

My complaint to the Secretary of the Department suggested that the 'public servant who advises Minister Cobb about who he should or should not accept (regardless of the recommendations made by the DIMIA case officers) has been in the same office since the days of Mr Ruddock ... continues the culture of exclusion at all costs. ... Several advocates have had very bad encounters with this woman and in fact I have told a couple of MPs of my experience of being ridiculed and belittled. I believe that my conversations with [that woman] may have in fact, seriously jeopardised the decisions that went against the two families'. In conclusion, I said, 'There is a lot more I could say about people who get accepted and those scoundrels in society ripping off people on Bridging Visas, some of whom are temporary themselves, and yet never "caught" by those vigilant "compliance officers". But seriously, I am tired of the façade, tired of the rhetoric and tired of the injustice dealt to good-living honest people, under the umbrella of "the law"'. I added in desperation, 'if I do not hear from you by the close of tomorrow, I will be obliged to forward this information to the Federal Ombudsman and the UN Human Rights Commission in Geneva'. Sometimes advocates had to take desperate measures. The reply was prompt. I was not the only one to complain about that woman. Ten weeks later Vasyl and Sabina received temporary residents' visas which secured Mikhaila a place in the high school.

We had to get the two older children, Yeva and Maxim, to Australia as soon as possible. They needed to leave quietly. No goodbyes to friends. Maxim was close to the age of army conscription. Vasyl's brother had been medically discharged from the army and died a young man as a result of exposure to dangerous gases. Vasyl didn't want this to happen to his son. They arrived within two months.

Vasyl's employer sponsored him for a permanent skilled visa and the whole family received permanent visas the following year. Vasyl has already enjoyed long service leave in the company that had employed him about fifteen years previously. Their son Maxim completed a degree in aeronautics and now lives and works in Singapore. Yeva is employed in financial management and owns her own unit. Mikhaila's designer clothes, which her mother Sabina makes, are published in glossy international magazines.

The delegate who assessed Orlondo's protection claims in the first instance, Ian Inglet, concluded 'that the harm feared by the applicant is of sufficient gravity as to constitute persecution'. But later he decided Judith Mullhead's compelling grounds for recommendation to seek the minister's intervention didn't meet the guidelines. 'New information' could be continually infected by the delegate's original negative assessment.

The same delegate, Ian Inglet, made this second negative finding on Orlando and Belicia's protection case. It would seem that the original unfavourable assessment became the reference point for all further submissions. If this is the acceptable process, there is an obvious conflict of interest in referring new information back to the original assessor. They didn't want to accept that a wrong decision had been made in the first place, a decision exposed in Orlando and Belicia's case where Inglet was not prepared to follow the contrary advice of Judith Mullhead and, possibly the judge in the court.

Every ministerial refusal was another nail in the coffin for people seeking protection. I personally delivered the bad news. Tears became sobs. There were long silences. When I spoke of returning to their home country, I was met with frustration and anger, and a profound sense of powerlessness. Over the years, I had come to know each family and we had discussed this possibility every time I delivered a negative message. Each time, the reaction was the same, but it was even more intense this time. Not because I had given them to believe they would be successful. I never did. All we could do was try. This produced a flicker of hope, a little less despair. I warned them that it was within the law to request the minister's compassion, but we could never be sure that compassion would be forthcoming.

They knew the tribunal decisions and the first decisions were obviously wrong. They had been misrepresented many times. They weren't ignorant, uneducated people. They had suffered human rights discrimination in their own countries. Jaime and Dmytro had studied human rights law at university. Naldo's son and Orlondo stood up for the human rights of young women trapped in sexual slavery. Marco fought for the rights of people in his community as an intelligence officer. They imagined Australia would be different. They discovered that, in Australia, they had no accessible avenue because there was no human rights law.

There was something weird about these decisions. The family were given no reasons. The minister said 'No' and that was that. It was incomprehensible, childish. They needed to understand. They deserved an explanation.

I had no words to comfort these despairing people. All hope of a peaceful, safe future had been blown away again. When I heard the words 'I'm tired', I became worried. 'I'm tired' carried a sinister message.

~~~~~~~~

13. **Pushing back against ministerial power**

More often than not it was a waste of time devoting resources to researching and writing submissions for protection claims. I made requests to ministers Andrews (6), Cobb (4), Evans (8), McGauren (3), Robb (1), Ruddock (13) and Vanstone (16) about the people whose stories are outlined here. There were many more that I haven't documented. There were thousands of people seeking protection each year whose claims were discarded, thanks to the systemic bias within the assessment and review procedures.

There is no obligation for the minister to heed the advice of departmental officers on 'cases falling within the ambit of (these) Guidelines'. Fortunately, some departmental officers recognised this, as they were prepared to keep trying to win what was becoming a lottery. An in-confidence DIMIA Ministerial Submission Minute about Nankunda noted that they considered the request met 'the relevant guidelines for referral because of compassionate circumstances regarding Nankunda's psychological state, physical disability and the possibility that she may face a significant threat to her personal security, human rights or human dignity on return to her country of origin'. Despite this constructive assessment, and even after the Deputy Director's submission and the former judge's letter, Minister Vanstone did not make a favourable decision.

She also refused requests for Orlondo and Belicia and Sabina and Vasyl. I wrote directly to the Departmental Secretary protesting that, on two separate occasions, the decision about Sabina and Vasyl was made in Canberra, against the advice of the departmental case officers. The latest decision, apparently made just before Christmas, had not yet been communicated to the family. I explained how, over the years, I had developed positive relationships with departmental staff in Canberra and Sydney and I knew for sure that one woman was not going to let this case through, despite the recommendations and options presented by the referral team on two separate occasions, and despite many letters from various MPs, including Bruce Baird, who told me they were *the most deserving case that he had ever come across*.

When departmental staff are satisfied that there is adequate evidence to suggest granting protection, the minister's refusal does not eliminate the need for protection. It merely undermines the authority of departmental officers, the ministry within the government, and community's trust in parliament. People seeking protection and advocates have a right to be treated with fairness and respect. Departmental assessors, tribunal reviewers and parliamentarians are people, just like the rest of us. They have a job to do, as do we all. Parliamentarians expect us to be fair, hardworking, honest citizens, and people living in Australia expect the same of them.

These cases highlight the importance of complaints. It seems that there was enough dissatisfaction to initiate a departmental reaction to one minister's non-compellable powers. An internal email from the Complex Case Support Section, Canberra, to the Manager of the Ministerial Intervention Unit, Sydney read: 'Apologies in advance for harassing you, but grateful if you could let me know if you've made any progress in relation to the intervention cases that Mr Cobb declined to intervene on just before Christmas, but the clients have not yet been advised'. The officer in Canberra said she thought something had been worked out with Mr Cobb's office, 'but the reshuffle has probably thrown a spanner in the works'!

By the end of January, Mr Cobb found himself no longer assisting Ms Vanstone. Another internal email provided further information about Nankunda's claims, as an officer from the Ministerial Intervention Unit in NSW justified withholding the negative decision of Mr Cobb who had been removed from office. This officer, in an internal email to a person in the NSW Deputy State Director's Office, attached 'the letter notifying Nankunda of the Minister's decision in her s417 request. Minister Cobb decided not to intervene in this case, however, notification of the decision was put on hold'. He then described how Nankunda had 'been diagnosed with severe PTSD and major depressive illness' pointing out that 'this request has received a high level of community support including support from (inter alia) Joanna Gash MP, Petro Georgio MP'.

Tensions regarding ministerial decision-making plagued lawyers and sometimes the court. Jane Lee reported in the *Sydney Morning Herald* that:

> Debbie Mortimer, SC, said Mr Bowen's decision should be quashed as it was "entirely arbitrary and entirely devoid of any rational consideration". She said the immigration department had made arrangements to remove him well before Mr Bowen had made his decision.[68]

Mortimer's dissatisfaction was colourfully expressed:

> For the minister to detain someone for years and then say, "You know what, I don't have to look at it" [he is saying] I can look at Mickey Mouse, what side of the bed I got out of, or just say, "I don't like the look of him". It can be totally irrational.

According to Lee, Mortimer then argued that

---

68. Lee, J, 2012, 'Minister's decision to deport Afghan man "irrational"'. *Sydney Morning Herald*, 3 November, https://www.smh.com.au/politics/federal/ministers-decision-to-deport-afghan-man-irrational-20121102-28ppn.html. Accessed May 2022.

> the whole point of this at a factual level is that the minister's decision is full of propositions that it doesn't matter what we say or how good our arguments are, there is a juggernaut on this man's removal.

Mortimer concluded that,

> the minister just says, "I'm going to remove this man," and it's in those circumstances we ask for an injunction.

Lee went on to say,

> Mr Donaghue, the Government's Solicitor submitted that Mr Bowen had no duty to exercise this power under the Migration Act: "The minister may elect to 'stop' considering exercising the power." He also said an offshore-entry person had "no right" to compel the minister to use the power.

For more than a decade, the Migration Act has been systematically exploited, despite public objections. Whether the person arrives by plane or by boat, nobody has a right to compel the minister to use their power, not even members of the same political party, the minister's delegated departmental assessors or so-called independent tribunal reviewers – and regardless of the evidence.

The Senate Legal and Constitutional Committee noted that ministerial discretion regarding international non-refoulement obligations was inadequate: 'Reliance on a non-reviewable and non-compellable discretion is an unacceptable means for determining the fate of persons claiming protection under Australia's international obligations'. The committee claimed that discretionary 'Ministerial powers alone were an insufficient safety net to ensure compliance' with international obligations. It also argued that 'Australia's non-refoulement obligations … are not discretionary and subject to few, if any, exceptions'. By granting ministerial discretions that are neither compellable nor, for practical purposes, reviewable by the courts, the Migration Act threatens the principle of the separation of powers between parliament and the judiciary. Only a few migration law experts 'have mastered the ever-changing complex provisions'.

Shamefully, the Migration Act allows for the misuse of ministerial powers. Where a minister gives directives setting out procedures to be followed in arriving at conclusions, the minister is abusing their power if they ignore the evidence in the directives. It could not have been the intention of the Migration Act to create an opportunity for ministers to misuse the Migration Act, but that is what is happening. It is in the public interest for there to be safeguards to protect the integrity of the Migration Act. As it stands, the Migration Act is an illustration of systemic privilege that confirms ongoing structural exclusion. Fairness is an illusion.

That the minister is not required to explain their actions indicates little respect for people whose claims have been rejected. Furthermore, the minister exhibits disdain for employees with the responsibility of deciding to refer favourable cases. Departmental assessors, advocates, lawyers and people seeking protection need to know what is lacking in their ministerial submissions and what doesn't meet the guidelines. For the Migration Act to be effective, the minister's decisions need to be transparent. Without transparency, perceptions of systemic bias are reinforced and conspiracy theories abound.

Perhaps Mr Cobb's decision to refuse the whole batch of submissions was to intimidate departmental personnel into limiting favourable referrals. One advocate, in her anxiety to understand the minister's negative decision, surmised, perhaps wrongly, that Nankunda's submissions were rejected because of claims of bias directed at departmental assessors. An in-confidence minute to Minister Vanstone reported that the Deputy Director 'alleged that this information was not appropriately assessed against the s48b guidelines because of bias by a departmental officer'. Conscientious departmental officers should not shoulder the blame for inadequate or inappropriate decisions made by Mickey Mouse ministers granted infallibility by elected members of parliament through policies they themselves have voted upon.

~~~~~~~~

A submission on behalf of Nankunda by the former judge was scathing. He understood that the extraordinarily strong evidence of the death of Nankunda's mother and 'the highly suspicious circumstances relating to it was not available before those involved in the prior determinations'. He pointed out that:

> an appellant authority may well understand how the tribunal at first instance came to its decision but can conclude that that decision was unlikely had the full evidence been able to be presented.

No amount of evidence could convince the decision-makers. The Refugee Advice and Casework Service (RACS) made a further submission in which Nankunda's claim included 'substantive and credible information'. The submission stated Nankunda received a letter from her uncle, detailing her mother's arrest and detention by the government. RACS maintained that Nankunda's uncle identified the main reason for her detention was to discover 'Nankunda's whereabouts and whether she was supporting the rebels and her not revealing Nankunda's plans which were known to her'. Her uncle reiterated what Nankunda's mother had told her, that she should 'never return' or 'she will be killed'.

Her consultant psychiatrist submitted that Nankunda had suffered repeated bouts of abdominal pain, vomiting and that a laparoscopy at the hospital 'confirmed pelvic inflammatory disease, no doubt a result of abuse in custody'. He added, 'of most concern to me was her depression and severe post-traumatic stress disorder', concluding 'I dread to think what will become of her should she be made to return'.

In July that year Onshore Protection sent the disappointing but familiar notice regarding the s48b request which indicated that the submission was refused as not meeting the guidelines for referral to the minister. A cold, cynical and, given the above information, sinister departmental email was circulated:

> The RRT found the client's original claims to be implausible and that: she was not a credible witness. It may be the claims made subsequently have been contrived, including letters from her uncle and [...] coach. If her mother was in fact killed, there is little evidence to show that this was a result of detention and abuse by the authorities – she may have been the victim of a random crime unrelated to her daughter's claimed activities.

If this departmental officer accessed tribunal reviewer Ros Redberry's decision, he could also have accessed Angelina Pilon's initial decision, where Nankunda alluded to her abuse by claiming she was afraid of rape and the 'safe house' or 'community house'. The above email indicates the level of scepticism within the department, and it also illustrates the way the system is cruelly structured to foster negative decision-making. This is a further example of the reliance of some departmental officers upon the earliest decisions to defend their biased stance. They prefer this to assessing the new material on its merits. The psychiatrist's and medical practitioner's credible reports and the legally proven credibility of witnesses were overlooked.

More than a year after her earlier submission, the Deputy Director was still arguing with immigration personnel in Canberra. She had been in touch with an advocate who knew her case well. The Deputy Director was worried that in any 48B procedure, the facts relevant to Nankunda's 'case may not be properly looked at'. In the FOI document, the next paragraph was redacted. Nevertheless, the Deputy Director's submission went on to say that Nankunda's case 'has many complications – not least of all the fact that the MRU [Ministerial Intervention Unit (MIU)] queried the credentials of the lawyers who had given affidavits from witnesses to her mother's torture and murder and Nankunda's own co-opting to spy and consequent torture'. She continued to express her frustration by stating that 'when asked about verification by the MRU [MIU], Nankunda was at a loss and unable to acknowledge any of this as she was not in a professional position to have the information'. The Deputy Director added that 'subsequently, the Law Council in her country verified the status of the lawyers as completely above board. These documents have been presented and must be taken seriously in future considerations of her case'.

This complaint indicates departmental negative bias towards lawyers outside Australia. It also illustrates the bewilderment of advocates at the ineptitude of assessors and reviewers about cross-cultural claims and the implausibility of the decisions of departmental officers. The Deputy Director's scepticism was confirmed when she received the advocate's comment that, 'Nankunda faces the long process of review under s48B which may fail similarly in the hands of unbelieving "judges" who know little about life in that country'. The Deputy Director concluded her submission: 'should she be dealt with by an officer with the mentality of the one I experienced this will not happen. Over to you'.

Not confident that the department would respond positively, the Deputy Director expressed her frustration to the Secretary of the Department. She said, 'again and again, I fail to understand why officers processing the claims of African refugees and asylum seekers cannot do more to become fully aware of the prevailing and historic conditions and political situations on the African continent'. She claimed that 'reading some of the judgements in this young woman's case I am stunned at how ignorant Australians can be of the underbelly of corruption and intrigue that oppresses the societies' of these countries. She informed the department that Nankunda had 'tried to kill herself at one point rather than be forcibly returned. Her history of abuse is horrific'. She added that in her experience,

> as I have told you, of the 48B process – with an officer who had obviously made up his mind to reject the applicants regardless of the clear evidence in their favour – leaves me very sceptical of what may happen to Nankunda in a 48B hearing.

I knew how the Deputy Director felt. I had written to the Secretary of the Department telling him I was 'tired of the façade, tired of the rhetoric and tired of the injustice dealt to good-living honest people, under the umbrella of the law'. Many other advocates were too.

An encouraging email to the Deputy Director was circulated by an immigration officer, indicating there were problems within the department. He wrote that 'the Department is currently evaluating compliance against policy and procedures in relation to the application of s48B. We are also in the process of strengthening training for onshore protection case officers'. He concluded reassuringly, inviting the Deputy Director to let him know 'if you feel at any stage of the process that there is actual, or indeed perceived, bias in relation to any of the officers concerned. I will have the claims investigated and issues addressed'.

Finally, an in-confidence, undated memo noted that Human Rights Watch recognised that fear of persecution if returned, 'if accepted to be well-founded, is supported by country information'.

Despite all this information and human rights country reports, Nankunda's claims weren't accepted. She was granted neither a refugee nor humanitarian visa. While she was granted a permanent visa recognising her need for protection, she was left to live with the fact that Australian authorities never validated her genuine refugee claims of politically motivated persecution resulting in rape and torture.

It seems that the department's evaluation of 'compliance against policy and procedures' was ineffectual. Years after this cohort's assessments, Professor William Maley, an expert on Afghanistan politics, said,

> It is very important that the standard of reviewing of asylum applications be drastically improved. Poor primary decision-making … is likely to clog up both the courts and the detention centres and contribute to an atmosphere of despair.[69]

~~~~~~~~

A postscript. Nankunda, nursing in a large Sydney hospital, is happily married with four children. When she was visiting a friend recently, a mutual friend arrived from England. The moment they set eyes on each other, they hugged each other tightly, their grief developing into sobbing. Nankunda's hosts, her husband and children didn't understand. On the journey home her husband told her he was mystified. Usually, when people met after a long time, they were full of joy, not overcome with grief.

Although married for almost ten years, Nankunda had never mentioned her painful past to her husband. The time was right to fill in the gaps. She explained that the visitor had been in the room next to her in the 'safe house'. Full of fear of what would become of each of them, they listened helplessly to each other's screams. They were terrified. Who would be next? The two friends validated each other's experience. For Nankunda and her friend, it was liberating. Her husband did not dismiss Nankunda's story as 'implausible'.

Social and political commentator, Waleed Aly, summed up the immigration department situation:

69. Quoted in Needham, K, 2011, 'Legal errors reverse more than half of refugee rulings', *Sydney Morning Herald*, 4 October, https://www.smh.com.au/national/legal-errors-reverse-more-than-half-of-refugee-rulings-20111003-1l5du.html. Accessed May 2022.

this is a culture of belligerence, trickling down from the political leadership. Again, just like White Australia. It's a culture that sees the sneaky denial of rights as a virtue. A culture that sheds tears for those who die at sea trying to get here, but barely blinks when people are killed after being sent home. A culture that watches a detainee attempt suicide, and dozens of people give up on the idea of asylum, and then chalks that up as a win.[70]

~~~~~~~~

Some departmental officers remain fixated on inappropriate or inaccurate tribunal review conclusions of 'implausibility'. The procedure of assessment of protection claims is structured so that early negative decisions, later found to contain serious errors, remain the basis of unfavourable outcomes. Only when people seeking protection, advocates, lawyers and judges consistently challenged these attitudes and values was there any measure of success for a limited number of lucky people seeking protection.

The constant accessing by reviewers of past files, some of which were nine years old, as in the case of Orlondo's family, creates a dynamic whereby subsequent assessments and tribunal reviews are not critically examined in the light of new information. This practice confirms structural bias in contaminated assessment and review processes.

Furthermore, two problems lay at the heart of numerous and repetitive ministerial requests. First, responsibility rested with departmental officers. Some made poor and inappropriate decisions at the earliest stages of the application for protection assessment, and others were dogged in upholding their colleagues' decisions. Secondly, the Migration Act allowed the minister to act irresponsibly towards the UNHCR Convention on Refugees and Australia's responsibilities regarding other UN Treaty obligations. Attempts to address numerous, repetitive ministerial requests with restrictive regulations about the number of requests allowed were inadequate. They didn't overcome the problem of people's protection needs but, instead, forced them to live without legal status and to be exploited in the workforce.

The negative attitude towards people seeking protection arriving from unfamiliar cultures and countries where some suffered unimaginable violence speaks of a cruel system. This system is insufficiently mature and flexible to broaden its cultural base and accept people with different beliefs and values.

The effect of unfair, unfavourable decision-making reached across the Department of Immigration, the Refugee Review Tribunal, the courts,

70. Aly, W, 2012, 'Land of the fair go takes refuge from the helpless', *Sydney Morning Herald*, 19 October, https://www.smh.com.au/politics/federal/land-of-the-fair-go-takes-refuge-from-the-helpless-20121018-27ts7.html. Accessed May 2022.

migration law and the minister's office. The Legal and Constitutional References Committee heard criticism that was 'directed at the Migration Act's failure to provide for requests for protection on humanitarian grounds to be undertaken at the primary stage of application'. This committee also regretted the fact that the government 'had chosen to ignore the recommendations made' by the 2000 and 2004 inquiries.

This cohort's requests to the minister might not have been necessary if the initial assessments had not been unsound. The tribunal reviews were not honest assessments. The courts lacked jurisdiction to examine all errors (non-jurisdictional errors) or the power to decide on the merits of the claims. If claims had been examined carefully and fairly, people seeking protection, lawyers and advocates would not have found it necessary to pursue rejected claims. Regrettably, we must conclude that the Migration Act is flawed because of the manner in which ministerial power is harnessed. The role of advocates has emerged as crucial to people seeking Australia's protection obtaining the security owed to them under Australia's commitment to the UN Refugees Convention and other UN treaties.

The complexity of the processes also bears scrutiny – whether a decision is made by the delegate (the person who made the first negative assessment) or a member (the person who reviewed the negative assessment) or the court (the person who judged the person who reviewed the assessment). Try viewing these scenarios from the perspective of a person from a non-English speaking country sitting in the hot seat, or friends sitting on the very ordinary seats behind, observing.

When the decision-maker enters the room laden with folders or wearing something strange on their head, the subordinates must stand and bow to these pretend gods. This fake process is meant to create an atmosphere of respect for the decision that 'The Court', or 'The Tribunal' will make. In truth, it is an act of intimidation, especially when people seeking protection have suffered serious harm from authority figures.

Tribunal decisions never mention the person who made the decision within the decision itself. The decision-maker is not required to own the review. They aren't accountable for the honesty and fairness of their review, but for the lawfulness of the decision. The decision usually reports that 'it found' or 'it concluded'. This is a clever way of distancing the decision from the person making it.

'The Court' can find that the member, the reviewer, made jurisdictional errors. Reviewers, however, can make non-jurisdictional errors. Strangely, while the reviewer is allowed to make mistakes, people seeking protection are often not. When a person suffering post-traumatic stress makes an error, reviewers like Ros Redberry will not tolerate mistakes. There is no leeway.

Years after the event, the person seeking a review of a negative decision is expected to remember exact details. The reviewer will question them about two dates that might have been mentioned for the same event, or whether a car outside the house was blue or dark blue – bizarre minutiae which can lead to confusion, and the reviewer claiming in their decision that a person was 'inconsistent' or 'not credible'. Thus, a negative decision is reached without jurisdictional error.

The law is discussed and debated *ad nauseam* while the merits of a person's claim for deserving Australia's protection sit on the shelf gathering dust. Who or what is this law that is so revered, and to which people have to stand and bow solemnly? Parliaments endorse laws. Members introduce them into parliament for other members to ratify so that somebody's mad, unfair idea can be made law.

Hence, a decision-maker like Redberry can distance herself from her inadequate decisions. The process allows her to pretend she was not actually making the decision but, rather, 'The Tribunal' did it. The buck stops with those who create the laws so decision-makers can sleep peacefully.

Then again, parliamentarians also sleep easy because the foreigners who speak foreign languages are not real Australian people. Their laws are not to protect strangers but Australians. The protection claims of the aliens are insignificant in the context of maintaining a safe and secure place for real Australian people.

No amount of judges and lawyers dressing up or legal paraphernalia can engender respect for the law. A few people in the Department, an occasional Tribunal reviewer and some lawyers and barristers have earned respect through what they say and do. Nobody can insist that 'the law must be respected' if the law is cruel, exclusive and sniffs of racism. International human rights law is respected, inclusive, fair and egalitarian. Regrettably, it is not embedded in the Australian legal system.

People come to Australia carrying the baggage of their previous corrupt legal systems. They struggle for years to gain protection in a legal system which is foreign to them and foreign to international human rights law. It is left to a few departmental officials and tribunal reviewers, some fair-minded lawyers and hundreds of Australian advocates to stand up for these aliens as friends.

~~~~~~~

14. A humanitarian visa story

The story of the unfair and inappropriate decisions of one family's lengthy and traumatising experience reveals the inflexibility of the restrictive legal process and the social and economic costs that arise when a case is not assessed and/or reviewed in strict compliance with Australia's international obligations. Orlando and Belicia had run out of options. All possibilities to pursue protection claims had been exhausted. Their case demonstrates the complexities of protection determinations for people seeking protection who fall outside the Australian government's interpretation of the Convention definition.

In determining Orlando's case, Ian Inglet found that the harm feared was sufficiently grave to constitute persecution. However, he claimed that the reasons for the persecution did not indicate Orlando 'is to be harmed because of his race, religion, nationality, membership of a particular social group or his political opinion'. Inglet concluded that the harm to be inflicted 'is criminal in intent'.

Orlando's mother, Herminia, his wife, Belicia and their two children, Latoya and Adella, arrived a year after Orlando. They submitted an application in Belicia's name, but the details were inadequate and sometimes inaccurate. For example, the grounds for leaving were given as 'to escape injury or death' despite Belicia's claim that a close family member had been brutally raped and murdered. Although she had a formal education, her profession was noted as 'domestic'. Officer, Bill Brown, found serious risk of harm, but no Convention grounds. In a study of decisions around this period, Kneebone argued that Australian legislation affecting a 'Refugee Woman' is 'contrary to international human rights standards'.

A third application was lodged seven years after Belicia's original application on behalf of Latoya, Adella and their grandmother, Herminia. In her refugee determination assessment and consistent with Ian Inglet, delegate Serina O'Keefe found the reason for harm was 'criminal activity'. Consistent with Inglet and Brown, O'Keefe could not 'link the feared persecution to any Convention reason'. Despite the passage of almost eight years, the fear of returning to the country from which the family fled as a result of persecution remained clearly evident.

I became involved when Orlando and his family came to my office seeking assistance. Because the trauma manifested in their behaviour, and their fear of being returned to the country they fled were tangible, I believed that there had to be some means by which such families could access Australia's protection. I read all the decisions the tribunal and the courts had made. Requests to the minister had been rejected and a complaint initiated at the United Nations.

At the time, apart from the non-compellable power of the minister (Section 417), there was no process in the Act to grant permanent legal status for people arriving by plane seeking protection whose cases did not fit Australia's narrow interpretation of the Refugees Convention definition of a refugee. Had there been alternative policies for families such as this at the initial application determination stage, or had the tribunal reviewer had the authority to decide on the basis of humanitarian considerations, the family would have been settled into society eight years earlier.

Over most of a decade and at great personal sacrifice, Orlondo, Belicia and their family endured government-sponsored unemployment, the 'no-work' condition on their bridging visas.

Their pathway to protection necessitated serious costs to the taxpayer because of the engagement of six members of parliament in the immigration portfolio; three delegates of the minister at the initial application stage; four tribunal reviewers; lawyers representing the minister in the Federal and High Courts and, on one occasion, Legal Aid representing the children; public servants in the Ministerial Intervention Unit, the Compliance Office, the Freedom of Information Office, the Attorney General's Office, the International Obligations and Interventions Office and the Government Debt Collectors; the staff of the 'Dob-In an Illegal' desk; detention centre staff, and staff at the Australian Embassy in Geneva.

During the ten years that the Australian Government rejected the case, the family's resilience was strengthened by their fear of being returned. Different representatives of the minister contradicted each other's decisions and delegates' assessments, and public servants overrode tribunal reviewers' advice. Negative interpretations of guidelines and intimidation by public servants have long-lasting effects. Insidiously, decisions are actually made at the departmental level and either handed on to the minister through advisory notes or finalised in the department on the basis of personal interpretations of guidelines, rendering ministerial authority tokenistic.

All three initial application assessments recognised fear of criminal activity, a fear that falls outside the delegates' jurisdiction regarding protection decisions. Initial assessors and tribunal reviewers don't have the delegation to grant humanitarian visas but, at times, assessors and public servants do make decisions that override tribunal reviewers' recommendations.

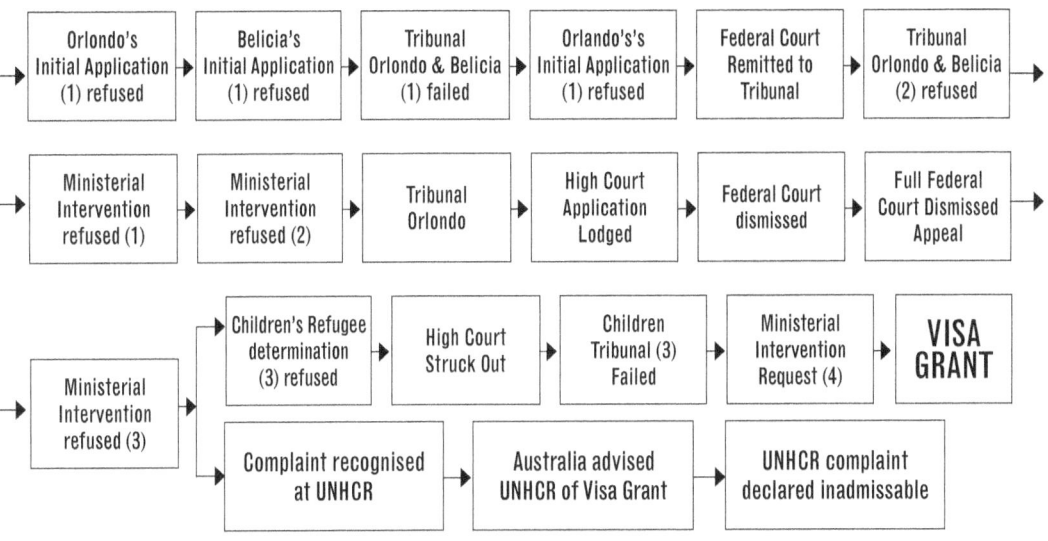

Orlondo and family's pathway to protection 1997–2008
Source: Decisions for all members of this family

Separate applications for review were lodged about the assessment of Orlondo's and Belicia's protection applications but the tribunal conducted one review for both cases. This decision helped the government but was problematic for the family, given their different claims. At the first tribunal hearing, Judith Mullhead found that Orlondo and Belicia's accounts of their experiences in their country of origin appeared 'plausible'. But she concluded that their explanations about conditions in that country were 'unreliable'.

Mullhead went on to say that she was sympathetic to Orlondo and Belicia's situation. She recognised that their lives had been 'dramatically altered by circumstances over which they have had little control'. She even accepted that their fear of harm was well-founded. But she couldn't bring herself to admit that their fear of harm was owing to a Convention reason. Mullhead recognised the violence perpetrated on close family members and the 'power of agents of harm' in their country. She concluded that Orlondo and Belicia's case was one in which *compelling humanitarian grounds* are raised. She then pointed out the limitations of her role in determining whether Orlondo and Belicia satisfied the criteria for protection visas. Consideration on other grounds was solely within the minister's discretion.

Tribunal reviewers don't decide on visas for protection on humanitarian grounds. And yet, if the minister thinks it is in the public interest, they may substitute for a decision of the tribunal under Section 415 another decision that is more favourable to the person, *whether or not the tribunal had the power to make that other decision.* S415(4) of The Act states that 'to avoid doubt, the Tribunal must not, by varying a decision or setting a decision aside and substituting a new decision, purport to make a decision that is not authorised by the Act or the regulations'. However, neither the reviewer nor the minister made the decision about Orlondo and Belicia. Inglet, a public servant, decided not to forward Mullhead's recommendation to Minister Ruddock.

While Mullhead decided not to grant a protection visa, she wrote a note to the State Director NSW alerting him to the final decision and stating that: 'The Tribunal has no authority to consider humanitarian claims. This case may raise such claims'.

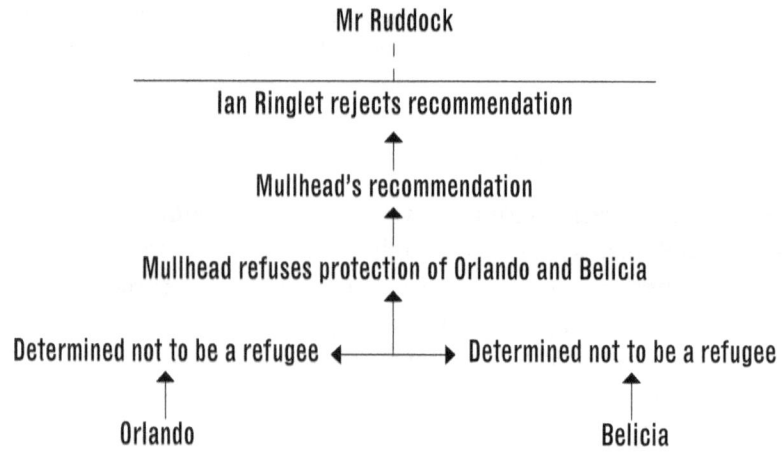

Recommendation for humanitarian consideration: 1997–1999
Source: The Parents' Decisions

Five days after the tribunal decision, Ian Inglet stated that Orlondo and Belicia's case 'had been considered under the Ministerial guidelines for stay in Australia on Humanitarian Grounds'. He concluded that it did not 'satisfy the requirements for consideration of the exercise of Mr Ruddock's discretion under Section 417(1) of the Act'. Contrary to Mullhead's recommendation, Inglet chose not to take the case to Mr Ruddock, although it was within his power to do so.

The guidelines don't oblige public servants or delegates to honour tribunal reviewers' assessments of 'compelling humanitarian grounds'. Eight years of persistent negotiations with the department might have been avoided had Inglet responded to the guideline rather than override Mullhead's assessment. The department exhibits little consistency in interpreting guidelines and no clarity on the status of recommendations by tribunal reviewers and departmental officers. Orlondo and Belicia appealed Mullhead's review in the Federal Court. The judge set aside the tribunal decision and remitted Orlondo and Belicia's case to the tribunal for redetermination. He concluded that:

> ... the Tribunal member erred in holding in this case that "family membership will only be relevant for the purposes of the Convention where there is a link to a broader relevant group".

There apparently being no question but that [Orlondo's family] were within a particular social group that might properly be described as [Orlondo's] family, the critical question for the Tribunal was whether the persecution they feared arose out of their membership of that group. The Tribunal failed to consider that issue.

He also set aside the decision on Belicia's application for redetermination. A second tribunal reviewer, Sally Bland, subjected the family to cross-examination of material that had already been recognised as plausible in the previous determination and decided that Orlondo was not a 'credible witness', discounting Mullhead's finding of plausibility. Since a tribunal reviewer is not obliged to accept earlier decisions in favour of the family, Bland chose to overlook Mullhead's and the judge's earlier conclusions. The adversarial character of tribunal hearings is difficult to reconcile with the UNHCR's guidelines on 'benefit of the doubt' and the independence of Australia's merits review.

The second hearing could have been avoided had the Migration Act included access to an alternative (complementary) visa for non-Convention people seeking protection. Since Mullhead had no authority to decide on humanitarian cases, her decision was disregarded by Bland, but eight years later, Minister Andrews granted a humanitarian visa. Often the tribunal process is an expensive formality because the minister cannot consider intervening without a review at the tribunal. The third tribunal experience was a waste of resources.

Rather than exploring the effects of trauma on a person's ability to remember and present logically, Bland concluded that Orlondo was not credible. And yet memory disturbance affects survivors to varying and fluctuating degrees. It has been found that trauma survivors can be reluctant to disclose trauma in unfamiliar settings. Coffey claimed that

> given the range of possible reasons for delayed disclosure, it is of concern that the Tribunal sometimes draws with apparent alacrity adverse conclusions on the basis of the inconsistencies in the applicant's account. ... irrespective of whether the later submission contradicted or supplemented the earlier claims.

Bland stated Orlondo's oral evidence was 'often confused' but gave no indication that she understood a person's ability to respond when traumatised. She noted confusion about the years certain events occurred, that her questions to Orlondo had to be repeated or rephrased, and that he was hesitant about many responses.

Bland recognised the difficulty of obtaining details of events that took place almost five years earlier. Orlondo had fled the country after surviving an attempted abduction and his wife had been seriously traumatised in a violent situation. With limited English and no treatment for trauma, he had confronted the failure of his and his family's initial assessment, a tribunal review and a Federal Court appeal, proceedings foreign to him. He had also experienced regular distressing visits to the compliance office for visa renewal and, lacking permission to work, he had nothing to occupy himself apart from ruminating on his traumatic experiences. When the tribunal fails to consider the effects of trauma, its conclusions are likely to be prejudiced.

Coffey also explored the problems of communication at the tribunal. Difficulties occur 'where assessment of demeanour in the context of cross-cultural communication, where the applicant speaks through an interpreter, where the applicant comes from a culture with norms of verbal and non-verbal expression that the Tribunal member is unfamiliar with, where the applicant is in a sub-ordinate position to the member and may have been subject to abuse and torture by authorities in his or her own country'.[71] He concluded that the influence of demeanour could conceal unintended bias.

In an analysis of tribunal determinations, Kneebone has argued for 'a more inquisitorial approach' which would allow reviewers to follow up answers to questions rather than employing a test of credibility approach that can confirm a preconceived view as to the decision. This would make possible reviewer bias more transparent.

In Orlondo's case, the issue the court remitted to the tribunal had nothing to do with Orlondo's credibility. It concerned whether or not the family could be recognised as Convention refugees because of their membership of a persecuted social group. At this second hearing, Sally Bland was satisfied that Orlondo and Belicia's claimed fear of persecution was not well-founded, so the issue of Convention ground was not addressed.

A person seeking protection rarely presents an organised account of their life in the context of Convention-related persecution. Evaluating their credibility on the basis of their demeanour, the consistency of their

71. Coffey, 2003, op. cit.

account, and whether aspects of their experience appear 'implausible' doesn't reliably measure the merits of their claims. Genuine people are disbelieved on the basis of 'unreliability'. Someone who fails primarily on credibility grounds has their claims discounted, whereas a non-Convention person seeking protection who experienced gross violations of human rights, but is assessed as credible, may put their claims before other forums.

Whether Bland's view was objective or caught up in a culture of negativity and performance rating is impossible to say. She rendered a disservice to Orlando and Belicia when she didn't respond to the court's request to address the issue of Convention possibilities. She ignored the findings of Mullhead, whose problem was the limitations of the definition rather than implausibility. Bland was also unaware of her own potential for prejudice by focusing on credibility. According to the Migration Act, Bland was bound to 'act according to the substantial justice and merits of the case' and not be 'bound by technicalities, legal forms or rules of evidence'. She was in danger of undermining the concept of 'substantial justice' in choosing to reject the conclusions of earlier ministerial representatives.

~~~~~~~~

People seeking Australia's protection who apply for ministerial intervention are not allowed to earn a living or access Medicare unless the minister is personally considering their request. According to a 2007 government fact sheet, people 'who are in Australia lawfully but working in breach of their visa conditions' and non-citizens working without a visa deny Australian citizens and permanent residents the opportunity to obtain a job. Locating and removing illegal workers is 'an additional burden on the taxpayer' and employers are disadvantaged if they employ legal workers because they may not be in a position to compete with 'those who employ and under-pay illegal workers'. Further, illegal workers may be subject to exploitation and organised criminal activity.

In the government's own estimation, being employed while holding a 'no-work' visa condition allows rogue employers to underpay and exploit people who arrive by plane seeking protection. Illegal activities by employers and employees arising from the 'no-work' clause question the usefulness of this law. Employers can terminate 'illegal' workers without remuneration for completed work and the 'dob-in an illegal' telephone line encourages suspicion in the community. Moreover, if the employer wants to terminate a 'lawful' person working illegally, all they need to do is contact the Department of Immigration. This was what happened to this family.

How effective is a lawful sanction that doesn't allow a person to work to support their family for a substantial period of time, and how does such a law sit with our international obligations? If someone is further traumatised because unemployment prevents them from caring for their family, is this not a form of torture? Even though existing jurisprudence relating to torture does not support this suggestion, the question should not be ignored where the imposition of 'no work' is both punishment and intimidatory. Further punishments include the denial of the right to access Centrelink (unemployment, disability or special) benefits, Medicare, funded settlement services, English programs, translating and interpreting services and public housing. The Convention Against Torture Article 1 describes torture as:

> any act by which severe pain or suffering, whether physical or mental, is intentionally inflicted on a person for such purposes as obtaining from him or a third person information or a confession, punishing him for an act he or a third person has committed or is suspected of having committed, or intimidating or coercing him or a third person, or for any reason based on discrimination of any kind, when such pain or suffering is inflicted by or at the instigation of or with the consent or acquiescence of a public official or other person acting in an official capacity. It does not include pain or suffering arising only from, inherent in or incidental to lawful sanctions.

The operative word is *lawful*. Is it lawful for domestic law to withhold basic human rights as a punishment for not leaving the country voluntarily, or as an intimidatory tool to cause people to return to a country where they fear further persecution? Article 31 of the Refugee Convention states: 'Contracting States shall not impose penalties, on account of their illegal entry or presence, on refugees who, coming directly from a territory where their life or freedom was threatened'. The International Covenant on Civil and Political Rights (ICCPR) Article 7 states that 'no one shall be subjected to torture or to cruel, inhuman or degrading treatment or punishment'.

It could be argued that living under conditions of forced unemployment was penalty or punishment for appealing decisions rather than leaving the country, and that government-sponsored unemployment is inhumane or degrading treatment that could subject people to abusive employers and dehumanise able-bodied people by preventing them from fulfilling their obligations to their families.

Article 27(2) of the Convention on the Rights of the Child (CROC) states that 'the parent(s) or others responsible for the child have the primary responsibility to secure, within their abilities and financial capacities, the conditions of living necessary for the child's development'. When Section 41(2)(b) of the Act restricts a person from working, it inhibits parents' rights and responsibilities. At what point will a state evaluate the degree of suffering inflicted by the lawful sanctions of the 'no-work' visa condition and laws that permit 'pain and suffering arising only from, inherent in or incidental to lawful sanctions'?

People who have exhausted their legal possibilities and, without permission, exercised their basic human right to support themselves, are methodically sought out by a dedicated compliance office. The duties of immigration compliance officers include 'preventing illegal work' and detaining and removing 'unlawful' non-citizens.

An 'integrity visit' to Orlondo's family by the compliance team found the 'occupants of the premises were not at home'. On the advice of another departmental officer, the company was keen to have him removed from their worksite and alerted the departmental investigators. The Compliance East Field Team executed a search warrant. Orlondo admitted to working which meant that, although lawfully living in the community, he was in breach of his visa conditions. He was required to report the following day to the compliance office where his Bridging Visa E was cancelled. He was granted another BVE immediately 'on the basis of an outstanding request' under s417 of the Migration Act and, from then on was required to report weekly to the compliance office.

Because Orlondo exercised his authority under the United Nations Conventions to work in order to provide food and shelter for his wife and children, he contravened Australian visa conditions. Since Orlondo had arrived in Australia he had not been permitted to work. This amounted to having to exist with his family in an overcrowded unit in sub-standard conditions for four years, accepting other people's payment for rent, electricity and other bills and to beg for his children to be educated free. This one breach is significant in relation to further decisions regarding the family's attempts to gain protection.

Two days after the execution of the search warrant, the 'outstanding s417 request' was assessed by case officers as 'Guidelines Not Met'. A brief prepared for the minister emphasised Bland's prejudiced findings of implausibility, as a result of Belicia not mentioning the death of a close family member in the initial application and Bland's decision regarding relocation.

The brief recommended that the minister *not* consider exercising his power under s417 because, in the opinion of the public servant, the 'case does not meet the Guidelines and the circumstances are neither exceptional nor unique'. The minister chose to follow the advice and the public servant chose to ignore a set of facts that could have resulted in a more positive brief. In this case the negative perspective presented in the ministerial brief could have influenced strongly the fate of this family's intervention request. This process effectively allowed public servants to act with ministerial authority and illustrates how public perceptions of ministerial tokenism can arise. In her report on the appropriate use of ministerial powers, Proust found a lack of trust in the judicial system and the public service 'to get migration issues right'.

The brief was prepared in such a way that the bureaucrats pre-empted the decision of the minister. Briefs can be produced from a range of contrasting decisions, depending on what public servants perceive the minister might be looking for, rather than fidelity to, the spirit of 'care and compassion' suggested in Ruddock's guidelines and the spirit of s417 of the Act, which requires the minister to act in the public interest. There is no legal definition of 'public interest'. The public servant could have focused on the decision of tribunal member Mullhead's recommendation for humanitarian consideration, pointing out the contradictions in the public servant's conclusions as to why the recommendation was not taken up, the Federal Court findings, and the different plausibility findings of Mullhead and Bland. In this case, the biased ministerial brief and the visa condition breach resulted in the minister's refusal to consider a humanitarian visa.

In her report, Proust touches on 'concerns about issues relating to culture' and concludes that 'if there are deeper cultural issues at play, then it will take time, changes to the way the Department operates, and perhaps some people change before a level of confidence in the Department returns'.[72]

Orlondo's lawyer submitted a further request asking for consideration, arguing that there had been dramatic changes with the new president in Orlondo's country of origin and a threat of a campaign of terror, that the USA still had grave concerns regarding human rights abuses, the validity of the first tribunal member's finding of 'compelling humanitarian grounds', and clear signs of 'post-traumatic stress disorder'. He concluded that given clarification of the current political extremities and reactions that prevail in their country, we 'contend that this case warrants re-consideration and referral to the Minister'.

The lawyer submitted sections of Mr Ruddock's own guidelines detailing reasons for claiming there were 'Unique and Exceptional Circumstances' including a significant threat to personal security, experience of torture or trauma or having been subjected to a systemic program of harassment. He argued that there were 'clearly unintended consequences of legislation', that Orlondo and his family had spent around 5 years integrating into the Australian community, and the psychological

---

72. Proust, 2008, op. cit.

fragility of the parents who had two children under twelve years of age. The public servant who assessed the submission concluded that their case remained outside the ambit of the guidelines.

Since new information was presented (unsuccessfully) regarding the political situation in the second request, the definition of 'additional information' in Ruddock's guidelines ought to be clarified. Apart from this, a number of guidelines could have been perceived as 'being met'. The first ministerial request decision was made only a few days after the execution of the search warrant, so the bureaucrats must have relied upon the guideline about the 'degree to which the person co-operated with the department and complied with any reporting or *other conditions of a visa*' (my emphasis).

This was confirmed in a file note reporting on events following the execution of the search warrant. After a Bridging Visa E was granted, the request for ministerial intervention was assessed as 'Guidelines not met'. Orlondo and Belicia's application was forwarded to the minister's office and the outcome was 'Power not considered'. The decision was sent to Orlondo and Belicia. A second ministerial request was lodged. When the family approached the compliance office, Orlondo was detained. An s48b request was lodged and assessed as 'Not met'; subsequent application not allowed. The decision was communicated to Orlondo and Belicia.

This one subsection of one Guideline (5.1.5) took precedence over Australia's treaty obligations in the decision of the two requests to the minister. The response to the s48b request indicated that public servants overlooked the 'additional information' in preference to the breach of the 'no-work' condition and the desire to detain. This incident revealed the priority departmental officials placed on the breach of the 'no-work' visa condition. Neither 'new information' nor Australia's treaty obligations could override Guideline 5.1.5. The family were in danger of being deported. Contravening a minuscule clause of a guideline took precedence over Australia's non-refoulement obligations regarding fear of persecution on return, 'whether or not they have been formally recognised as refugees'.

Ian Inglet had enough material in the guidelines to justify consideration of a second request. There remained a question as to why a public servant was justified in concluding that 'the purported further application/request is considered **NOT** to meet the Guidelines'. The fact that these ministerial discretions cannot be delegated is no reason for the department to refrain from making recommendations that do meet the Guidelines.

In a letter to Orlondo and Belicia, Inglet stated that their request to allow a further application was not referred to the minister. He stated that the minister, 'does not wish to consider whether to exercise his power again unless additional information is provided'. Inglet judged that information regarding the dramatic changes in the country and grave US concerns were either not new or not relevant. He found that Mullhead's compelling humanitarian grounds and claims of post-traumatic stress were not something the minister should respond to 'with care and compassion' in 'serving the public interest'. A further ministerial request was made (and rejected) which included updated psychological assessments, two UNHCR country reports, material on the effects of post-traumatic stress, and numerous letters of support from the family's faith community.

When determining whether to forward cases to the minister, ministerial or departmental officials can be exposed to unacceptable or undesirable practices. A migration agent, businessman or church official could put energy into fostering a close relationship with the minister or staff. Equally, a migration agent could antagonise a case officer. In a publicised example, Dante Tan made a $10,000 donation to Mr Ruddock's electorate campaign. Mr Tan was granted a visa but Minister Ruddock later had his visa revoked.

~~~~~~~~

Following the execution of the search warrant, Orlondo and Belicia presented at the compliance office. They were advised that the minister had declined to intervene on their behalf. They were then told that the only condition on which a further bridging visa could be given was their willingness to undertake departure arrangements. The department was prepared to purchase the tickets if the family 'requested removal'. Although the compliance officer reported that the parents began to cry and 'stated assertively that there was no way they would go home', there is no evidence that departmental officials questioned the fact that these people were genuinely afraid to return. Orlondo was immediately detained in the Villawood camp for three months. Belicia and the children were required to organise flights to their country of origin. Orlondo was eventually released on a $5,000 bond because his advocate submitted an appeal to the High Court. Belicia was put on an $8,000 bond. A friend in their church community loaned them the money.

An advocate's version of what seems to be this same interview revealed that Orlondo and Belicia felt intimidated. The advocate asserted that Orlondo and his family had felt harassed, intimidated and threatened. They had no alternative but to sign a document without legal assistance. The advocate felt that it was an abuse of power. He expressed his frustration to the Assistant Manager Compliance Field Operations (East), maintaining that people seeking protection had the legitimate expectation that departmental officers and tribunal reviewers would 'genuinely assess their applications'.

Criticism that powers entrusted to the minister were being abused was emerging. In his report of this period, Palmer found that there was no automatic process of review sufficient to provide confidence to the government, the secretary of the department or the public 'that the power to detain a person on reasonable suspicion of being an unlawful non-citizen under s.189(1) of the Commonwealth's Migration Act 1958 is being exercised lawfully, justifiably and with integrity'. He went on to say that 'the speed of change in the immigration detention environment since 2000 has led to policy, procedures and enabling structures being developed on the run'.[73] This created challenges for the department and its compliance and immigration detention staff.

If children aged seven and ten were removed along with their traumatised parents, the decisions of public servants are protected by a note in the guidelines which quotes Article 3 of the Convention on the Rights of the Child (CROC). The guidelines states that 'in all actions concerning children, whether undertaken by public or private social welfare institutions, courts of law, administrative authorities or legislative bodies, the best interests of the child shall be a primary consideration'.

However, the guidelines include a bracketed rider: 'Note: this must be balanced against any countervailing considerations'. It is not clear what the 'countervailing considerations' might have been. It could not have been in 'the best interests of the child' to return them with psychologically traumatised parents to a place which they had left as three- and six-year-olds. They fled following the horrific rape and murder of a close family member with whom they were living. The 'countervailing consideration' in this case seemed to be that the family were to be deported because one parent was accessing his basic human rights to house, feed and clothe his family, while living in a state of government-sponsored unemployment.

In making the decision that, 'there are no issues which engage Australia's obligations under the ICCPR, CEDAW, CROC and CAT' two public servants clearly overlooked Article 3 of CAT regarding non-refoulement obligations. While public servants may dismiss the plausibility factor, it would be difficult to find reason for dismissing the flagrant violations of human rights in Article 3(2) and, the 'substantial grounds' in Article 3(1) of CAT, given the more recent country information. They also overlooked the Conclusion No. 6 (XXVIII) (1997) of the Executive Committee of the United Nations High Commission for Refugees which reaffirmed the fundamental

---

73. Palmer, 2005, op. cit.

importance of the observance of the principle of non-refoulement – both at the border and within the territory of a state – of persons who may be subjected to persecution if returned to their country of origin irrespective of whether or not they have been formally recognised as refugees.

Since Orlando and Belicia couldn't pay for tickets to a country to which they were afraid to return, the threat of detention and the offer to pay for plane tickets on the condition that they request removal indicated that coercion was used to persuade them to comply. Although detained, Orlando never requested removal and this was noted on every departmental removal document. He was listed as an 'overstayer' rather than a person seeking protection. Orlando was consistently unwilling to be returned and, according to Article 3 of CAT, the family should not be refouled.

Two further findings in Palmer's report are worth noting. He concluded that there is a serious cultural problem within the department's 'immigration compliance and detention areas: urgent reform is necessary. The combination of pressure in these areas and the framework' within which departmental officers had been required to operate 'has given rise to a culture that is overly self-protective and defensive, a culture largely unwilling to challenge organisational norms or to engage in genuine self-criticism or analysis'. Palmer stated that departmental officers 'are authorised to exercise exceptional, even extraordinary, powers. That they should be permitted and expected to do so without adequate training, without proper management and oversight, with poor information systems, and with no genuine quality assurance and constraints on the exercise of these powers is of concern. The fact that this situation has been allowed to continue unchecked and unreviewed for several years is difficult to understand'.[74]

The appeals Orlando and Belicia lodged in the High Court and the Federal Court were dismissed or withdrawn. Ministerial intervention requests were rejected or mislaid. There was a successful tribunal hearing for Orlando to be released from detention. A complaint was lodged and accepted with the UNHRC in Geneva. A further determination application was made on behalf of the children, so that they could all remain legal – as filing a complaint with UNHRC is not a condition for a bridging visa. This was refused by Serina O'Keefe and, again, Carmel Petitie at the tribunal upheld O'Keefe's decision. Each refusal resulted in a letter suggesting the family prepare to leave Australia. After failed attempts to speak to the minister personally, a further complaint was made to the department regarding the abuse of power in the minister's office.

Belicia made a complaint to the UNHRC. Initially, the department didn't comply with the timeline set by the UNHRC in providing their

---

74. Palmer, 2005, op. cit.

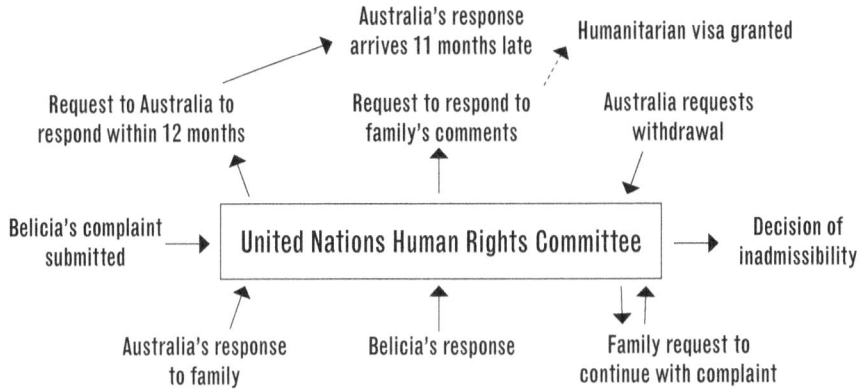

UNHRC Petitions Unit process
Source: Correspondence in relation to UNHRC complaint

response. The complaints process and the interaction between Belicia, the UNHRC and the government was a long drawn-out process.

Rather than respond to Belicia's extensive submission, Minister Andrews granted a humanitarian visa, the same visa the first tribunal member, Mullhead, had trusted the department would consider eight years earlier. The department notified UNHRC of Andrews's decision. It then requested UNHRC to invite Belicia to withdraw the case.

Clearly, the Australian Government had little respect for the Committee. The UNHCR Petitions Unit took no notice of the delays, obviously extending the deadline for the response and continuing the process. Under Rule 97 of the Committee's Rules of Procedure, the response should have been made 11 months earlier. Ignoring the request to respond to the family's further comments, the Australian Permanent Mission in Geneva advised that 'the authors of the Communication were granted permanent Refugee and Humanitarian visas', adding: 'In recognition of this development, the Australian Government respectfully requests the [UNHRC] Committee to ask the authors whether they would consider withdrawing their communication'.

Since there was no mention of Australia's obligations to foster basic human rights for people seeking protection, Belicia and Orlondo felt that nothing would change for others in similar predicaments. There was no evidence either that the Australian Government had responded to the family's further response regarding the government's Admissibility and Merits Submission to the UNHRC. The family's withdrawal was conditional. They felt that the systematic failures revealed by their case should be explained by the Australian Government to the international community to ensure best practice by Australia in the future.

Suggesting that this 'very aggressive' letter would upset the Australian Government when forwarded, and could have 'implications' for the family, the Petitions Unit at UNHRC made a phone call requesting Belicia and Orlando to withdraw the response. Although shocked by the request, in order to keep the communication alive, Belicia and Orlando rewrote the reply without withdrawing from the process. The response from the Petitions Unit was curt: 'Fine – we have taken note of Belicia's request'. The statement went on to say: 'with all due respect, however, I take the liberty to point out that in virtually all similar cases concerning Australia, consideration of the complaint was discontinued after the issuance of a humanitarian residence permit. The Committee considered that the complainants' claims had become moot'.

With an underlying intimidatory tone, the notification continued: 'We are not convinced that Belicia is not doing herself and her family a disfavour by insisting on continuation of the case'. Condescendingly, the UNHRC officer finished with: 'We are happy to explain this to her on the phone, from Spanish-speaking lawyer in this office'.

Shortly afterwards, the claims were declared inadmissible and the family was notified of the decision. What else could they do? Australia makes a significant financial contribution to the upkeep of the UN Human Rights office and you can't bite the hand that feeds you. The Australian Government is off the hook again! Accountability is secondary to cruelty.

It must be said, though, that the newly elected government at the time did take some of its UN obligations seriously. After a year in office, it made significant changes to refugee/protection policy and, in 2011, the *Migration Amendment (Complementary Protection) Act 2011* brought significant changes to the *Migration Act 1958 (Cth)*. This change provides protection for those who are not refugees according to the Act, but who can't return to their home country because they will suffer certain types of harm that engage Australia's other protection obligations.

UNHRC ignored its own procedural rules when Australia failed to comply under Rule 97. The UN Complaints process was further undermined by the manner in which the UNHRC Complaints Committee requested withdrawal of the case. For the Complaints Committee, provision of a visa seemed to dissolve human rights breaches regarding individual cases, a short-term solution that failed to address the policy issues for future non-Convention people seeking Australia's protection.

Belicia, Orlando and their advisers felt that the 'similar cases' that were withdrawn once permanent protection was granted had not changed the system for families such as theirs. It was important politically to continue with the case in order to encourage those within the then newly elected government who might be contemplating modifications to the Migration Act. A decision of admissibility would have encouraged and challenged the new government to examine the previous government's policies under a human rights prism.

The Migration Act bestows extraordinary powers on the minister, and yet public servants had been allowed significant leeway to forward, or not forward, advice to the minister. This resulted in contradictions and inconsistencies when interpreting the guidelines. 'New information' seemed to exclude extenuating circumstances in updated country information, country advice and information on the effects of trauma on a person's ability to present 'credible' factual evidence. Breach of the 'no-work' condition restricted basic human rights and was a significant barrier in providing humanitarian treatment.

~~~~~~~~

This case demonstrates the complexities of protection determinations for people seeking protection who fall outside the Convention definition. Without access to a fair and just system for assessing protection claims, Australia runs the risk of deporting people to danger. For Orlando and Belicia and their family, immigration policy bordered on systemic bias. It failed to recognise the needs of non-Convention people seeking protection through a proactive policy. It failed to provide avenues for non-Convention people seeking protection to be assessed on the *merits* of their 'humanitarian needs' in a fair and just manner, according to UN human rights standards. It granted non-compellable power to one individual who was not required to consider the opinions of members of other democratic institutions including delegates of the minister, tribunal reviewers or judges in the courts. It granted a major decision-making role to public servants whose interpretations of ministerial guidelines were inconsistent, and it relied heavily on advice and decisions of public servants, creating a tokenistic role for the minister.

After Orlando and Belicia received their protection visas, the *Migration Amendment (Complementary Protection) Act 2011* was passed and, in March 2012, new applications for protection could be assessed under this legislation, but it was not retrospective. Some who had already been refused protection successfully challenged this aspect of the law in 2013 and later that year, the High Court disallowed the government's application to appeal.

John von Doussa, a former judge and president of the Australian Human Rights Commission, reflecting on a decision he made in court (the infamous case of the indefinite detention of Mr Al Kateb) wrote:

although international law prohibits inhumane and arbitrary detention, Australian law does not. The results are troubling. As a judge, I felt the decision at which I arrived was both legally correct and morally reprehensible.[75]

He went on to say that 'after five years at the commission, I can no longer in good conscience support the familiar refrain that rights are best protected by the common law and Parliament'. He continued that he was then convinced of the need to ensure 'that all three arms of government – the Executive, the Legislature and the Judiciary – take care when they make decisions that have an impact on basic human rights'. He said the best way was 'to introduce a statutory charter of rights'.

Triggs argues that a legislated charter of rights would encourage compliance without resorting to litigation. Where a case proceeds to court a charter would send a law that is incompatible with rights back to parliament for amendment and reform. This 'dialogue model' preserves the supremacy of parliament and representative democracy.[76]

Without a model like that suggested by Triggs, a charter of rights might protect detainees and less visible cohorts of people seeking Australia's protection, but it will not change structural exclusionary policies and practices that have evolved since colonisation. Belicia and Orlando's protection journey illustrates how the powers of the government frustrate the responsibilities of the court to uphold international law.

~~~~~~~~

75. Von Doussa, J, 2008, 'Bill of rights is essential to best serve human rights', *Sydney Morning Herald,* 9 October. https://humanrights.gov.au/about/news/opinions/bill-rights-essential-best-serve-human-rights-2008. Accessed March 2022.
76. Triggs op. cit., p.282.

15. Exceptions: historical and contemporary

In 2002, Minister Ruddock concluded that people who were unsuccessful in seeking protection abused the judicial process by misusing the court procedures 'to delay their stay and frustrate their removal from Australia', arguing that these factors justified introducing a privative clause into migration legislation to restrict access to the courts.[77] Ruddock claimed that, despite the introduction of the Refugee Review Tribunal, the volume of cases before the courts was not reduced. He also complained that there had been a rise in litigation costs from $5.8 million in 1995–1996 to $15 million in 2000–2001.

The legal and political context of seeking protection in Australia needs to be seen against a background of governmental practices, designed by successive colonial governments, to regard the needs of British 'settlers' as paramount and to 'except' Indigenous peoples from those governments' duty to govern fairly. Two hundred years of legal exceptions from the general law resulted in oppressive treatment of Indigenous peoples who were not even counted as part of the population or allowed in many cases to own property or have entitlement to the few constitutional rights the Australian Constitution has provided. This occurred under Federal and State regimes until the passing of the Racial Discrimination Act and the High Court's Mabo decision. Aborigines were people 'without the law'. Members of parliament were never innocent bystanders in the treatment of Indigenous peoples, nor are they now in the treatment of refugees who are similarly regarded as somehow outside and, *prima facie*, unacceptable in Australia.

All too often that perception is reinforced by reaction to the 'race' of people struggling to gain protection, as a consequence of Australia's laws being founded on this exception. Colonial state laws and the Federal Constitution were formulated at a time when the original Australians were classified as an inferior race, and left out of the process. The Migration Act and the Citizenship Act were constructed during a time of deliberate rejection of any concept that Australian Indigenous peoples were equally human. They had no rights as citizens, let alone rights to self-determination or sovereignty as the first Australians.

~~~~~~~~

There are tensions between the Judiciary and Federal Parliament in maintaining fairness and justice for people seeking protection. For people arriving by plane, 'membership of a particular social group' was a pertinent persecution category in the Refugees Convention in relation to assessments of protection claims. The 1951 Convention relating to the Status of Refugees and the 1967 Protocol are the key legal documents in defining who is a refugee, their rights, and the legal obligations of states. The Canadian Immigration and Refugee Board (1991),[78] and the United Nations High Commission for Refugees' (UNHCR) (2002) guidelines for assessing protection claims through membership of a particular social group are also significant.[79]

In the US justice system, if a person witnesses a crime and does nothing to try to stop it, that person is guilty by association. Protecting the vulnerable in society should not be a choice but a moral obligation. Australians don't have this obligation. It is not enshrined in our legal system.[80]

To understand contemporary refugee and protection policy we need to appreciate the legal approach to Indigenous Australian citizens in the era of the emergence of Western democracy from a juridico-classical tradition regarding the human being to one of biopolitical sovereignty.[81] Australia's Indigenous peoples and persecuted people seeking protection have a common identity whereby both social groups consist of sovereign human beings or sovereign citizens within other cultures. They are politically placed outside the boundaries of Australian citizenship in the sovereign state in which they find themselves. Legislatively, when the power of the sovereign state usurps the power of the courts, these two social groups are abandoned by the law. In our failure to protect human rights, there is a litany of instances where Australia reveals a dysfunctional parliament and disempowered courts. These instances include indefinite detention of people seeking protection, Aboriginal deaths in custody, domestic violence, racism in the delivery of health services, and gender inequality.[82]

The Magna Carta of 1215 stated that: 'No free man may be arrested, imprisoned, dispossessed of his goods, or placed outside the law, or molested in any way'.[83] In 1679 the writ of *habeas corpus* that first recorded bare life, or the very fact of existence itself as the new political subject stated: 'We command that you have before us to show, at Westminster, that body X, by whatsoever name he may be called therein, which is held in 'your custody.'[84] The corpus (the body) became the new subject of politics, 'not the free man and his statutes and prerogatives'. Agamben argues that the assertion and presentation of this 'body' was the birth of democracy where *habeas corpus* assumed the form of law and became inseparable from Western democracy. However, in the title of the French declaration on 'The Rights of Man and Citizen' in 1789, it is unclear whether 'man' and 'citizen' form a unitary system in which the first is always included in the second. Agamben points out that as a consequence of this ambiguity 'the "rights of an Englishman" when preferred to the inalienable rights of man acquires an unsuspected profundity'.[85] Historically, this is the period between the British invasion of Indigenous Australians' territorial lands (1788) and the declaration of *terra nullius,* or land without owners (1835). In 1828, Governor Arthur of Tasmania proclaimed martial law, which was tantamount to a declaration of war against Aboriginal peoples. During the three years in which martial law remained in force, the military were entitled to shoot on sight any Aboriginal person in the settled districts.[86]

This purported 'civil war' is related to the chaos created by the colonial occupation of land, lawlessness on the part of early 'settlers', and a constituted British law abandoning the original law regarding the rights of all citizens. The colonial invaders caused the chaos in Tasmania. By suspending the rule of law protecting *all* human beings and creating a legal exception, some human beings could be killed with impunity.

It is not possible to discuss Australia's contemporary policies and practices without at least acknowledging the profound exclusionary legal exceptions of white Australia's past. Historically, Australian exclusionary policy-making has its foundation in the 'exception', 'something that is included solely through an exclusion'. After occupying the land of Australia's Indigenous peoples for forty-seven years, British authorities declared the non-existence of Indigenous ownership of their land with the *terra nullius* proclamation of 1835.[87] In 1837, England's House of Commons Select Committee on Aborigines questioned the legitimacy of the Colonial Office's proclamation. They recognised that Indigenous Australians and their territorial rights were excluded from settler Australia's social structures and discourses. They noted that these Indigenous people

77. Ruddock, 2002, op. cit., p.4.
78. Canadian Immigration Refugee Board, op. cit.
79. UNHCR 2002, op. cit.
80. Smith, L, 2014, 'Ex-Immigration officer: is there asylum seeker blood on my hands?', *Crikey: Independent Media, Independent Minds*. Now available at http://sievx.com/articles/28LifeJackets/20140130Smith.html. Accessed March 2022
81. Natural born citizenship: The United States law defines citizenship for Indigenous Americans as 'Any Indian or Eskimo born in the United States, provided being a citizen of the U.S. does not impair the person's status as a citizen of the tribe' (J Spurgeon, 2013, 'Defining 'Natural Born Citizen': The Debate Over Who Qualifies To Run For President'). Indigenous Australians deserve recognition of their original citizenship also.
82. Triggs op. cit., p.278.
83. Agamben op. cit., p.73.
84. Holt op. cit., p.90 defines 'bare life' as 'the very fact of existence itself'.
85. Agamben op. cit., p.75.
86. Ryan quoted in Bourke, C & Cox, H, 1994, 'Two Laws: One Land', in C Bourke, E Bourke & W Edwards (eds), *Aboriginal Australia*, University of Queensland Press, St Lucia, pp.49-64, p.49.
87. Thompson, S, 2013, (Curator) *Objects through Time*, Migration Heritage Centre 2006-2013, http://www.migrationheritage.nsw.gov.au/exhibition/objectsthroughtime/bourketerra/. Accessed March 2022.

'unoffending as they were towards us, have as might have been expected, suffered in an aggravated degree'. The office went on to state that, 'in the formation of these settlements it does not appear that the territorial rights of the natives were considered'. They recognised that 'the effects have consequently been dreadful beyond example, both in the diminution of their numbers and in their demoralization'.[88]

However, the legal exception was not overturned. Indigenous Australians were excluded from the legal processes and settler Australians 'proceeded without concessions to traditional culture, settlement patterns or land use' to appropriate land.[89]

Australia's Constitution was enacted in 1901, after 113 years of unresolved coexistence between two very different social groups – one which believed it had never ceded sovereignty and, as first owners and occupiers, had sovereign rights, and the other which believed that it was superior, and that Indigenous peoples had no right to sovereignty beyond the Australian sovereign state that was instituted at Federation.

In the process of establishing political sovereignty, George Reid, Leader of the Opposition in 1901, argued in parliament that the reason for excluding Indigenous peoples was based on problems 'caused by coloured people in the United States'. He declared: 'the Opposition wants the new Australia to be a land for the finest products of the Anglo-Saxon race'.[90] The formation of Anglo-Australia's legislation included the British and their descendants on the basis of an exclusion. Through a legal exception, the original sovereign citizens of the country could not rely on the legal protection granted to generations of settler Australians.

This exception was extended to other non-Anglo people in 1901. After having lived and worked alongside other 'settlers' and Australia's Indigenous peoples for many years, non-Anglo people were deported solely to preserve the lifestyle of generations of British. These non-Anglo people included Chinese indentured labourers (1840s), Afghan cameleers (1838), and Pacific Islanders abducted to work in banana plantations and cane fields (1868).[91] In the House of Representatives of the Australian Parliament in 1901, Alfred Deakin contended in his argument to restrict Asian immigration that: 'It is not the bad qualities, but the good qualities of these alien races that make them dangerous to us ... It is their inexhaustible energy, their power of applying themselves to new tasks, their endurance, and low standard of living that make them such competitors'.[92]

The Australian legal system is grounded in these early discriminatory and exclusionary policies and practices. The legal exception encompassed Germans during World War One (1919). Many Australian-born Germans who had committed no crime were held in military-run camps and then deported. There were around 38,000 Germans in Australia in 1901. During both First and Second World Wars, German, Italian and later Japanese internees were harshly treated in camps in rural Australia.[93] This expulsion further 'reinforced rather than contradicted the White Australia Policy by clarifying that "white" meant British'.[94]

In 1937, the sovereignty of Australia's Indigenous peoples was once again not recognised by the political system and its constituted parliament. Australian citizenship was created on the basis of an exception. The *Australian Citizenship Act of 1948* excepted Indigenous people, failing to recognise their rights as citizens. It created a type of citizenship that could include and exclude, as distinct from all-inclusive sovereign citizenship.

Like the *terra nullius* fiction, the 'dictation test' (administered in any language), a sham immigration determination process, was introduced. This restricted non-Anglo/European people from entering Australia for 72 years after Federation. The dictation test was abolished in the same year as the introduction of the *Migration Act (1958)* but was in use for 57 years. The White Australia Policy was law from 1901 to 1973. The exception had become the norm. For 185 years (1788–1973), Anglo/European Australians legally excluded people who were either Indigenous to Australia or non-Anglo/European. In 1967, as a result of years of intense lobbying, Indigenous Australians were included in the census. Their original sovereignty remains unrecognised in Australia's Constitution.

In 1992, Eddie Mabo, a Murray Islander, had his family's traditional title to land recognised by the High Court. Justice Brennan stated that 'the fiction by which the rights and interests of indigenous inhabitants in land

---

88. quoted in Pittock, B, 1972, 'Aboriginal Land Rights', in F Stevens (ed), *Racism: The Australian Experience,* 2nd Vol, ANZ Books Company, pp.199-208.
89. Reynolds, H, 1987, *Frontier,* Allen & Unwin Pty Ltd., St Leonards, NSW, p.194.
90. McDonald, P, 2019, 'Migration to Australia: From Asian Exclusion to Asian Predominance', *Revue Europeenne des Migrations Internationales* vol. 35, https://journals.openedition.org/remi/12695. Accessed March 2022.
91. Chinese indentured labourers (1840s) Jones, P, 2005, 'Chinese-Australian Journeys: Records on Travel, Migration and Settlement, 1860-1975', National Archives of Australia; Flinders Ranges Research 2013, The Afghan Camelmen, http://www.southaustralianhistory.com.au/afghans.htm. Accessed July 2013; Pacific Islanders abducted for banana plantations and cane fields (1868) Giuliani, G, 2011, 'Throwaway Labour. Blackbirding and a White Australia', The *Journal of the European Association of Studies on Australia,* vol. 2, no.2, pp.98-112.
92. Clancy, L, 2004, *Culture and Customs of Australia,* Greenwood Publishing Group, p.12. Accessed March 2022
93. Manne, R & Corlette, D, 2004, *Sending Them Home: Refugees and the new Politics of Indifference, Quarterly Essay* Issue 13, pp.1-95; Mares, P, 2001, *Borderline: Australia's treatment of refugees and asylum seekers,* University of New South Wales Press Ltd, Sydney.
94. Bashford, A & Strange, C, 2002, 'Asylum-Seekers and National Histories of Detention', *Australian Journal of Politics and History,* vol. 48, no. 4, pp.509-527, p.519.

were treated as non-existent' was 'an unjust and discriminatory doctrine'.[95] In 1992, Prime Minister Paul Keating announced that it was time 'to bring the dispossessed out of the shadows, to recognise that they are part of us, and that we cannot give Indigenous Australians up without giving up many of our own most deeply held values, much of our own identity – and our own humanity'. The same year during which he partially included Indigenous Australians, Keating introduced mandatory detention for people seeking protection who arrived by boat. [96]

~~~~~~~~

From 1860, a legal exception allowed the forced removal of Indigenous children that resulted in them being institutionalised or adopted by white Australian couples. The forced removal of Indigenous children under the *Assimilation Act (1937)* was focused on the merging of 'half-caste' children into Australian society through a policy of white adoption. However, Indigenous children were also separated from their families and institutionalised in homes designed to provide labour as 'farm hands' and 'housemaids'. This process of exclusion and inclusion by successive governments occurred for around 100 years, until the late 1960s.[97] Legal exceptions were also introduced to allow unaccompanied children in state care to be sent to Australia from England without the permission of their families from 1911 to 1912, and from 1947 to 1967. [98] From the 1940s to the 1980s, legislation created by predominately male authorities[99] allowed Anglo-Australian babies to be taken from their unmarried mothers for adoption by married couples.[100] Hundreds of children were victims of family separation and dispossession. During this period, the exception had been extended beyond the exclusions of Indigenous Australians and non-Anglo people to excluding vulnerable people in the Anglo-Australian community.

 The next step is that of excluding yet another social group of vulnerable 'outsiders'. White superiority in Australia developed the embedded notion of 'we know what's best', and this is still evident today in our legal and political frameworks. We as a society should remain vigilant in countering smaller steps that lead to people dying in camps: the adoption by parliament of laws that breach fundamental freedoms; the expansion of executive discretions that are not subject to challenge in the courts; the use of populist slogans and the politics of fear to win elections; the demonisation of 'other' races and religions; attacks on civil society advocates for human rights; restrictions on freedom of speech and the media; and marginalisation of the judiciary.

~~~~~~~~

From the 1990s, refugee children with or without parents could be incarcerated in isolated adult detention camps on the Australian mainland or on neighbouring islands. Like the Germans in 1919 or Australia's Indigenous people condemned to reserves, they had committed no crime. They had arrived by boat seeking protection.

Creating exceptions to exclude vulnerable people is a structural problem in Australia. Boat arrival people seeking protection are now prevented from having their claims examined in Australia. A former detention camp staffer, G Lake described how his 'instructions (from the Minister for Immigration's office) were to find families with children as young as possible (because we need to send a message to people smugglers that children, even young children, weren't exempt)'. Lake said, 'we couldn't transfer children under seven, as they couldn't be inoculated against Japanese Encephalitis or Malaria, so I had to choose children who looked young, to send a message to people smugglers'. He began to question his own actions even though he was acting under instructions from the minister's office. He said, 'as I was looking at the names of these young children, knowing that I was sending them to a place where they had no hope for the future, I found myself crossing an ethical line that I simply couldn't live with'.[101]

This statement illustrates the gap between the parliamentary legislators who repeatedly make laws and regulations which except the rights of sovereign human beings and, those employed to enact the lawful exceptions. Australia moved from making exceptions for Indigenous children to British children to children of unmarried mothers to 'young' children. Later the Navy intercepted boats at sea and transported potential

---

95. quoted in Reynolds, H, 2000, 'Indigenous social welfare: From a low priority to recognition and reconciliation', in A McMahon, J Thomson & C Williams (eds), *Understanding the Australian Welfare State: Key documents and themes,* Tertiary Press, Croydon, Victoria, pp.97-135, p.124.
96. Indigenous Australians continue to experience discrimination regarding health and education services and policing and incarceration.
97. Human Rights and Equal Opportunity Commission (HREOC), 1997, *Bringing Them Home: A guide to the findings and recommendations of the National Inquiry into the separation of Aboriginal and Torres Strait Islanders children from their families.* Sydney.
98. Molong Historical Society, Child Migration to Australia, http://www.migrationheritage.nsw.gov.au/exhibition/fairbridge-farm-school/child-migration-to-australia/. Accessed March 2022.
99. The first woman to enter the Australian Parliament was in 1943.
100. Senate Community Affairs References Committee Report 2012, *Commonwealth Contribution to Former Forced Adoption Policies and Practices.* https://www.aph.gov.au/parliamentary_business/committees/senate/community_affairs/completed_inquiries/2010-13/commcontribformerforcedadoption/report/index Accessed March 2022
101. Lake, G, 2013, 'Have you got any bodybags? We've run out', Bible Society. http://www.biblesociety.org.au/news/bodybags-weve-run. Accessed March 2022.

people seeking protection back to the country where they boarded the boat. Smith, another former immigration officer wrote that,

> ultimately, I chose to leave the department rather than to continue to implement policies that: sent people back to their homelands risking their death; allowed people to drown in Australian and Indonesian waters; and detained people indefinitely in harsh conditions, with limited access to water, food and medical treatment. Unequivocally, we Australians are causing severe mental and physical harm to fellow human beings.[102]

Just as the myth of *terra nullius* seriously impacted on the lives of Australia's Indigenous peoples, contemporary fictional stories have been created to justify further legislation excepting vulnerable people and enhancing political support. To cite two: people seeking protection throwing their children overboard;[103] and the deployment of the military to protect Australian sovereign borders when there is no imminent threat of war.[104] The language of war was introduced and opposition to the arrival of people seeking protection was successfully labelled 'a war against people smugglers', although only a few ever came near our borders.[105] Most remained in Indonesia. Since 2000, all people seeking protection who arranged or participated in arranging passages for family and friends have been labelled 'people smugglers'. Regardless of their motives, if caught they have been given substantial custodial sentences. Through mandatory sentencing, successive governments have prevented the courts from distinguishing between the motivations of the carefully planned, controlled voyage of people seeking protection and the unprincipled, indiscriminate, profiteering people-smuggler business.[106]

~~~~~~~~

Australia's treatment of vulnerable people includes myths about land not owned by the inhabitants of the country and children taken from their parents. Immigration history includes incarceration of non-Anglo people not charged with a crime, a fake and unfair dictation test, accusations that people seeking protection drowned their babies, and fantasy wars. A further piece in the puzzle of Australian legal exceptions is the creation of a process for *not* determining protection for people who arrived by plane in need of a safe place to raise their children.

There is little evidence to suggest that anything has been done legislatively to introduce a process whereby further parliamentary discriminatory exceptions relating to vulnerable persons' sovereign rights can be prevented in the future. The public has had to rely on the courts, especially the High Court, where a few successful cases, such as the failure of the government to implement legislation regarding the 'Malaysian solution', a proposal whereby Australian parliamentarians would actually legislate to 'swap' people seeking protection:[107] in other words, Malaysia would take some people who arrived by boat and, in return, Australia would take some refugees from their camps.[108] This was another form of people trafficking, but the motivation was not profit or prostitution but political gain.

~~~~~~~~

102. Smith op. cit.
103. Parliamentary Inquiry 2002, 'A Certain Maritime Incident', https://www.aph.gov.au/Parliamentary_Business/Committees/Senate/Former_Committees/maritimeincident/report/index Accessed March 2022; Fickling, D, 2002, *Australia lied about refugees throwing children overboard*, Senate inquiry's finding, http://www.dawn.com/2002/10/25/int3.htm. Accessed March 2022. https://www.theguardian.com/world/2002/oct/24/australia.immigration. Accessed March 2022.
104. Raschella, A, 2013, 'Former SAS commander breaks silence on Tampa'. https://www.abc.net.au/news/2011-07-07/former-sas-commander-breaks-silence-on-tampa/2785164. Accessed March 2022.
105. ABC News 2014, 'Prime Minister Tony Abbott likens campaign against people smugglers to "war"'. Updated Tue 4 Feb 2014, 6:02pm AEDT, http://www.abc.net.au/news/2014-01-10/abbott-likens-campaign-against-people-smugglers-to-war/5193546 Accessed March 2022; Packham, B, 2013, 'We're winning war against boats: Coalition', *The Australian,* Nov 1, 2013.
106. For portrayals of both types of People Smugglers see De Crespigny, R, 2012, *The People Smuggler: the true story of Ali Al Jenabi, the 'Oskar Schindler of Asia'*, Penguin Group, Australia.
107. *M70/2011 v Minister for Immigration and Citizenship [2011]* https://www.hcourt.gov.au/cases/case-m70/2011. Accessed March 2022.
108. The *Sydney Morning Herald*, 2011. 'Gillard announces Malaysian solution', https://www.smh.com.au/national/gillard-announces-malaysian-solution-20110507-1ed0h.html. Accessed March 2022.

16. Contested boundaries: the court and the parliament

Refugee law as expressed in the Migration Act is relatively new and is continuing to evolve. From Federation to 1977, migration issues were resolved through administrative discretion – the exercise of professional expertise and judgement, as opposed to strict adherence to regulations or statutes, in making a decision or performing official acts or duties. Until 1958, entry into Australia was dependent on a dictation test in any European language. During the era of the *Immigration Restriction Act (1901)* or the White Australia Policy (1901–1973), the *Migration Act 1958 (Cth)* was passed and, while creating a new legislative structure, it retained administrative discretion.[109]

The Federal Court was created in 1977 to review administrative decisions. The grounds for review included error of law; breach of natural justice; improper exercise of power; unreasonableness; jurisdiction to make decisions; and decisions that were not authorised.[110] The White Australia Policy was officially abolished in 1973 but, ten years later, the ghosts of xenophobic attitudes had not been put to bed. Justice Gageler, the Solicitor General in 2010, has observed that, in 1983, the *Migration Act (1958)* was amended 'to become anchored in the legislative power of the Commonwealth Parliament to make laws with respect to "aliens" rather than the legislative power to make laws with respect to "immigration"'.[111]

Thirty years later, the substance of the Refugees Convention was incorporated into Australian domestic law through the *Migration Act 1989* which provided: merits review of migration decisions; the need for visa applications; and the duty to detain and deport.[112] Justice Sackville pointed out that 'the role of the courts is to interpret and apply the Refugees Convention, insofar as it has been incorporated into Australian domestic law, regardless of political controversies that any given decision may generate'.[113] Sackville claimed that the Migration Act amendments in early 2000 had allowed parliament to 'legislate in a manner inconsistent with Australia's obligations under the *Convention*'. Sackville cited examples such as: excision of islands; s91R redefines the 'causation' requirement; and s91S risk of persecution by association with another family member as not well-founded fear by reason of membership of a particular social group.[114]

By 1994, Labor Party Immigration Minister, Nick Bolkus limited the scope of judicial review to jurisdictional error through the introduction of Part 8 of the Migration Act. This meant that no merits review was allowed in the courts. A judge could no longer decide that an appellant deserved protection on the basis of misunderstandings or mistaken judgements on the part of the assessor but could only make decisions regarding the reviewer's legal errors. Grounds for review were restricted and decisions reviewable by the Federal Court were limited. According to Gageler, the government's intention was to restrict the scope of judicial review, preferring 'credible independent merits review' to erosion by 'narrow judicial interpretations'. Grounds for review were more restrictive than the 1977 Administrative Decisions (Judicial Review) (ADJR) Act and, except for bias, they excluded 'breach of rules of natural justice'.[115]

The Federal Magistrates Court, renamed Federal Circuit Court of Australia in 2013, was established in 1999 to 'provide a simple and accessible alternative to litigation in the Federal Court' and Family Court, and to relieve their workloads. The first appeals were filed in the Federal Magistrates Court in 2000 but it wasn't until 2003 that people in my study began accessing this court.

Between 1999 and 2003 at least 23 immigration cases had been heard in the full High Court. Justice Sackville claimed that most of them involved 'persons claiming to satisfy the *Convention* definition of "refugee" and therefore to be entitled to protection visas'.[116] Generally, the High Court examined whether or not the lower court properly applied the law and, if found in favour of the appellant, the case was 'sent back to the Federal Court for reconsideration in accordance with the law'.[117] In theory, people could apply directly to the High Court if they believed they were badly affected by a migration decision. Appeals regarding breaches of procedural fairness and the *Wednesbury*[118] 'unreasonable' cases ceased in the Federal Court, but they could be addressed in the High Court where 'prohibition' and 'mandamus' writs were available to common law to

---

109. Gageler, op. cit., pp.92-105.
110. Sackville, 2003, Gageler, 2010.
111. In 2012 he was elevated to the High Court.
112. Gageler op. cit.
113. Sackville op. cit., p.13.
114. Sackville op. cit., pp.8,9.
115. Gageler op. cit., pp.98,99.
116. Sackville op.cit., p.1.
117. Burn, J & Reich, A, 2001, *The Migration Kit: A Practical Guide to Australia's Immigration Law*, 6th edn, The Immigration Advice and Rights Centre, The Federation Press, NSW, p.666.
118. In *Associated Provincial Picture Houses v. Wednesbury Corporation* [1948] the principle has been asserted that 'the making of the decision was an "improper exercise of power" in that it was "an exercise of power that [was] so unreasonable that no reasonable person could have so exercised the power"' (Gageler 2010, p.94).

correct jurisdictional error.[119] Gageler explained that 'to grant prohibition to restrain a Commonwealth officer acting on a decision which manifests jurisdictional error is to do no more than the constitutional duty of a court to declare and enforce the law'.[120]

Amendments to Part 8 of the *Migration Act 1989* were introduced in 2001 to review privative clause decisions, a decision of an administrative character made under the Migration Act. Gageler points out that in this amendment, one privative clause decision under the Ruddock/Howard government was to be final and conclusive; not challenged, appealed against, reviewed, quashed or called into question in any court; not subject to prohibition, *mandamus* injunction, declaration or *certiorari* in any court on any account; on the provisos that the decision-maker was acting in good faith; was acting within their authority; and did not exceed constitutional limits.[121] The case of *Plaintiff S157/2002* in 2003 challenged a privative clause that 'attempts to shield Refugee Review Tribunal decisions from judicial review except on very narrow grounds'. Sackville claimed that if the privative clause had claimed to protect decisions of the Refugee Review Tribunal against judicial review for jurisdictional error, it would get into trouble for failing to do what is required by s75(v) of the *Constitution*.

Sackville concluded that the decision regarding *Plaintiff S157/2002* established 'the central role played by Chapter III of the *Constitution* and s75(v) in maintaining the rule of law in Australia' and marked the 'constitutionalisation of refugee law in Australia'.[122] At this time, Justice Sackville believed that the High Court marked out a protected field of judicial review into which 'Parliament may not intrude'.[123] Gageler noted the High Court's respect for the basic right to the entitlement to fair procedures in administrative decision-making.

Given the potency of the White Australia Policy, it is possible that determinations breaching conventions have resulted in the introduction of legal restrictions. A privative clause that further excludes access to justice through the courts for people seeking protection who arrived by plane is one example. Policies introduced for expediency rather than fairness and basic rights illustrate a continuing history of exclusionary law-making and legal exceptions which result in a bias towards protecting reviewers over people seeking review of protection assessments. Such policies accentuate the vital role of vigilant courts. A Senate Select Committee in 1973 considered this input from the Vietnamese community:

> on one side of the room is someone familiar with English and Australian law. On the other side is a person who doesn't even recognise the Sydney Opera House, and who may be scared of governmental authorities. The former minutely drills down to find apparent inconsistencies to reject

the latter's credibility, while trusting any and all materials adverse to the latter. With no lawyer to defend them against the onslaught, innocent and honest people can be turned by tribunal members into liars. That is what we have seen happen to Vietnamese applicants.[124]

One problem for people seeking review of a negative assessment in my study was the mental gymnastics required for the leap from the inquisitorial tribunal process to the adversarial court procedures. Clearly, those who were unrepresented did not understand the difference in procedures between the tribunal and the court or could not afford to engage lawyers to argue on their behalf. Under the inquisitorial process at the tribunal one person, the member or reviewer, questions the person seeking review of their assessment. At court, unrepresented people appealing a tribunal review found themselves confronted with a decision-maker (the judge) who weighed up arguments presented by themselves and the legal team representing the government and tribunal. At the tribunal, there was a greater reliance on written evidence. The reviewer had knowledge of all aspects of the case, and thus could be influenced by outside issues. The tribunal review decisions indicated that the reviewer was aware of past records which 'could mean that biases are formed', and records could be outdated or inaccurate.[125] For the person seeking protection in this new and foreign environment, an adversarial procedure normally provided legal representatives to argue the person's case and, if necessary, expert witnesses to support them. In the adversarial process, claims are openly debated

---

119. Traditionally, anyone seeking judicial review had to use the common law procedure of seeking the issue of a 'prerogative writ'. The High Court now calls them 'constitutional writs' ('**writs**'). There are three main types of writ which are relevant to judicial review: mandamus, certiorari and prohibition. 1. **Mandamus** is an order issued by the court against a tribunal, public body or official requiring it to perform a duty which it has failed to perform. 2. **Prohibition** is an order to a tribunal, public body or official requiring it to cease proceedings. An order for prohibition should be sought where a body has failed to exercise its *jurisdiction* properly or failed to provide *natural justice* and its proceedings are continuing. 3. **Certiorari** is an order setting aside a decision (technically, the record of the decision-maker is removed to the court and the court then quashes the decision and expunges it from the record). An order for certiorari would be sought where a decision has been made unlawfully and the decision should be set aside. Generally, an order for certiorari is sought in combination with an order for mandamus, i.e., an order for certiorari setting aside the decision and an order for mandamus requiring the decision-maker to make the decision again (McKenzie, 2012).
120. Gageler op. cit., p.101.
121. Gageler op. cit., p.102.
122. *Plaintiff S157/2002 v Commonwealth* (2003) 195 ALR 24
123. Sackville op. cit., p.6,7.
124. Vietnamese Community of Australia 2003, Submission by the Vietnamese Community of Australia to the Senate Select Committee on Ministerial discretion in migration matters, Western Australia, p.4.
125. Beazer, M, Humphreys, M & Filippin L 2010, 'Justice and Outcomes', *11e Legal Studies for VCE Unit 3 and 4*.

and decisions made within the boundaries of Australian legal restrictions of international refugee law. Consistent with the history of exclusionary legislation, Australia's immigration policy has been weighted against 'the other', the person arriving by plane seeking protection, appealing tribunal review decisions in the courts, especially when unrepresented.

Justice Sackville has pointed out that, in defence of reviewers whose decisions were being tested in the courts, complying with procedural fairness principles was an 'onerous requirement' for the tribunal. This is pertinent, since a high proportion of reviewers were not qualified lawyers.[126] Reviewers' caseloads were heavy and they needed to comply with 'rigorous procedural standards'.[127] Justice McHugh alluded to a further tension for reviewers when he concluded that 'Review of a Public Servant's decision by an administrative tribunal, whose members do not have the same security of tenure and independence as judges, is no substitute for review by a court'.[128]

A reviewer's fear of losing tenure can contribute to negative outcomes for the person seeking protection. It has been argued that 'the concept of loss aversion is certainly the most significant contribution of psychology to behavioural economics. This is odd, because the idea that people evaluate many outcomes as gains and losses, and that losses loom larger than gains, surprises no one'.[129]

Justice Sackville claimed that tensions have developed over the years between the courts and the Commonwealth Executive,[130] and the Federal Parliament, with judicial review of refugee cases generating the most conflict.[131] Justice Gageler pointed out that for the year ending June 1983 migration law litigation accounted for 6% of all Federal Court cases determined. Twenty years later, for the year ending June 2004, migration law litigation accounted for around 49% of Federal Court determinations, 46% of cases determined by single judges and 54% by Full Courts. For the minister and the judiciary, this increase in appeals was concerning.[132]

Justice McHugh strongly argued that people seeking protection had a right to test tribunal decisions. He stated that 'even a national emergency should not be a sufficient basis for refusing to permit the courts to examine the legality of the conduct of the Executive Government'.[133] He had little concern for Minister Ruddock's 'abuse' argument where he affirmed that '30 percent of applicants' abusing the system is no reason for denying the possible success of others' judicial reviews. He claimed that thirty per cent of applicants extending their stay was 'a small price for a just and prosperous country to pay for maintaining the rule of law'.[134]

The tension between the courts and the Executive intensified with Ruddock's restrictions of the rights of people seeking protection. Guy and

Hocking argued that privative clauses would exclude the jurisdiction of courts to review tribunal decisions.[135] From 2001 to 2003, the legitimacy of the privative clause was tested in the courts. Attempts were made to protect the interests of the individual through judicial review where executive action was 'prevented from exceeding the powers and functions assigned to the executive by law'.[136] The judges had reasons for concern, as Ruddock's rationale for introducing a privative clause seemed blatantly discriminatory. He specifically intended to reduce 'the grounds on which the courts can set aside decisions' which affects the quality of assessments. Ruddock intended to 'facilitate faster resolution of court cases' and decrease 'delays in removal of non-citizens' and lower costs.[137]

Expediency was no excuse for changing the law to restrict access to International Refugee Convention benchmarks. Ruddock was prepared to lower the standards for reviewers and at the same time lift the bar on the grounds for protection for those people seeking protection. In quoting Sir William Wade, whom he believed to be 'the doyen of administrative lawyers', Justice McHugh warned that 'to exempt a public authority from the jurisdiction of the courts of law is, to that extent, to grant dictatorial power'.[138]

Aware of tensions around the separation of powers, Ruddock relied upon the then Chief Justice of the High Court, Justice Gleeson: 'It is for Parliaments to decide what controversies are justiciable, and to create, and

126. Biographical data for RRT and MRT Members is available in the RRT/MRT Annual Reports 2000-2001 to 2010-2011.
127. Sackville op. cit., p.3.
128. McHugh, M 2002, 'Tensions between the Executive and the Judiciary', Australian Bar Association Conference, Paris, p 9. http://www.hcourt.gov.au/assets/publications/speeches/former-justices/mchughj/mchughj_paris.htm Accessed March 2022
129. Kahneman op. cit., p.300.
130. The Executive Government consists of the Cabinet and the Ministry led by the Prime Minister. The Ministry is derived from the party or parties that command a majority in the House of Representatives. Constitutionally, the Governor-General heads the Executive Government, but in practice the Governor-General acts on the advice of the Prime Minister. Cabinet and Minsitry https://australianpolitics.com/executive/ministry Accessed March 2022.
131. Sackville op. cit., p.4.
132. Gageler 2010.
133. The Executive government in this respect are those public servants delegated to act on the Minister's behalf as well as review tribunal officials engaged in accordance with the Migration Act.
134. McHugh op. cit., p.9.
135. Guy, S & Hocking, B 2008, 'Migration Act and the constitutionality of privative clauses', *Australian Journal of Administrative Law,* vol.16, no.1, pp.21-44.
136. Spigelman, J 2004, 'Integrity and Privative Clauses', The Third Lecture in the 2004 National Lecture Series for the Australian Institute of Administrative Law, Brisbane, Supreme Court of NSW, Index to compilation of speeches delivered by the Hon. J J Spigelman, AC, Chief Justice of NSW in 2004 pp 25-41 https://www.supremecourt.justice.nsw.gov.au/Documents/Publications/Speeches/Pre-2015%20Speeches/Spigelman/spigelman_speeches_2004.pdf Accessed March 2022.
137. Ruddock 2002 op. cit., p.4.
138. McHugh op. cit., p.9.

where appropriate, limit, the facilities for the resolution of justiciable controversies'.

Ruddock believed that 'it would simply be unsustainable and unacceptable to allow the ever-increasing immigration litigation load to grow unchecked'. With little regard for the genuineness of the protection claims, Ruddock remained determined to overcome High Court opposition. He declared that the government would 'have to look for alternative ways of tackling the abuse of judicial review processes in migration matters'.[139]

Ruddock's obsession with checking people seeking protection litigation raised tensions with his need to be seen as legitimately fair and non-discriminatory in the eyes of the judiciary. The introduction of the privative clause legislation revealed the government's resistance to fair and just outcomes for people arriving by plane who came legally and applied for protection through the proper channels. McHugh complained that the persistence of tension in the migration area damaged public confidence. His concern was that the courts were being undermined by the government's continual criticism. This was diminishing 'public confidence in the integrity and impartiality of the judges'. He also feared that continuing conflict would undermine the rule of law if the Executive Government pressured 'the legislature to take the extreme step of reducing or abolishing judicial review'.[140]

Abolishing judicial review would also undermine Australia's international obligations that the courts attempt to safeguard, in a culture of negatively geared assessments. Mike Scrafton claims that, as a senior defence official, he had extensive experience with national security and strategic policy issues. At some time, he headed up a section in the Determination of Refugee status branch within the Department of Immigration and Multicultural Affairs. He described the long-standing difficulties experienced by people seeking protection in his submission to the expert panel.[141] He suggested that the initial assessors were infected by the above tensions. Within the immigration department culture's 'barrier mentality', Scrafton claimed the 'denial of access to the unworthy potential citizens infused the determination process'. The attitudes that were the drivers of immigration policy in general 'were transposed on to refugee determination' assessments, adversely affecting the protection of genuine refugees.[142] This reflected Palmer's earlier conclusions regarding the Department of Immigration's management of detention. Palmer found a focus on process to the detriment of quality outcomes: 'quantitative yardsticks rather than qualitative measures', or quotas of negative decisions rather than fair outcomes that respect human dignity.[143]

Scrafton's 'barrier mentality' concept might also include a negatively geared assessment policy that emphasised 'quantitative yardsticks'. The more cases that failed possibly resulted in higher performance ratings for reviewers. The source of prolific court appeals that became an economic liability for the minister may have been the focus on quantitative yardsticks.

Fortunately for people seeking protection and their advocates, some courts persisted in attempting to administer justice. Gageler concluded that categories of jurisdictional error not only overlapped 'but could never be stated exhaustively'. The standard requirement for decision-making to reach a 'state of satisfaction' was not only on the basis of 'error of law' or unreasonableness, but also 'where a decision-maker arrived at a primary finding of fact by an illogical process of reasoning or failed at the factual level to understand the nature of the case being put'.[144]

The High Court reminded parliament that there were boundaries to law-making that were restrictive when it came to safeguarding the rights of people seeking protection in Australia. The legislature may change the substantive rules of law. However, under the separation of powers, it is questionable as to whether the legislature can 'prevent the courts from examining the legality of the conduct of those who are bound by those rules of law'. Justice McHugh exhorted the judiciary to publicly resist 'any attempt by the Legislature or the Executive to undermine the rule of law'.[145]

~~~~~~~~

Further tension has since arisen over the implementation of Complementary Protection legislation introduced in 2012. Complementary protection is the term used to describe a category of protection for people who are not refugees as defined in the Refugees Convention, but who also cannot be returned to their home country because there is a real risk that they would suffer certain types of harm under Australia's international *non-refoulement* obligations.[146] People arriving by plane could immediately submit new protection applications but only fifty-five had received visas by December 2013. In 2013, the Labor government tried to appeal a successful

139. Ruddock 2002 op. cit., p5.
140. McHugh op. cit., p.9.
141. A panel set up by the Gillard Labor government in relation to finding a solution to the problem of people coming to Australia by boat, some of whom drowned before reaching their Australian destination.
142. Scrafton, M 2012, Submission to Expert Panel on Asylum Seekers.
143. Palmer op. cit., p.171.
144. Gageler op. cit., p.101.
145. McHugh op. cit., p.10.
146. Australian Government 2012, Fact Sheet 61a, Complementary Protection.

court challenge regarding the retrospectivity of the legislation, but the High Court did not allow the appeal.[147] While Chris Evans, a Labor Immigration Minister, saw his discretionary powers as 'an incredible waste of ministerial time', and also lamented that he was single-handedly '"playing God" with asylum seekers' futures', the Coalition Government intended to repeal the legislation. At the end of 2013, the government introduced the *Migration Amendment (Regaining Control over Australia's Protection Obligations) Bill 2013* which, if passed, would provide no guarantee that 'people at risk of torture, death or serious human rights violations will be protected from removal from Australia'.[148] There would be no check or balance on the non-compellable decisions the minister makes. As was the case prior to 2012, such decisions are made with impunity. In 2014, the Australian Human Rights Commission recommended that the bill not be passed.

Introducing legislation to restrict access to the law, rather than acting on the causes of the assessment and tribunal review discrepancies that result in the need for judicial appeals, could be perceived as a systemic abuse of Executive power and an attempt to usurp the powers of the court. The tension between the Executive and the courts is justified in so far as the court has endeavoured to avoid discriminatory conduct. Because of Australia's lack of human rights protections in law, it is essential to maintain its powers, which reach all sovereign citizens who have inalienable rights, and not merely Australian citizens. If this does not occur, the courts lose public confidence and respect. Responsible citizens and advocates are faced with a dilemma: collude with parliamentarians who create cruel, inhumane laws or challenge those laws and parliamentarians by acting according to conscience.

~~~~~~~~

Because of the nature of their allegations, 'member of a particular social group' (MPSG) was the most appropriate category for the majority of protection claims in the cohort of people seeking protection who were participants in my research. However, while MPSG might be the group with the least clarity, it is also the area of the most controversy.[149] In 1991, the Canadian Immigration and Refugee Board (CIRB) produced a framework for analysis which outlined a number of basic considerations for claiming MPSG. These are listed as: (1) a member is unable to disassociate from the group; (2) affiliation is fundamental to the person's identity and human dignity; (3) irrelevance of group size; (4) a group criminal record doesn't automatically exclude the claimant from protection; (5) the overriding objective is the protection of group members who have a well-founded fear of persecution; (6) the claimant is not required to show that he/she has been 'singled out' or 'targeted'; and (7) the crucial test is whether the claimant's fears are sufficiently serious to constitute persecution. In determining how a group is defined the following points were listed: (a) an internal characteristic, which might be 1) innate (gender, colour, kinship ties, etc); 2) immutable (past economic or social status, etc); or 3) fundamental to members' identity/human dignity; or (b) external perceptions, society's perceptions of the group.[150] The CIRB believed that, in order to protect groups or individuals without claims that relate to the other four grounds for protection in the Refugees Convention definition, a broad and liberal interpretation must be applied to membership of a particular social group.

Guidelines published by UNHCR provide 'legal interpretative guidance on assessing claims which assert that a claimant has a well-founded fear of being persecuted for reasons of his or her membership of a particular social group'. The major points include that: a social group cannot be defined exclusively by having been targeted/persecuted; there is no specific list of social groups because of the diverse and changing nature of groups in various societies and the evolving international human rights forums; and The Convention grounds are not mutually exclusive. There can be eligibility on more than one ground.

In determining what constitutes a social group, two approaches emerge in the guidelines: the 'protected characteristics' (immutability) approach which means that the characteristic is so fundamental to human dignity that a person should not be compelled to forsake it – women, homosexuals, and families each constitute a particular social group in this context. The second approach is 'social perception', meaning that common characteristics make them a cognizable group in the community or sets them apart – women, homosexuals and families. While the two approaches can converge, at times 'the social perception standard might recognise as social groups associations based on a characteristic that is neither immutable nor fundamental to human dignity – such as perhaps, occupation or social class'.

---

147. *SZGIZ v Minister for Immigration and Citizenship* [2013] FCAFC 71.
148. McAdam, J, 2013, 'Playing God on asylum seekers is unacceptable', *The Drum: Analysis and Opinion on Issues of the Day*, http://www.abc.net.au/news/2013-12-05/mcadam-playing-god-on-asylum-seekers-is-unacceptable/5137794 Accessed March 2022.
149. Foster, M, 2012, *The Ground with the Least Clarity. A Comparative Study of Jurisprudential Developments relating to 'Membership of a Particular Social Group'*, Legal and Protection Policy Research Series, UNHCR, https://www.unhcr.org/en-au/protection/globalconsult/4f7d8d189/25-ground-clarity-comparative-study-jurisprudential-developments-relating.html. Accessed March 2022.
150. Canadian Immigration Refugee Board op. cit., p.2.

Incorporating the two approaches, the UNHCR defined a particular social group as 'a group of persons who share a common characteristic other than their risk of being persecuted, or who are perceived as a group by society. The characteristic will often be one which is innate, unchangeable, or which is otherwise fundamental to identity, conscience or the exercise of one's human rights'.[151]

Other factors in the UNHCR (2002) guidelines that are relevant to this cohort of people include: owning a shop or participating in a certain occupation; persecutory action toward a group; there is no requirement for group cohesiveness – members of a particular group need not know each other or associate with each other as a group; it is not necessary to demonstrate that all members of a particular social group are at risk of persecution.[152] The causal link is regarded as established if a non-state actor inflicts or threatens persecution based on a Convention ground, and the State is unwilling or unable to protect the claimant. Examples of inflicting or threatening persecution include being fired because of homosexuality or being extorted in a protection racket.

The 1991 CIRB framework for MPSG was effective when the claims of my study's cohort of people seeking protection were first submitted for determination. The later UNHCR (2002) guidelines confirm the validity of the CIRB guidelines at the time of the refugee determinations and reviews.

White Australia has a long and persistent history of making exceptions for particular social groups. Legal exceptions have been made on the basis of race (Australia's Indigenous people, Germans and others) and vulnerability (Indigenous children, Anglo-Australian children and Anglo-Australian single mothers). Despite the attitude of the Australian Parliament and the Executive, the courts have attempted to maintain some form of fairness and justice. While the parliament has apologised on some occasions, there has been no substantial parliamentary reparation in the form of the creation of legislation that ensures that unfair, discriminatory and racist exceptions will not be repeated in the future.

~~~~~~~~

151. UNHCR 2002, op. cit., para 1, 9, 11.
152. Ibid, para 13-15; 17-20.
153. Migrants and Refugees: Towards a Better World, 2014, *Message of Pope Francis for the World Day of Migrants and Refugees*, Vatican Press. https://www.vatican.va/content/francesco/en/messages/migration/documents/papa-francesco_20130805_world-migrants-day.html. Accessed March 2022.

17. Cultural erosion: systemic discrimination

> While it is true that migrations often reveal failures and shortcomings on the part of States and the international community, they also point to the aspiration of humanity to enjoy a unity marked by respect for differences, by attitudes of acceptance and hospitality which enable an equitable sharing of the world's goods, and by the protection and the advancement of the dignity and centrality of each human being.[153]

Questioning the way in which Federal law and policy introduce legislation that restricts the power of the courts, and exploring the manner in which decision-makers are absolved of the subsequent violence that the introduced laws cause, reveals aggressive systemic discrimination.

As we have seen, the authority of the Australian refugee assessment system to comply with the UN definition of a refugee may be influenced by the discretion and bias of individual immigration ministers. When parliamentary powers undermine the power of the Courts injustices are legitimized and the perpetrators of that injustice are protected. By prohibiting a court review of the 'merits' of a case, the government is able to change the law to suit its own purposes, to favour the executive bodies such as the tribunal and to defend its own negative decisions in the Courts. By insisting on 'errors in law' only, and not the 'merits of the case', the government can legitimately condone errors of fact.

Further, and because of the time taken to determine a protection claim, immigration policy in Australia does not provide a fair, economical and efficient process. Over many years, the cohort of persecuted sovereign citizens whose stories are told in this book has had to fight for their human rights to be protected. In many cases, government policy seems to work against this protection. By restricting the UNHCR definition of a member of a particular social group such as 'the family' the Australian parliament does not act responsibly towards the UN conventions or have consideration for the time it takes to reach a protection result.

Federal law and policy that exclude people who arrive by plane from seeking protection and from accessing rights that other Australians take for granted is discriminatory and contrary to international human rights standards. A policy that assists certain sections of the electorate to maintain the historical racism to which this country is heir is also contrary to international human rights standards. In reaching beyond its legitimacy, the Parliament has undermined the power of the courts by increasing its parliamentary power over people seeking protection. Making such exceptions legal has cruel consequences for people seeking asylum whether or not they arrive by plane or by boat. Granting decision makers immunity from prosecution, be they parliamentarians, their delegates, immigration or military personnel is an aberration of democracy and contrary to the Westminster system.

At present, 'the pendulum has swung too far' – away from principled decision-making on the part of the tribunal, 'so that judicial review of cases on their facts is merited'.[154] The quality of Australia's immigration policy has been prejudiced by historical and ongoing systemic exclusion. Legal exceptions were consistently made in Indigenous, immigration, and refugee policy during the nineteenth, twentieth and now the twenty-first century. This, in itself, indicates that a thorough independent investigation into the separation of powers between the parliament and the courts is long overdue.

Structural discrimination is demonstrated through bias apparent in four main areas: the reluctance of decision-makers to recognise protection needs; the restrictive annual quotas regarding people seeking protection; the inability of the court to acknowledge the merits of protection claims; and the failure of decision-makers to recognise Australia's obligations to adhere to international treaties.

Through the immigration minister's authority to delegate, extraordinary powers are conferred upon public servants who may or may not have the capacity to appropriately perform the authorised duties. Not all responsibility for unjust assessments can be laid at the feet of delegates/assessors or departmental personnel. Just or unjust officials are obliged to abide by the policies enacted by the parliament which, in certain circumstances, results in people with valid visas being denied protection. Assessors themselves, at risk of receiving a low performance rating, are between a rock and a hard place when formulating their decisions and are further victims of an unjust law.

Decision-makers often assess claims through the prism of an ordered and functioning society, rational behaviour and choice. In my study, if the reviewers didn't understand a situation that was outside their cultural experience they could claim 'implausibility'. Surely this is a primary finding of fact by an illogical process of reasoning. In the decisions of Ros Redberry and Sally Bland, 'implausibility' impacted on credibility findings for Orlando and Belicia, Jaime and Ladonna, and Nankunda. Had Redberry taken the fear of rape and of gender-related violence into consideration, it would have further strengthened Nankunda's review appeal. Had her fears been aired then, her claims would have been plausible. Another convenient omission on the part of the reviewer in this case was the relevant information regarding a member of a particular social group – women who fear persecution. It was opportunistic on Redberry's part to rely on the tried and tested implausibility factor. Nankunda's counsel did not pick up what may have been jurisdictional error, which is the omission of relevant material about the fear of rape and torture. An independent judge might well conclude that such a claim related to the merits of the case, which is not within the jurisdiction of the court.

Contemporary law-making in Australia has evolved from patterns of excluding people who did not advantage the Empire's goals and pursuits. This practice has resulted in a legislative system that violates the rights of sovereign citizens. The legislative power of parliament creates laws that advantage the political environment (the electorate), rather than protect marginalised sovereign citizens. The function of parliament and judges is to provide checks and balances against the inevitability of executive overreach. The institutional failure of parliament over the past decade or so poses risks to our individual liberties. Piece by piece, legislation passed by compliant federal parliaments has facilitated a creeping expansion of executive powers and non-compellable or reviewable discretions of federal government.

Elected members have acted outside parliament's jurisdiction and restricted the authority of the court to properly administer justice. In doing this, the parliament usurped the powers of the court regarding refugee law. In limiting the courts' ability to administer justice, the rights of sovereign citizens of other countries who came to Australia to lawfully seek protection, were excluded. Through parliament's manipulation of sections of the Migration Act to favour the independent executive body, the tribunals' reviewers have been granted immunity from the subsequent violence resulting from their non-jurisdictional errors. The abuse of power,[155] or the failure to exercise power,[156] on the part of reviewers during the assessment procedure is not always able to be challenged in the court. Through modification of the Migration Act, judges and lawyers are given legal space to divert from traditional court principles regarding the 'inalienable and indefensible' rights of all human beings. The requirement that the courts accept tribunal reviewers' 'non-jurisdictional' mistakes and, in the light of

---

154. Psihogios-Billington, M 2009, 'A Case for Justice: Position Paper on the Legal Process of Seeking Asylum in Australia', *Asylum Seeker Resource Centre*, North Melbourne, p.26.
155. For example, acting in bad faith, or for an improper purpose, or taking into account an irrelevant consideration.
156. Impeding discretion and acting inflexibly on a policy, for example, the avoidance of examining claims regarding persecuted 'members of a particular social group'.

such mistakes, the inability of the courts to review the merits of protection claims are examples of parliament's discriminatory powers that undermine the authority of the court.

~~~~~~~~

People seeking Australia's protection are demonised in the media and by government when categorising and stereotyping are employed against people arriving by plane seeking protection. Categorisation and stereotyping are 'things we do in talk in order to accomplish social actions such as blaming, accusing, excusing, persuading, justifying, etc.' and excepting.[157] This is apparent in the scrutiny of the assessment procedures, reviews and decisions when, for example, claims were made out to be 'implausible'.

Categorisation and stereotyping lead to objectification, distortion, bias and prejudice. The notions that Indigenous Australians were not landowners at the time of colonisation, that people who arrive by boat seeking protection are illegal and possibly terrorists, that people who arrive by plane seeking protection are labelled 'economic' refugees rather than 'persecuted' refugees are examples of strategic constructions based on an exclusionary ideology. Indigenous Australians and people seeking Australia's protection were captured by the stereotyping of public discourse, usually in pejorative terms and through negative associations. The way exclusionary discourse and strategies of governments continue to be nurtured and cultivated is through a system of Australian federal law and policy that consistently amends the Migration Act.

In the context of seeking protection, people who are non-Australian citizens are the disadvantaged 'outsiders'. In my study this group consisted of multiple ethnicities, citizens of other countries but not of European heritage. Laws and regulations were based on race when they were specifically directed to disadvantage them but did not affect the general Australian population of 'legitimate' citizens. The necessity for people arriving by plane seeking permanent protection to pay the equivalent education fees to those who temporarily visit Australia on student visas, rather than the fees paid by Australian citizens, is discriminatory. People prevented from working and supporting their families or accessing Medicare benefits do not access the rights of the broader Australian community. The distribution of social resources which regularly and systematically disadvantage some ethnic and racial groups, but advantages others, is institutional racism.

157. LeCouteur, A & Augoustinos, M, 2001, 'The Language of Prejudice and Racism', in M Augoustinos, & KJ Reynolds (eds), *Understanding Prejudice, Racism, and Social Conflict*, SAGE Publications Ltd, London, pp.215-230, p.215.

It is through social and political discourse that discriminatory and exclusionary practices are prepared, promulgated and legitimised. Covert institutional racism was evident in the procedures of assessing and reviewing protection claims of people seeking a safe country in which to raise their children. In a cross-cultural environment, in some cases, core claims were not given sufficient attention and, in most cases, assessors in consulting the USA human rights reports avoided specific human rights reports of particular and pertinent countries. Apart from the UN Refugee Convention definition there was no access to other UN treaties that, for example, would affect a decision about returning a person to danger. Australian domestic law was preferred to that of international law despite Australia's international obligations as signatories to UN Conventions and Treaties. In reviewing decisions, tribunal personnel were discriminatory when they did not consider the specific protection needs of women with respect to gender-based violence or the best interests of children.

Some tribunal reviewers alleged 'implausibility' when people made claims that related to their specific cultural environment. Tribunal reviewers also made assumptions about the credibility of people from different cultural backgrounds despite the confusing experience of negotiating a foreign legal procedure and language difficulties. When new information was introduced as a result of discussions regarding the earlier written claims, reviewers refused to accommodate it. When for example Belicia, a traumatised woman, did not mention the very recent brutal rape and murder of her sister on her application form, Sally Bland dismissed this very relevant information. When people presented legitimate documents that were verified by notaries or lawyers or state protection offices outside Australia, these were dismissed as fraudulent. When tribunal reviewers had the opportunity to build a case for refusing protection prior to the hearing, based on documentation beyond that of the specific case claims, this would indicate procedural bias.

There was evidence of racial profiling in the case of Africans whose refugee determination decisions had to be sent to the Canberra office for scrutiny. There was extreme racial prejudice manifested in the manner in which Ros Redberry reviewed Nankunda's protection claims, and in comments in internal departmental email chains. At the outset, Redberry paid no attention to Nankunda's psychological condition. Redberry couldn't comprehend the cultural complexities of Nankunda's claims, dismissing them as 'implausible'. Also, she constructed a bizarre explanation for the documentation Nankunda submitted to support her claims.

Systemic bias is evident in the procedures where tribunal reviewers are not bound to ask questions which means that information that could be significant does not necessarily emerge at the hearings. When further information does emerge in the lengthy process of determining protection, departmental assessors and tribunal reviewers question the person seeking protection in relation to the inconsistency of not presenting vital information earlier, rather than exploring the relevancy of the information to the protection claim.

The ministerial intervention assessments exposed cynicism within the Department of Immigration towards people seeking Australia's protection, and a strong resistance to overturning earlier decisions whether they were those of ministers, assessors or reviewers. Institutional racism was clearly evident in the execution of the minister's powers under the Migration Act, to advantage the minister and disadvantage the non-citizen person seeking protection. Decisions to grant humanitarian or other types of permanent visas were haphazard and decisions not to grant some form of protection were sometimes irresponsible. The fact that there is no ministerial accountability or redress for the person seeking protection when a minister doesn't recognise legitimate claims for protection means that the Migration Act allows an inadequate response to Australia's obligations not to return people to danger.

Racism is 'deeply embedded in our language, our institutions and our culture', damaging 'its victims, its perpetrators and the society which sustains, tolerates or ignores it. It corrodes our culture and marginalises and punishes whole categories of people for no reason other than the accident of their birth'.[158] In Australia many people, particularly those of British and European heritage, have difficulty understanding the cumulative and devastating effects of racism on the lives of those who experience racism, and the continuing impact upon modern Australian society that lacks this recognition. Australia's contemporary form of racism, as manifested in the assessment and reviews of protection claims in my study, is culturally based. It is still governed by the values, beliefs and assumptions of a white Anglo-Australian 'colonial' culture, shifting to a postcolonial and post multicultural society that consistently excludes Indigenous cultural influences. Racism in Australia continuously confers both dominance and privilege through socially divisive inclusion and exclusion. In a tolerant and compassionate multicultural society difference should be the norm rather than an enemy that needs to be purged.[159]

158. McConnochie, K, Hollinsworth, D & Pettman, J, 1988, *Race & Racism in Australia*, Social Science Press, Wentworth Falls, NSW, p.253.
159. Kivel, P, 2002, *Uprooting Racism: How white people can work for racial justice*, New Society Publishers, Gabriola Island, Canada.

My study found that excluding the non-Anglo 'Other' sustained normative structures and power relations that retain prejudice and discrimination as the norm embedded in Australian institutions, cultural life and in party politics. Through legislated policies that unfairly victimise a particularly vulnerable social group, the cruelty of institutional racial prejudice is exposed. Successive Australian governments have gained almost unfettered power to make laws that result in harmful practices directed at people who are non-Australian citizens and more precisely, non-European. My empirical study involved people seeking protection from South America, South Asia, the Ex-Soviet Bloc and Africa, all with quite different cultural backgrounds to those of British or European heritage.

The way some people who arrived by plane seeking protection met almost insurmountable resistance to acknowledging claims of persecution throughout the whole of the refugee application system over many years, signifies a strong resistance to non-Anglo-Saxons. Orlondo and Belicia struggled to penetrate the perceptions of white Australians at all levels of the refugee determination process and their eventual success only came in convincing the Europeans at the International Human Rights Committee. The impact of racial attitudes and values in the way this cohort of non-Australian citizens were seriously deprived of basic human rights by Australian institutions, is indicative of the deprivation of rights afforded Indigenous Australians.

Some individual Australian citizens from a range of cultural backgrounds risked stepping beyond the boundaries of discriminatory laws and social mores by consciously and morally responding to the medical, educational, legal or socio-economic needs of people seeking protection. Undertakings that countered racism were particularly evident in the persistent one-to-one relationships between people seeking protection who arrived by plane and some activists and lawyers in their endeavours to infiltrate the impervious exclusionary policies and practices within the Department of Immigration.

The intricacies of racism were more pronounced in the institutional procedural assessments and reviews where resistance to honest evaluations of claims and ever increasing and not so subtle, discriminatory legal restrictions were exposed. The negative assessments of those seeking protection are a by-product of a structure of exclusionary policies and practices set in place during the colonial era. In excluding Australia's Indigenous peoples from the legal system, biopolitics was introduced. Discrimination based on racial difference was strengthened with laws that were essentially apartheid, introduced at the time of Australian Federation in 1901. Federal law and policy have fostered institutionalised methods for discriminating and excluding through controlling legislative procedures, making it difficult for the courts to legitimately administer justice. Some examples include the human right to access the court. The privative clause that restricted access to the courts for people seeking protection was racist. The prevention of the court to examine the merits of the case of a person seeking protection advantages the Tribunal reviewer, and the Tribunal's institutional racism. Preventing family members from being recognised as members of a particular social group where one family member was persecuted, is also racist in that it specifically disadvantages the non-Australian citizen. The allowance of non-jurisdictional errors prejudices the person seeking protection and advantages the Tribunal reviewer. When a judge does not consider the importance of legal assistance for unrepresented people seeking protection, the judge is advantaging the Australian defendant. When the government defends the independent body's decisions to refuse protection and, appeals the independent body's decisions to grant protection, this could be perceived to be interference with the independence of the tribunal, with the government favouring tribunal reviewers and disadvantaging non-Australian citizens.

In Australia, racism is the instrument by which biopolitics has emerged and flourished, and fosters parliamentary legislation that is discriminatory, resulting in violent outcomes for marginalised social groups. No system is perfect, but this analysis of assessment and review procedures may contribute to a fairer and more inclusive assessment system for people arriving by plane who seek a place to live free of persecution. But this is contingent upon a parliament's willingness to remit power to decide protection claims to the court. Where there is a willingness, it is possible to enable the restoration of access to human rights, not only for people arriving by plane, but for all people seeking protection, through developing a system that protects, includes and is non-discriminatory.

~~~~~~~~

18. **If only: achieving fairness**

My intimate engagement with the refugee determination process as a citizen advocating on behalf of people seeking our protection has enabled me to consider at length what remedies for this inhumane system need to be put in place. The strategic suggestions for addressing racism and achieving fairness I outline below are based on the findings in my study and my experiences of advocacy for these groups of people arriving by plane seeking protection in Australian society.

Achieving an assessment reasonably free of politics

An initial strategy is to provide well qualified, competent assessors at the outset of the refugee determination assessment process. The very first assessment of a protection claim is vital, and my study has shown that serious mistakes can be made at this point. To avoid drawn-out legal procedures and expensive reviews, it would be far fairer and more efficient economically to ensure that each person applying for protection is assisted in preparing their claims by free legal practitioners well versed in international refugee law. This should ensure that important information is not excluded in the assessment and decision, and would avoid perceptions of superficiality or tokenism. These initiatives may also avoid issues such as embellishment of claims, fraudulent claims and omission of significant information on behalf of both the person seeking protection and the decision-maker.

Women and children have distinct rights that cannot necessarily be accessed when an application is submitted as a family unit in the father's or husband's name. Access to such rights was not accommodated in the decisions of all the people in my study. In the interests of fairness, making available the opportunity for different family members to present individual protection claims, and have these claims assessed separately and according to appropriate UN guidelines, would deliver justice to members of these marginalised groups.

A separate office or Peoples' Protection Assessment Centre to determine protection claims, independent of the Department of Immigration, would be beneficial. To achieve some objectivity, the centre could be accountable to a board consisting of a dedicated Australian Human Rights Committee (AHRC) member, an international lawyer and a representative from the UNHCR Canberra office.

If a person who arrives by plane seeking protection is assessed as not needing protection, and later fails at the tribunal or in the courts and subsequently makes a request for humanitarian consideration, such requests should also be prepared at a place outside the immigration department, for example, at the Peoples' Protection Assessment Centre. It would be more appropriate to have claims for humanitarian consideration assessed by AHRC or a dedicated member of the Board of the proposed Peoples' Protection Assessment Centre rather than by a minister constrained by the politics of preventing the arrival of people seeking protection. In the interest of transparency, if the minister makes a decision, they should provide a detailed explanation.

It is not easy to gain entry to Australia. If people seeking protection who arrive by plane access fair assessments and are found to be in need of protection, there should not be an annual quota on the number accepted as refugees. This is not unrealistic as the numbers are not large and could be included in the overall intake of skilled migrant numbers, protecting the separate annual quota for refugees accepted from overseas camps.

If KPIs were based on the number of *positive* decisions made, departmental assessors and advocates would no longer suffer the toxic culture which has developed within the Department of Immigration.

Awareness of personal racism

An anti-racism strategy for all Australians is the second strategic initiative. Decision-makers lack experience in recognising personal racist attitudes and practices when engaged in cross-cultural dialogue.

It would improve the quality of decisions made in a cross-cultural environment if all decision-makers involved in decisions and policies about refugees and people seeking protection, be they public servants, tribunal reviewers, judges or parliamentarians, had compulsory training in recognising personal racist attitudes and values. Similarly, journalists and editors reporting on cross-cultural incidences should take part in training to assist them to recognise personal racist attitudes and values. Compulsory racism awareness subject components in schools and tertiary institutions would help avoid racially affected assessments in the future. Relevant bodies to scrutinise decisions for racist elements could be established for each level of the decision-making procedure.

If Australia had human rights legislation, parliamentarians might not have introduced restrictive and discriminatory legislation directed at people seeking protection who arrive by boat or plane.

Reviewers' responses to trauma

A third suggestion is to improve skills for identifying psychologically vulnerable people applying for protection with training and education. Assessors in the public service, the tribunal, the judiciary and the minister's office sometimes lacked these skills. Decision-makers would benefit from training in recognising trauma, reporting it in decisions and responding appropriately to traumatised people seeking protection.

Assessing individual protection claims

A fourth strategy is to have a second application for refugee determination from the same family assessed by a person different from the delegate who made the original family assessment. This would eliminate the potential for a conflict of interest on the part of the assessor. If people applying for protection were assessed on the individual's claims without access to previous families' files, this would avoid circumstantial interference and a perception of bias towards a past unfavourable decision. It would be fairer if an assessor or reviewer did not make a decision on the basis of the material relating to other members of the family which had already been assessed and found wanting. A decision based only on information in the individual's application form should be informed by relevant guidelines, country human rights information, UN documents, departmental regulations, and the interview transcript. This would result in greater fairness in the primary stages of assessment.

Achieving fairness at decision reviews

A fifth strategy is achieving acceptable levels of fairness in decision reviews. The tribunal was the most problematic section of the application for protection process. Several reviewers were not legally qualified or experienced in cross-cultural dialogue. In many cases, the decisions arrived at were deceitful and the decisions of children and women were not assessed in their own right or according to specific international guidelines. It is impossible to imagine a review tribunal independent of the Department of Immigration or of political persuasion, so a more just, practical and economical approach would be to abandon this step in the application process, replacing it with a dedicated court for people seeking protection (Peoples' Protection Court) similar to the Children/Family court. This would eliminate confusion for people facing first an inquisitorial, then an adversarial process. It would also avoid immigration ministers engaging parliamentary 'has beens' in the tribunal process.[160]

Should the tribunal continue to function, as with initial refugee determination assessments outlined above, review decisions should be

---

160. Six days before Prime Minister, Scott Morrison, called the 2022 federal election it was announced that 6 of 19 new appointments to the Administrative Appeals Tribunal were former Liberal government staff or former Liberal Party candidates. In addition to immigration appeals, the Tribunal is responsible for appeals against government decisions in areas including social security, the national disability insurance scheme and freedom of information. Since 2013, eighty-five former liberal candidates and staffers have been appointed by the Liberal-National Party.

made on assessments of the merit of individual's claims, not historical documents from government files relating to the negative findings on other family members or other internal departmental documents. Reviewers should only have access to the interview and the individual's application form, the adverse decision, the tape of the compulsory interview, as well as a wide range of country information including human rights reports and UN documents.

Court appeals

A sixth strategy is to allow The Peoples' Protection Court to reinstate powers such as the ability to rule on the merits of the claims and abandonment of the non-jurisdictional error and other restrictive clauses in the Migration Act. This court would scrutinise particular cases rather than relying on previous failed decisions of other family members. In the interest of balanced judgements in appeals, all people seeking protection should be assisted by a qualified immigration lawyer and, if necessary, that this be provided by Legal Aid. This would ensure that the very serious claims of persecution and protection needs would be given adequate scrutiny by appropriately qualified personnel.

In the event that the tribunal is disbanded, if a person seeking protection fails at the first court of appeal, a second appeal before three judges could be allowed. If this is unsuccessful, appeal to the High Court should remain a possibility, as it is in the broader Australian community. Because of the high volume of appeals, this dedicated court should not have jurisdiction for other immigration appeal matters.

There are also problems that surfaced regarding the power of the parliament to introduce laws with cruel consequences. An independent body such as the Australian Human Rights Commission should be given the power to provide scrutiny over potential legislation to ensure that laws remain within the boundaries of Australia's international obligations to refugees and to basic human rights. In the absence of human rights legislation, and since it is the parliamentarians that are the offenders, this scrutiny should not be the lone responsibility of a parliamentary committee.

Bridging visas consistent with Australia's human rights obligations

Strategy seven is the provision of bridging visas in line with human rights obligations. In my study people applying for protection who requested ministerial intervention were granted bridging visas. They had to present at the compliance office to renew the visa, sometimes weekly, at the outset, then three-monthly. To avoid unnecessary trauma, it would be both compassionate and fair to grant one bridging visa until the procedure is complete. Furthermore, they should be granted a dedicated work/study visa that is sufficient to cover their stay in Australia until the assessment procedure has completed its course of reviews and if necessary, responses to their requests to the minister (or another appropriate body).

People seeking protection pursued their claims in the courts and had their work rights rescinded once they failed at the tribunal. To ensure equal access to human rights, all those applying for court reviews should be allowed to work until their application for protection is completed, regardless of whether they participate in other court appeals such as class actions or take their case to the UN Human Rights Committee.

People who arrive by plane seeking protection are not the same as economic migrants or overseas students. During the protection examination procedure, parents of school-age children should be charged school fees equivalent to those of Australian citizens at all levels of the education system, not overseas student fee rates.

Expanding visa opportunities

To avoid lengthy, expensive court appeals and given the potential for skilled and qualified people arriving by plane seeking protection becoming employed, the range of accessible visas onshore should be expanded. This would include not only the partner visa, but also skilled, sponsored and carer visas. This would allow people seeking safety who were refused protection, to apply for an appropriate visa without having to go offshore. These types of visas have been granted previously by the minister when they did not wish to grant a humanitarian visa. As we saw, Vasyl's employer was willing to sponsor his permanent skilled visa.

If visas were available onshore, some people may not consider the refugee pathway at all. However, access to the abovementioned visas should only be available to people fleeing violent situations if they fail the refugee determination assessment. For this cohort, these visas should be assessed in liaison with and on the recommendation of the proposed Peoples' Protection Assessment Centre. Visitors without appropriate protection claims who were not prepared to wait their turn for such a visa to be processed would not qualify.

~~~~~~~~

19. A society in peril: privilege and injustice

> The problem with only responding in a humanitarian as opposed to a conscious way that addresses structural issues, is that questions of justice are unaddressed, so that while the symptoms may be ameliorated, the causes of the problem are at best ignored and at worst legitimated or colluded with.[161]

~~~~~~~~

Recent Labor government apologies made to Australia's Indigenous peoples (2008), to British/Australian people (2009), and Australian adults taken from their mothers at birth (2013) are signs that the Australian parliament has the capacity to realise in hindsight that the lawful 'exception' seriously harms citizens who are excluded. However, there is little evidence to suggest that anything has been done to institute changes in the legal system in order to prevent parliament's exclusionary recidivism affecting people seeking protection and others at risk. Since the introduction of mandatory detention in 1992, ever increasing restrictions have been placed on migration law. Historical discriminatory laws have also enabled people seeking protection, in particular those arriving by plane, to be excluded from laws and human rights that mainstream Australians take for granted. Such legal and citizenship exclusions are contrary to international obligations to allow equal access to socio-economic and inalienable human rights.

Australian Governments with bipartisan support have introduced laws, policies and procedures that have adversely affected the persecution claims of people seeking protection. These practices prevent the court from undertaking a merits review of claims, and protect reviewers through the introduction of non-jurisdictional errors. Lawmakers, in the various colonial governments that existed before Federation, and even twentieth century parliamentary democracy in Australia, created or perpetuated the myth of *terra nullius*, claiming Australia was uninhabited or the inhabitants were not the landowners at the time of the British incursion. As a result of a society suffering from invasion paranoia, contemporary parliamentary leaders have created an ideology of 'border protection' to seek to legitimise Parliament's legislative exceptions regarding the inalienable rights of people seeking protection arriving by planes and boats. The deployment of the military to protect Australia's sovereign borders against unarmed persecuted people in often unseaworthy vessels and generating further peril and suffering in turning back the boats when they present no evidence of a military threat to Australia, should raise alarm for Australian citizens.

This military deployment can only be explained by examining Australia's biopolitical environment and concluding that it is the boundaries of sovereign power (parliament and the prime minister) that are being protected. One deceitful practice was revealed when a prime minister's confidant and strategist was quoted in the press saying, 'Kevin [Rudd] is now in PNG [Papua New Guinea], looking to do the deal on asylum seekers. My only concern is that people on the left will see it as a harsh measure. Having said that, it will almost certainly go down well with most people – particularly in Western Sydney, where the problem is felt most acutely'. He continued, explaining that they '*had to go to elaborate lengths to disguise the real purpose of this visit* – it's about visa simplification'. Richard Marles as trade minister, accompanied Rudd, as having Immigration Minister Tony Burke there would have caused 'too much commentary in the media'.[162] (my emphasis)

The Australian national armed forces (Army, Navy and Airforce) abandoned their powers to protect all people in, or on the way to, Australia in order to protect the powers of the prime minister and parliamentarians. Engaging the military for this purpose is misguided, deceitful and manipulative.

In contemporary Australia, the 'emergency has become the rule' and the declaration of 'a war' on people smugglers or people seeking Australia's protection, or illegals, is the justification for the 'emergency'. The restrictive and cruel refugee laws that parliamentarians constitute in the 'national interest' or 'public interest' are also a misappropriation of power which ultimately protects its own sovereignty. The deceitful methods and procedures evident in refugee determination and reviews of people who arrive by plane seeking protection, raises the issue of a misappropriation of power.

Parliamentarians' powers are rarely restrained when it comes to decisions about people seeking Australia's protection. Some past decisions are seriously questionable, as in the case of excising pieces of Australia's 'sovereign borders' and thus declaring some Australian territory 'not Australia for the purpose of migration'.

Barlow claimed that Australia's invasion paranoia has resulted in the powers of the parliamentarians gradually descending into a place of 'exemption chaos'. Land is excised from mainland Australia for this purpose.[163] Children are detained in camps and exposed to extreme violence. Adults are incarcerated without criminal records or any precise

---

161. Bretherton, L, 2010, *Christianity and Contemporary Politics*, Wiley-Blackwell, UK, p.141.
162. Morris, S, 2014, 'Rudd's backbench role in the Manus Island crisis', *The Saturday Paper* https://www.thesaturdaypaper.com.au/news/politics/2014/02/28/rudds-backbench-role-the-manus-island-crisis/1393550623111. Accessed March 2022.

understanding of the length of their imprisonment. Innocent, persecuted individuals are deported to places out of reach of Australia's lawyers, advocates and the media, and incarcerated in camps Australia has little control over. Detention camps are run by private companies with a code of secrecy to protect them from the violence they perpetrate on detained people seeking protection. This is the biopolitical environment in which people discussed in this book, who arrived by plane seeking a safe place to raise their children, sought a review of adverse protection assessments at the tribunal and in the courts.

~~~~~~~~

One example of parliamentarians' preparedness to question and rein in some of the immigration minister's power was the Complementary Protection legislation established in 2012, even if the retrospectivity of the law was contested (unsuccessfully) by the government. The courts, especially the High Court of Australia have made some attempts to maintain and sustain the separation of powers that is being undermined by the power of the parliament. One example of the courts' success was the prevention of parliament exchanging (trafficking) some persecuted sovereign people who arrived in Australia in boats, with some of Malaysia's persecuted people seeking protection. The courts' role in the case of people arriving by plane seeking protection was significant in its powerlessness. Because of restrictive legislation, all that could be done in most cases was to remit the case to the tribunal where the findings of the court could be abandoned. However, the numerous occasions in which the court's judges have provided an injunction, when government officials have planned to unfairly deport people arriving by boat seeking protection, cannot go unnoticed.

The changes resulting in regressive legislation exemplify the argument that exception is the rule of government in the area of refugee/protection determination, rather than fairness or equality for all under a citizenship contract. The violence of the 'exception' is confronted when the injustice of parliamentary power is interrogated through the law. This means relying on the court to reclaim its power more aggressively. The court owes this to every person who is mistreated by the powers of parliamentarians, whether they be Indigenous peoples, persecuted people seeking protection or other groups of excluded sovereign people including vulnerable Australian citizens. Only the courts and an independent assessment body can administer the justice people arriving by plane seeking protection deserve, because the general

163. Barlow, K, 2013, 'Parliament excises mainland from Migration zone', *ABC News*, http://www.abc.net.au/news/2013-05-16/parliament-excises-mainland-from-migration-zone/4693940; Accessed March 2022.

population has been infected by government bias about the inalienable rights of persecuted people who seek protection in Australia. Australia will only reclaim its dignified space in a global society through acknowledging international responsibilities and taking on board justified criticism that international bodies have been making over the past twenty years. The courts have a particular obligation not to abandon their power and responsibilities by allowing the power of parliamentarians to usurp them.

In a liberal democracy, people know when their rights are abused, and the hope is that every attempt by governing bodies to diminish their human, social and economic rights will be met with resistance and resilience. This counter-discourse on social and political exclusion will, I believe, happen regardless of the way the governing bodies publicly portray persecuted people seeking protection in order to convince the broader Australian community to fear them. The Museum of Australian Democracy claims that 'in a liberal democracy efforts are made to define and limit power, often by means of a written constitution. Checks and balances, such as the separation of the Parliament, senior government and judicial power, are instituted. In addition, there are conventions of behaviour and a legal system that complements the political system'. A pseudo-democracy develops when authorities or governments act outside their limits of power and this creates potential for aggressive discriminatory laws which are offensive and violent.

The media simultaneously depict brutality, highlighting the violence of the targeted people and the violence of the law. Mainstream Australians, the voters, are confused and afraid. Some are affected by vicarious trauma. The government then restores law and order by claiming they, and mainstream Australians, are the victims and the vulnerable people are the perpetrators, who are duly punished. This encourages mainstream Australians to feel somewhat safer because the government has stepped in and protected them but, at the same time, they feel more afraid of 'the other', the vulnerable group targeted by the inhumane laws. The vulnerable feel more unsafe and become more fearful of the all-powerful government, and so the process of fear is perpetuated without proper understanding of the experiences of the vulnerable or of disadvantaged people.

Waleed Aly, reflecting on the horrific uprising in the Manus Island camp where one person seeking Australia's protection had been murdered, wrote,

> when social behaviour repeats itself like this, we have two explanations open to us. One is that this is a coincidence of sorts: that it is nothing more than the misbehaviour of immoral individuals gaming the system, and that these individuals merely happen to pop up repeatedly. This is

very much the explanation favoured by officialdom – from both major parties – who immediately declare these rioters to have failed any decent character test.

His second explanation is,

> that there is something about the circumstances of detainees that generates this behaviour. Put any group of people through this wringer, and they will eventually respond with riotous protest. Such behaviour is not a function of defective personalities of individuals, but the inevitable human reaction to inhuman treatment: that the violence we've witnessed over and over is simply a product of the system.

This is a graphic picture of the consequences of the cruelty of the law perpetrated in Australia's name. Aly concludes that 'the political truth is that there is almost nothing any government could do that the electorate would deem too brutal, which is precisely how' we arrived at this point.[164]

The violence occurring in Australia's island detention camps is provoked by actions of parliamentarians. In incarcerating people who are not criminals in other states' territories, such as Papua New Guinea and Nauru, parliamentarians deem them unworthy of Australia's assessment system on the basis of sustaining political power, not compliance with international law. The ultimate expression of Australian biopolitics in 2014 resulted in the alleged murder of Reza Barati, an innocent persecuted person seeking Australia's protection in one of these island camps and, in the past, numerous suicides in other camps for which Australia is responsible. Less visible people arriving by plane seeking protection suffer severe depression and suicidal ideation as a result of the prolonged unfair system of assessment and review, and the repetitive denial of their credible persecution claims.

~~~~~~~~

This book has documented how and why some people arriving by plane seeking protection in Australia were refused protection. My commitment to equal access to human rights for every person made me, an Australian citizen, uncomfortable with the adverse decisions made about the protection claims of people arriving by plane. By analysing refugee determination assessment decisions, tribunal reviews and court appeals, my study found that the strategies for assessing claims and reviewers' decision-making techniques were unfair and unjust. Immigration laws and regulations were unfairly restrictive and rewarded negative outcomes.

Assessors and reviewers were adversely influenced by historical attitudes and values that nurture a biopolitical culture where the power of parliamentarians continually seeks to undermine the power of judges in the courts. People seeking safety, sovereign citizens from other cultures and countries, arrived by plane and sought Australia's protection. They were prevented from accessing their inalienable international human rights – rights available to Australia's privileged citizens – just as sovereign Indigenous Australians have been prevented for over two centuries. In introducing the biopolitics of modernity, the very natural life that is placed at the foundation of order vanishes into the figure of the citizen in whom 'rights are preserved' and where the principle of all sovereignty resides essentially in the nation.[165] Laws with violent consequences are condoned and perpetrators (assessors, reviewers and parliamentarians) are protected when implementing laws targeting 'non-Australian citizens'. In the process of introducing an exception to the law for non-Australian citizens, the truth of the law is assumed, thus expiating the guilt of the perpetrators of laws that result in violent consequences.

As a determined advocate, I too have been on the receiving end of perpetrators of violent laws, laws I find insulting. One family applied in 2000 and received protection eventually in 2013 after I defended myself against accusations of 'working illegally' by the tribunal manager. My credibility was also questioned by departmental assessors delegated by the minister, as evident in their ministerial submissions. These unfair allegations helped me to understand how people arriving by plane felt when their significant protection claims were consistently misrepresented. I can only imagine what might be happening to people who arrive by boat when I observe the outpouring of frustration in the detention camps. I have learnt that, in positioning myself as an advocate, it is necessary to be open to the possibility of being confronted by the power of the perpetrators of unjust laws.

My study has been undertaken in the hope that the research will bring about change in the way refugee and protection determination assessments are carried out. This book suggests small steps that can be taken so that fair and just decisions can be made about people arriving by plane who seek Australia's protection. Such steps could begin a movement away from laws with violent consequences and towards a more inclusive Australian society.

Questioning the fairness and injustice of the decisions of assessors and reviewers is but a small piece of the Australian unwelcoming refugee puzzle. The bigger picture extends beyond to one that which excludes men, women and children who arrive by boat. The horrific manner in which their

---

164. Aly, W, 2014, 'The whole point of detention for asylum seekers is horror, whether it is acknowledged or not', *Sydney Morning Herald*, 21 February, https://www.smh.com.au/opinion/the-whole-point-of-detention-for-asylum-seekers-is-horror-whether-it-is-acknowledged-or-not-20140220-333yw.html. Accessed March 2022.
165. Agamben op. cit., p.75.

protection claims are dismissed extends in turn to the broader Australian community, when the unbridled power of governments allows ever-increasing repressive legislation that could affect any vulnerable Australian citizen in future.

Australia has been excluding people 'legitimately' according to decision-makers' discriminatory legal standards and questionable moral and ethical practices since the beginning of the colonial period. The potentiality for laws that are cruel to disrupt Australia's multicultural society increases every time laws with violent consequences are introduced and implemented. The violence that occurred in Australia's island detention camps is a contemporary example of what could occur on a larger scale as a result of the unbridled power of successive parliamentarians who stealthily usurp power from the courts. Violence is the outcome of the actions of a government that expands the borders of its sovereign powers under the guise of a ruthless sovereign border protection policy.

Human rights law needs to be firmly embedded in the Australian legal system before societal change is possible. If parliamentarians continue to introduce laws with cruel and unfair consequences, judges will continue to be constrained, tribunal reviewers will continue to be morally corrupt, and departmental assessors will continue to improve their performance ratings through fake assessment practices. Immigration ministers will continue to be called upon to 'play God'. Human rights will continue to be inaccessible to people not only in the immigration sector, but in other areas including social security, banking, policing. Relationships with neighbouring countries including Papua New Guinea and Nauru will continue to be troubled.

Without reform, our democratic system will never measure up to the standards required internationally. Australia will be no better than countries our parliamentarians frequently criticise, often the very countries from which people flee in search of safety and protection. Australians will continue to live in a pretend world where human rights are believed to be accessible.

I have called these final observations 'privileged' but in truth, the time for privilege is over. Our national government expects us to respect the law and the democratic system, but respect needs to be earned and renewed. Australian society needs protection from ill-gotten powers that inflict unjust, illegitimate, grotesque laws, policies and practices on people in marginalised sectors of Australian society and that advantages mates, lobbyists and donors.

Gaining society's respect for what promises to be a reasonable democratic system is dependent upon whether or not human rights law is accessible to Australians, to others living within Australia, and to those for whom Australia is responsible beyond our geographic borders.

~~~~~~~~

Appendix

Below:

Visa history of people who participated in my research
Source: File documents.

	Visa on arrival	Author met after arrival	Time taken to get visa	Type of Permanent Visa obtained
Marco + Amora	Tourist	4 years	7.5 years	857 Skilled Sponsor
Sabina + Vasyl	Tourist	2 years	6.5 years	457 Business Long Stay TEMPORARY
Sofia + Olek	Tourist	10 years	11 years	Protection XA 866
Naldo + Maita	Tourist	8 years	9.5 years	835 Remaining Relative
Belicia + Orlondo	Tourist	7 years	10 years	202 Global Humanitarian
Nankunda	—	6 years	6 years	856 Employer Nomination
Polina + Dmytro	Tourist	8 years	13 years	XA or 202
Ladonna + Jaime	Tourist	8 years	10 years	202 Global Humanitarian
Grisha + Inna	Tourist	6 years	7 years	202 Global Humanitarian
Mateo	Tourist	11 years	12 years	151 Former Resident

Right:

The choices facing asylum seekers at each stage of the process

The diagram opposite is designed to illustrate the complexity rather than to elucidate the process. If the Department makes a negative decision, an independent body makes a negative decision, or the courts find against the asylum seekers they can approach the Minister or UNHCR or UNHRC. If the asylum seeker chooses not to follow the steps outlined (grey) alternative pathways are presented.

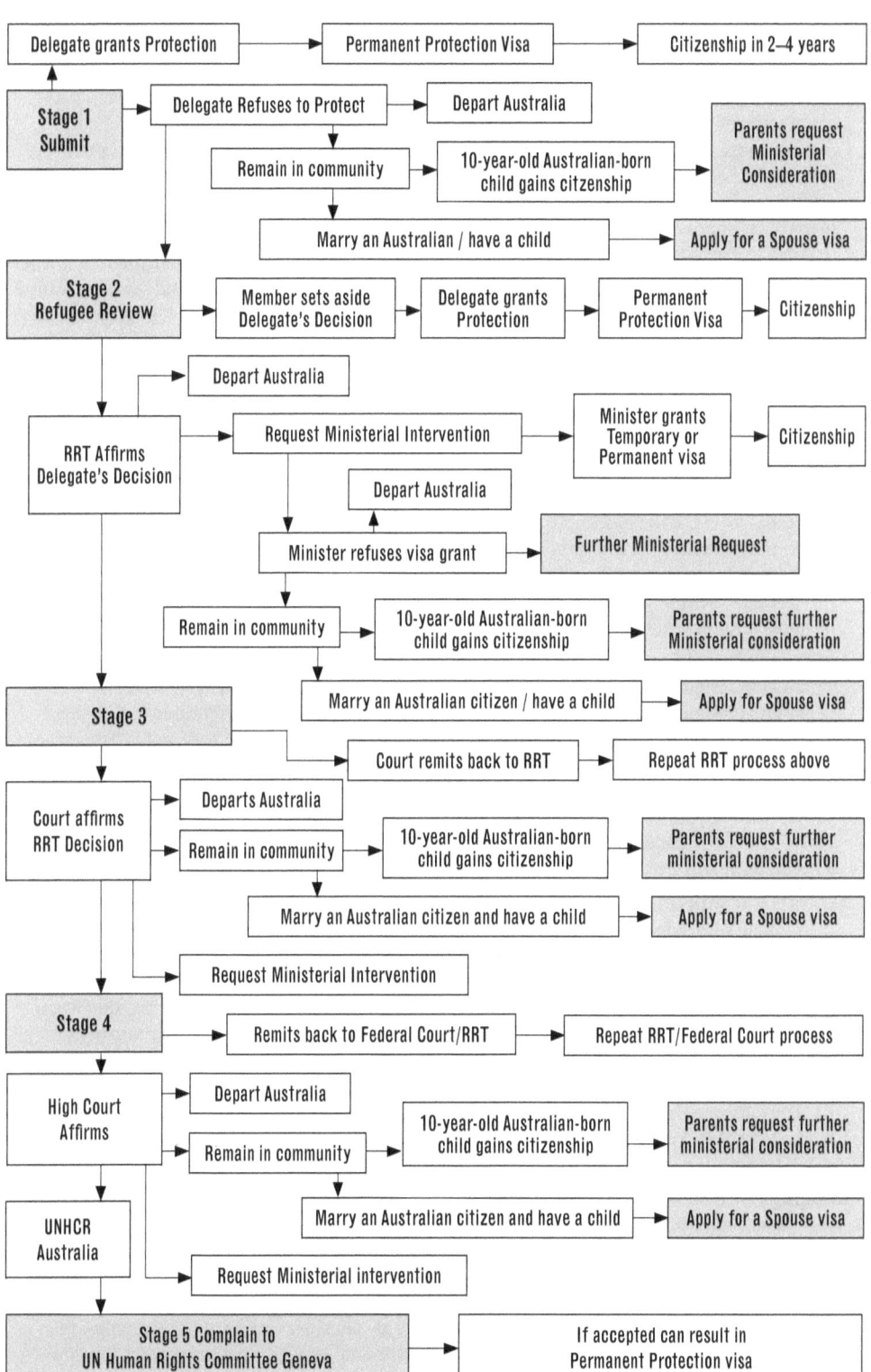

Glossary

s48B In most cases, if a person has been refused a protection visa, they are prevented from making another application for a protection visa. Under Section 48B of the *Migration Act 1958 (Cth)*, the minister can grant permission to make another protection visa application due to exceptional circumstances. The minister's policy is that permission will only be granted if there is new information or significant changes in circumstances after the protection visa refusal decision, sufficient to justify giving such permission.

s417 Section 417 of the *Migration Act 1958 (Cth)*, gives the minister the power to grant a visa to a person refused by the Administrative Appeals Tribunal's (AAT's) Migration and Refugee Division, if the minister thinks it is in 'the public interest' to grant them a visa. It is only possible to request the minister to use this power if the AAT has made a decision on an application for protection.

AAT/The Tribunal The Administrative Appeals Tribunal (referred to as 'the tribunal' in this book) provides independent merits review of government decisions, including migration and refugee visas and other visa-related decisions. However, the tribunal members are government appointed for fixed 5-year terms and are therefore dependent on government support for renewal of their appointments.

Assurance of Support (AOS) is a legal agreement made with Services Australia (Centrelink) to assist someone to obtain a visa to live in Australia. The assurer promises to pay back any income support that Services Australia may provide to the visa applicant. An assurer may need to give a bank guarantee through the Commonwealth Bank of Australia. The Assurance of Support period depends on the type of visa applied for. It can last 1, 2, 4 or 10 years.

Bridging visa E BE (subclass 051) is a temporary visa which can be issued to people (a) who have applied for protection and where a final decision hasn't been made; (b) whose protection visa application was denied and they have applied for an appeal of the decision at the tribunal, or a judicial review.

Character test Before a person is granted a permanent visa, they must pass a character test which includes Police Checks both in Australia and the former country of residence, and other considerations.

Centrelink is an arm of Services Australia, an Australian Government department. It is a delivery point for payments and services available to Australian families. It provides such payments as Parental Leave pay, Job Seeker payment, Youth Allowance, and Child Care Subsidy, none of which is accessible to people holding BVEs. However, access to Medicare can occur under certain circumstances, especially when a person has permission to work.

Complementary Protection The *Migration Amendment (Complementary Protection) Act 2011 (Cth)* passed by parliament in 2011 provides for the grant of protection visas to people who are not refugees under the Refugees Convention, but to whom Australia is required to provide protection under other international agreements to which Australia is a party. Persons are entitled to Complementary protection if they would otherwise be returned to a country where they would be subject to the death penalty or torture or other cruel or inhuman treatment or punishment.

Delegate Under the *Migration Act 1958 (Cth)*, the minister can delegate their power to make certain decisions to officers of the Department of Immigration. Such people are labelled 'Delegates'. However, I prefer to use 'Assessor', as the term 'Delegate' can appear to distance the decision-maker from the decision when, in reality, they are ordinary departmental employees assessing protection claims.

Federal Court The Federal Court of Australia is made up of judges appointed by the Commonwealth Government. Its processes are highly formal, and complicated legal procedures and complex language are used. For those unaccustomed to Australian court procedures, it can be very intimidating. It does not have the power to undertake a 'merits review' (see below) as is the case at the tribunal. This court only considers issues of law – whether the tribunal reviewer or a lower court interpreted the law correctly, and whether they followed the correct methods to assess the case. This court can decide if the procedures in making the decision outlined in the Migration Act and Regulations were followed; whether the decision-makers acted within their powers or improperly exercised their powers or made an error of law; made a decision induced by fraud or bias or had enough information to justify the decision. If an appeal of a tribunal decision is successful, the claims are sent back to the tribunal to be reviewed by a different person. The Federal Court also has the power to hear appeals in relation to decisions of single judges. Such appeals are heard by a panel of three judges.

High Court The High Court of Australia, the highest court in Australia, can accept appeals from persons who have exhausted appeal rights in lower courts. The High Court must 'grant leave' for the appeal to proceed. This is done in only a minority of cases raising special issues. If the appeal is successful, the case is sometimes sent back to the lower court for reconsideration in accordance with the law. The High Court also has original jurisdiction to hear cases involving constitutional law.

Humanitarian visa can be a Protection Visa (Class XA) (Subclass 866) which is granted to a person already lawfully in Australia. In successfully being granted a humanitarian visa, a person must be a refugee a defined by s.36 of the Migration Act, pass health and character tests, and sign the Australian Values Statement. The Protection Visa affords permanent residency status and allows a person to receive Medicare and Centrelink services. Other humanitarian visas pertinent to this study include the In-country Special Humanitarian Program Visa (Subclass 201) and the Global Special Humanitarian Program Visa ('SHP') (Subclass 202).

Judicial review is the review by a court of a decision made by a tribunal, to ensure that the decision is legal.

Jurisdiction is the authority of a court or tribunal to hear and determine cases. The jurisdictions of Federal Courts and the tribunal arise under the Australian Constitution (in the case of the High Court) or under Commonwealth legislation. For example, judges cannot decide if claims merit refugee status, but can decide if the tribunal reviewer followed the law in the way the decision was made, because the Migration Act defines their authority.

Jurisdictional error arises when a decision-maker exceeds the authority or power conferred upon them, takes into account irrelevant information, fails to take into account relevant information, or makes a completely unreasonable decision. The courts can only declare a decision invalid if there is a jurisdictional error. Some types of errors made by decision-makers are not jurisdictional error and cannot be overturned by the courts.

Key Performance Indicators (KPIs) are criteria whereby progress toward an intended result or level of achievement can be measured — usually within organisation or businesses. KPIs provide a focus for strategic and operational improvement and include setting targets or the desired level of performance (such as, in the case of the Department of Immigration, number of applicants for protection denied or allowed refugee status).

Magistrates Court The Federal Magistrates Court of Australia was established in 1999 and because the Federal Circuit Court of Australia in 2013. It was a court with jurisdiction over migration matters. The Court was created to deal with the increasing workload of the Federal Court and the Family Court by hearing the less complex cases for them and freeing those Courts to deal only with more complex cases. In 2021, these Courts were merged to for the Federal Circuit and Family Court of Australia.

Medicare is a government service that provides Australian residents with access to a wide range of health and hospital care at no cost or low cost.

Merits review A merits review is undertaken by a tribunal reviewer, formally called the 'Member' who can take a fresh look at the facts, law and policy relating to a particular decision. In most cases, The Administrative Appeals Tribunal (AAT) can look at new information that was not available to the original decision-maker. The tribunal reviewer can make a decision to confirm the original decision, to vary it, or to overturn the original decision. If the decision is overturned, the person seeking protection still needs to meet health and character criteria before a visa is granted.

Migration agent A migration agent provides immigration advice and assistance on a fee for service basis. In Australia, migration agents are registered with the Office of the Migration Agents Registration Authority (OMARA), which is part of the Department of Home Affairs. All qualified agents are authorised by the Australian government to provide their services.

Ministerial request If the tribunal merits review or court appeal is unsuccessful a person seeking protection can ask the minster for immigration to overturn the decision. The minister has the power to substitute 'a decision more favourable to the applicant' even if the person does not meet all the legal requirements. This power is non-compellable, non-reviewable, and non-delegable.

Newstart The Newstart Allowance is an Australian government income support payment providing financial assistance to unemployed people aged 22 years or more, until they become eligible for the aged pension. They must be participating in or willing to participate in approved activities and/or job search, and be prepared to enter into, comply with or vary an existing Job Plan.

Privative clause A privative clause is a provision in a statute that seeks to prevent an administrative action being challenged in court. An example is s. 474 of the Migration Act, which provides that most administrative decisions under the Migration Act are to be classed as privative clause decisions, and says that such decisions must not be challenged, appealed against, reviewed, quashed, or called into question in any court. However, the High Court has held that administrative decisions which are affected by 'jurisdictional error' are not decisions made under the Act, and therefore are not affected by privative clauses such as s. 474.

Pro bono Work, in particular legal work, which is undertaken at no cost to the person seeking assistance unless a successful outcome is obtained and costs can be recovered from another party, is said to be undertaken pro bono. Legal work is often undertaken pro bono for cases deemed 'in the public interest'.

Refugee A refugee is a person outside their country of origin or residence who is unable or unwilling to return to their country of origin because of a legitimate fear of persecution regarding their race, religion, nationality, group membership, or a political belief; who is not a war criminal and has not committed any serious non-political crime.

Relocation Depending on the circumstances of the particular claims, it may be reasonable for a person seeking protection to relocate in their country to a region where, objectively, there is no appreciable risk of occurrence of the feared persecution.

Reviewer The reviewer is the tribunal officer, formally known as 'the Member', who conducts a hearing, examines all the person's previous files, and makes a decision about the Refugee Status Determination that was previously made by the government clerk or Delegate.

Schedule Schedules are case summaries provided to the minister for personal consideration where the case falls outside the Ministerial Guidelines for consideration.

Set-aside rate is the average annual number of cases for which tribunal reviewers found in favour of the applicants.

State Parties State Parties referred to in this book are countries that have signed the various United Nations Conventions, such as the Refugee Convention and the Universal Declaration on Human Rights.

Supreme Court This is the highest court in each of Australia's eight States and Territories. These courts do not hear appeals from the Federal Magistrates Court, and do not deal with protection matters.

Tribunal See above under AAT.

~~~~~~~~

Bibliography

AAP, 2011, 'Gillard announces Malaysian solution', *Sydney Morning Herald*, 7 May, https://www.smh.com.au/national/gillard-announces-malaysian-solution-20110507-1ed0h.html. Accessed March 2022.

Agamben, G, 1998, *Homo Sacer: Sovereign Power and Bare Life*, translated by Daniel Hedler-Roazen, Stanford University Press, USA.

Aleinikoff, T A, 2003, 'Protected characteristics and social perceptions: an analysis of the meaning of 'membership of a particular social group', in E Feller et al (eds*), Refugee Protection in International Law: UNHCR Global Consultations on International Protection*, University Press, Cambridge, pp. 263-311.

Australian Government, 2003, 'Performance pay', *2002-2003 Annual Report*, Appendix 2, Department of Immigration and Multicultural and Indigenous Affairs.

Australian Government, 2012, Fact Sheet 61a, Complementary Protection, Department of Immigration, http://www.immi.gov.au/media/fact-sheets/61a-complementary.htm. Accessed 2013.

Bashford, A & Strange, C, 2002, 'Asylum-Seekers and National Histories of Detention', *Australian Journal of Politics and History*, vol. 48, no. 4, pp. 509-527.

Bergen, R K, 1993, 'Interviewing Survivors of Marital Rape' in C M Renzetti & R M Lee (eds), *Researching Sensitive Topics*, SAGE Publications, Newbury Park, London.

Bourke, C & Cox, H, 1994, 'Two Laws: One Land', in C Bourke, E Bourke & W Edwards (eds), *Aboriginal Australia*, University of Queensland Press, St Lucia, pp. 49-64.

Bretherton, L, 2010, *Christianity and Contemporary Politics*, Wiley-Blackwell, UK.

Briskman, L, Latham, S & Goddard, C, 2008, *Human Rights Overboard: Seeking Asylum in Australia*, Scribe, Melbourne.

Canadian Immigration Refugee Board (CIRB), 1991, 'Membership in a Particular Social Group as a Basis for a Well-founded Fear of Persecution: Framework of Analysis', *Refworld*, https://www.refworld.org/docid/3ae6b32510.html. Accessed March 2022.

Coffey, G, 2003, 'The Credibility of Credibility Evidence at the Refugee Review Tribunal', *International Journal of Refugee Law*, vol. 15, no. 3, pp. 337-417.

Department of Immigration and Multicultural Affairs (DIMA), 1996, *Refugee and Humanitarian Visa Applicants: Guidelines on Gender Issues for Decision Makers,* http://refugeestudies.org/UNHCR/66%20-%20Refugee%20and%20Humanitarian%20Visa%20Applicants.%20Guidelines%20on%20Gender%20Issues%20for%20Decision%20Makers..pdf, p.16, para 4.6. Accessed March 2022.

De Crespigny, R, 2012, *The People Smuggler: the true story of Ali Al Jenabi, the 'Oskar Schindler of Asia'*, Penguin Group, Australia.

Edwards, A, 2003, 'Age and gender dimensions in international refugee law', in E Feller et al (eds*), Refugee Protection in International Law: UNHCR Global Consultations on International Protection*, University Press, Cambridge, pp. 46-80.

Enright, C, 2012, *Anatomy of a Privative Clause*, Maitland Press, Newcastle NSW.

Feller, E, Turk, V & Nicholson, F, (eds*),* 2003, *Refugee Protection in International Law: UNHCR Global Consultations on International Protection*, University Press, Cambridge.

Fickling, D, 2002, 'Australia lied about refugees throwing children overboard', Senate inquiry's finding, https://www.dawn.com/news/63324/australia-lied-about-refugees-throwing-children-overboard-senate-inquiry-s-finding. Accessed March 2022.

Fleay, C, 2010, *Australia and Human Rights: Situating the Howard Government*, Cambridge Scholars Publishing, Newcastle upon Tyne.

Foster, M, 2012, 'The Ground with the Least Clarity. A Comparative Study of Jurisprudential Developments relating to "Membership of a Particular Social Group"', *Legal and Protection Policy Research Series*, UNHCR, https://www.unhcr.org/en-au/protection/globalconsult/4f7d8d189/25-ground-clarity-comparative-study-jurisprudential-developments-relating.html. Accessed March 2022.

Gageler, S, 2010, 'Impact of migration law on the development of Australian administrative law', *Journal of Administrative Law*, vol. 17, pp. 92-105.

Giuliani, G, 2011, 'Pacific Islanders abducted for banana plantations and cane fields (1868). Throwaway Labour. Blackbirding and a White Australia', *Journal of the European Association of Studies on Australia*, vol. 2, no.2, pp. 98-112.

Glendenning, P, Leavey C, Hetherton, M & Britt, M, 2006, *Deported to Danger II: The Continued Study of Australia's Rejected Asylum Seekers*, Edmund Rice Centre, Sydney.

Griffiths, P, 2001, 'Racism: whitewashing the class divide', https://openresearch-repository.anu.edu.au/bitstream/1885/42702/2/Anti-immigrant_racism.pdf. Accessed March 2022.

Guy, S & Hocking, B, 2008, 'Migration Act and the constitutionality of privative clauses', *Australian Journal of Administrative Law*, vol.16, no.1, pp. 21-44.

Haines, R, 2003, 'Gender-related persecution' in E Feller et al (eds*), Refugee Protection in International Law: UNHCR Global Consultations on International Protection*, University Press, Cambridge.

Hall, D E, 2004, *Subjectivity*, Routledge, Taylor and Francis Group, New York.

Hathaway, J C & Foster, M, 2003, 'Internal protection/relocation/flight alternative as an aspect of refugee status determination', in E Feller et al (eds*), Refugee Protection in International Law: UNHCR Global Consultations on International Protection*, University Press, Cambridge.

Holt, M, 2003, 'Biopolitics and the "Problem" of the Refugee', *Critical Perspectives on Refugee Policy in Australia*, https://www.deakin.edu.au/arts-ed/ccg/rsg/pdfs/matthew-holt.pdf pp 89-101, pp. 89–101. Accessed 2013.

Human Rights and Equal Opportunity Commission (HREOC), 1997, *Bringing Them Home: A guide to the findings and recommendations of the National Inquiry into the separation of Aboriginal and Torres Strait Islanders children from their families*, Sydney.

Humphreys, S, 2006, 'Legalizing Lawlessness: On Giorgio Agamben's State of Exception', *The European Journal of International Law*, vol. 17, no. 10, pp. 677–687.

Jones, P, 2005, 'Chinese-Australian Journeys: Records on Travel, Migration and Settlement, 1860-1975', National Archives of Australia.

Kahneman, D, 2011, *Thinking, Fast and Slow*, Farrar, Straus and Giroux, New York.

Kivel, P, 2002, *Uprooting Racism: How white people can work for racial justice*, New Society Publishers, Gabriola Island, Canada.

Klocker, N & Dunn, K M, 2003, 'Who's Driving the Asylum Debate? Newspaper and Government Representations of Asylum Seekers', *Media International Australia Incorporating Culture and Policy*, no. 109, November. http://www.uws.edu.au/__data/assets/pdf_file/0010/26956/A17.pdf. Accessed March 2022.

Kneebone, S, 2005, 'Women within the refugee construct: "Exclusionary Inclusion" in Policy and Practice – the Australian Experience', *International Journal of Refugee Law*, vol. 17, pp. 7-42.

Lake, G, 2013, 'Have you got any bodybags? We've run out', Bible Society, http://www.biblesociety.org.au/news/bodybags-weve-run. Accessed March 2022.

LeCouteur, A & Augoustinos, M, 2001, 'The Language of Prejudice and Racism', in M Augoustinos, & K J Reynolds (eds), *Understanding Prejudice, Racism, and Social Conflict*, SAGE Publications Ltd, London, pp. 215-230.

Lee, J, 2012, 'Minister's decision to deport Afghan man "irrational"', *Sydney Morning Herald*, 3 November, https://www.smh.com.au/politics/federal/ministers-decision-to-deport-afghan-man-irrational-20121102-28ppn.html. Accessed 2022.

Mackenzie, C, McDowell, C, & Pittaway, E, 2007, 'Beyond "Do No Harm": the challenge of constructing ethical relationships in refugee research', *Journal of Refugee Studies*, vol. 20, no. 2, pp. 299-319.

Manne, R & Corlette, D, 2004, 'Sending Them Home: Refugees and the new Politics of Indifference', *Quarterly Essay*, Issue 13, pp. 1-95.

Mares, P, 2001, *Borderline: Australia's treatment of refugees and asylum seekers*, University of New South Wales Press Ltd, Sydney.

Markus, A & Taylor, J, 2006, 'No work, no income, no Medicare: the Bridging Visa E regime', *People and Place*, vol. 14, no. 1, pp. 43–52.

McConnochie, K, Hollinsworth, D & Pettman, J, 1988, *Race & Racism in Australia*, Social Science Press, Wentworth Falls, NSW.

McHugh, M, 2002, 'Tensions between the Executive and the Judiciary', Australian Bar Association Conference, Paris, http://www.hcourt.gov.au/assets/publications/speeches/former-justices/mchughj/mchughj_paris.htm. Accessed March 2022.

Migration Review Tribunal-Refugee Review Tribunal, 2006, *Guidance on the Assessment of Credibility*, October, paragraphs 4.1 and 4.3.

Migration Review Tribunal and Refugee Review Tribunal, *Annual Reports 2006/2007-2010/2011.*

Moreton-Robinson, A, 1998, 'Witnessing Whiteness in the Wake of Wik', *Social Alternatives*, vol. 17, no. 2, pp. 11-14.

Palmer, M, 2005, *Inquiry into the Circumstances of the Immigration Detention of Cornelia Rau*, Report, Commonwealth of Australia, https://www.homeaffairs.gov.au/reports-and-pubs/files/palmer-report.pdf. Accessed March 2022.

Parliamentary Inquiry, 2002, 'The Children Overboard Incident', Chapter 2, https://www.aph.gov.au/Parliamentary_Business/Committees/Senate/Former_Committees/scrafton/report/c02. Accessed March 2022.

Pittock, B, 1972, 'Aboriginal Land Rights', in F Stevens (ed), *Racism: The Australian Experience*, vol. 2, ANZ Books Company, pp. 199-208.

Psihogios-Billington, M, 2009, 'A Case for Justice: Position Paper on the Legal Process of Seeking Asylum in Australia', Asylum Centre Resource Centre, North Melbourne.

Proust, E, 2008, *Report to the Minister of Immigration and Citizenship on the Appropriate Use of Ministerial Powers Under the Migration and Citizenship Acts and Migration Regulations,* https://nswbar.asn.au/circulars/july/proust.pdf. Accessed March 2022.

Refugee Review Tribunal, *Annual Reports, 2001/2002-2005/2006.*

Renzetti, C M & Lee, R M, 1993 (eds), *Researching Sensitive Topics*, SAGE Publications, Newbury Park, London.

Reynolds, H, 2000, 'Indigenous social welfare: From a low priority to recognition and reconciliation', in A McMahon, J Thomson & C Williams (eds), *Understanding the Australian Welfare State: Key documents and themes*, Tertiary Press, Croydon, Victoria, pp. 97-135.

Reynolds, H, 1987, *Frontier*, Allen & Unwin Pty Ltd., St Leonards, NSW.

Ruddock, P, 2002, 'Immigration Policy and the Separation of Powers', *Upholding the Australian Constitution*, vol. 14, The Samuel Griffith Society.

Sackville, R, 2003, 'Refugee law: the shifting balance', Judicial Conference of Australia, Darwin, Federal Court of Australia, http://classic.austlii.edu.au/au/journals/SydLawRw/2004/3.html. Accessed March 2022.

Scrafton, M, 2012, Submission to Expert Panel on Asylum Seekers. http://expertpanelonasylumseekers.dpmc.gov.au/published-submissions. Accessed 2013.

Senate Committee Report, 2012, *Commonwealth Contribution to Former Forced Adoption Policies and Practices*, https://www.aph.gov.au/Parliamentary_Business/Committees/Senate/Community_Affairs/Completed_inquiries/2010-13/commcontribformerforcedadoption/report/index. Accessed March 2022.

Senate Legal and Constitutional References Committee, 2006, 'Administration and operation of the *Migration Act 1958'*, Parliament House, Canberra, https://www.aph.gov.au/Parliamentary_Business/Committees/Senate/Legal_and_Constitutional_Affairs/Completed%20inquiries/2004-07/migration/report/index. Accessed March 2022.

Senate Committee on Ministerial Discretion in Migration Matters, 2005, Chapter 8, https://www.aph.gov.au/Parliamentary_Business/Committees/Senate/Former_Committees/minmig/report/index. Accessed March 2022.

Senate Select Committee on Ministerial Discretion in Migration Matters, 2003, Submission by the Vietnamese Community of Australia, Western Australia, p.4.

Shaw, M & Skelton, R, 2003, 'Ruddock may face inquiry on intervention', *The Age*, 7 June, http://www.theage.com.au/articles/2003/06/06/1054700391819.html. Accessed March 2022.

Skelton, R, 2006, 'How we wrongly locked away 60 people', *The Age*, 15 January, https://www.theage.com.au/national/how-we-wrongly-locked-away-60-people-20060115-ge1krr.html. Accessed March 2022.

Smith, L, 2014, 'Ex-Immigration officer: is there asylum seeker blood on my hands?', *Crikey: Independent Media, Independent Minds*, http://sievx.com/articles/28LifeJackets/20140130Smith.html. Accessed March 2022.

Spigelman, J, 2004, 'Integrity and Privative Clauses', The Third Lecture in the 2004 National Lecture Series for the Australian Institute of Administrative Law, Brisbane, Supreme Court of NSW, https://www.supremecourt.justice.nsw.gov.au/Documents/Publications/Speeches/Pre-2015%20Speeches/Spigelman/spigelman_speeches_2004.pdf. Accessed March 2022.

Spurgeon, J, 2013, 'Defining "Natural Born Citizen": The Debate Over Who Qualifies To Run For President', http://ivn.us/2013/08/13/defining-natural-born-citizen/. Accessed March 2022.

Thouless, R H, 1964, *Straight and Crooked Thinking*, (Revised Edition, 8th Print), Pan Books Ltd, London.

Thompson, S (Curator), 2013, *Objects through Time*, Migration Heritage Centre 2006-2013, http://www.migrationheritage.nsw.gov.au/exhibition/objectsthroughtime/bourketerra/. Accessed March 2022.

Triggs, G, 2020, *Speaking Up*. Melbourne University Press, Melbourne.

Turk, V & Nicholson, F, 2003, 'Refugee protection in international law: an overall perspective', in E Feller, et al (eds), *Refugee Protection in International Law: UNHCR Global Consultations on International Protection*, University Press, Cambridge.

UNHCR, 2002, *Guidelines on International Protection: 'Membership of a particular social group' within the context of Article 1A(2) of the 1951 Convention and/or its 1967 Protocol relating to the Status of Refugee*s, http://www.unhcr.org/3d58de2da.html. Accessed March 2022.

UNHCR, 2009, Guidelines on International Protection: Child Asylum Claims Under Articles 1(A)2 and 1(F) of the 1951 Convention and/or 1967 Protocol Relating to the Status of Refugees. https://www.unhcr.org/en-au/publications/legal/50ae46309/guidelines-international-protection-8-child-asylum-claims-under-articles.html. Accessed March 2022.

USLegal.com, http://definitions.uslegal.com/r/res-judicata/. Accessed March 2022.

Von Doussa, J, 2008, 'Bill of rights is essential to best serve human rights', *Sydney Morning Herald*, 9 October, https://humanrights.gov.au/about/news/opinions/bill-rights-essential-best-serve-human-rights-2008. Accessed March 2022.

Wilson, J P & So-kum Tang, C (eds), 2007, *Cross-Cultural Assessment of Psychological Trauma and PTSD*, 1st edition, Springer Publishing Company, USA.

Winant, H, 2000, 'Race and Race Theory', *Annual Review of Sociology*, vol. 26, pp.169-185.

~~~~~~~~

Index

A

AAT / Administrative Appeals Tribunal 24, 205 (fn)
Adella 37, 38, 64, 81, 82, 93, 123, 134, 157
Administrative Decision (Judicial Review) Act ADJR 185
Africa 48
African 48, 67, 79, 152, 199, 201
Agamben, G 119, 120, 128–130, 176
Akith 16, 41, 90
Albanese, Anthony 135, 136
Al Kateb 173
Aloysha 58, 83
Amora 29, 30, 47, 60, 62–64, 86, 117, 118, 124–126, 134, 141, 144
Andrews, Kevin 133
Andy 42, 140
Assurance of Support 63, 136
Australian Federal Police 133
AHRC / Australian Human Rights Commission 132, 173, 192, 203, 204, 206

B

Barati, Reza 212
Belicia 37, 38, 44, 56, 63, 66, 67, 73, 74, 78, 80, 81, 86, 89, 93, 95, 97, 117, 121, 123, 133–136, 141, 142, 146, 147, 158–163, 165, 167, 168, 170–174, 196, 199, 201
Bland, Sally 73, 74, 76, 78–80, 83, 89, 106, 123, 124, 138, 161–166, 196, 199
Boat(s) 7, 16, 22, 30, 129, 149, 180–183, 198, 204, 208, 210, 213, 214
Boat people 7
Bodham, Ben 68–70, 74, 96, 97, 100, 102, 104, 109
Bowen, Chris 53, 135 148 149
Bridging visa 31, 45, 54, 59, 64, 135, 137, 145, 158, 165 167, 168, 170, 206, 207
Brown, Bill 66, 157
Burke, Tony 136, 209

C

Centrelink 45, 63, 136, 164
Character test 212
Coalition 48, 50, 51, 192
Cobb, Minister 141, 142, 145, 147–150
Complementary Protection 41, 42, 120, 161, 172, 173, 191, 210
Constitution 8, 11, 21, 90, 126, 128, 129, 132, 149, 155, 175, 178, 179, 186, 211
Convention Against Torture CAT 46, 70, 80, 94, 164
Convention on the Rights of the Child 70, 99, 164, 169

D

Daryna 34, 69, 100, 101 103, 112
Delegate 20, 67, 68, 107, 145, 146, 155, 157, 158, 160, 173, 205, 213
Department (of Immigration) 9, 17, 22, 24, 44, 49, 54, 60, 68, 70, 72, 74, 80, 113, 114, 137, 143, 148, 163, 190, 200–205

D ...
Dicker, Diana 73, 81, 116, 117
Diego 42, 65
Dmytro 40, 41, 135, 136, 140, 216
Doussa, John von 173
Dutton, Peter 131

E
Evans, Chris 36, 51, 97, 127, 135, 139–141, 192

F
Faizon 42, 53
Federal Court 80, 115, 116, 120–125, 135, 138, 161, 162, 166, 170, 184, 185, 188

G
Georgina 43, 48
Gillard, Julia 131
Gleeson, Justice 189
Grisha 57, 58, 61, 63, 76, 82, 83, 102, 122, 144
Guidelines 40, 83, 86, 89, 99, 117, 122, 127, 133, 137, 139, 140, 142–147, 150, 151, 158, 160, 161, 165–169, 173, 176, 193, 194, 203, 205

H
Herminia 37, 63, 93, 133, 134, 157
High Court 8, 9, 10, 96, 110–116, 124, 138, 158, 168, 170, 173, 175, 179, 183, 185, 186, 189, 190–192, 206, 210
Hirst, Philip 74, 75, 78, 125
Howard, John 48–50, 95–97, 113, 131, 186
Humanitarian 62, 72, 81, 89, 109, 127, 132, 138–140, 153, 157–161, 166, 168, 171–173, 200, 203, 204, 207, 208
Humanitarian visa 63, 132, 139, 153, 157, 158, 161, 166, 171, 207

I
Implausibility 79, 85, 94, 105, 120, 121, 124, 152, 154, 163, 165, 196, 197, 199
Inglet, Ian 82, 89, 97, 106, 138, 145, 146, 157, 160, 167, 168
International Covenant on Civil and Political Rights ICCPR 92, 120, 164
International Covenant on Economic, Social and Cultural Rights 50, 60, 63
Itan 42, 91, 140

J
Jaime 51, 57, 58, 63, 73, 76–83, 95, 99, 106, 123, 138, 139, 146, 196
Judicial review 72, 115, 123–126, 184–190, 196
Julia 40, 41, 136
Jurisdictional Error 9, 10, 11, 80, 117–119, 122, 127, 155, 156, 184, 186, 191, 197, 202, 206, 207, 208
Justice Gageler 115, 126, 184–186, 188, 191

K

Keating, Paul 180
Key Performance Indicators (KPI) 52, 70
Kalyna 34, 50, 51, 64, 68–74, 96–109, 111, 112
Kneebone, Susan 157, 162

L

Labor (Party) 48, 97, 191, 194, 208
Ladonna 51, 56–63, 81, 92, 95, 99, 106, 123, 138, 139, 196
Latoya 37, 38, 61, 64, 81, 82, 93, 123, 134, 157
Lee, Jane, 148

M

McGauren, Minister 147
McHugh, Justice 188–191
Mabo 10, 175, 179
Magistrate's Court 119–121, 135, 185
Maita 35, 36, 62, 139
Marco 29, 30, 47, 56, 59, 62, 63, 73–79, 86, 117, 118, 124–126, 141, 144, 146
Mateo 43, 56–63, 76–80, 99
Medicare 33, 57, 58, 61–63, 65, 163, 164, 198
Merits review 76, 119, 121, 161, 184, 185, 208
Migration Act 7, 19, 58, 112, 132, 137, 141, 149, 150, 154, 155, 161, 163, 165, 169, 172, 173, 175, 179, 184, 186, 197, 198, 200
Migration agent 17, 82, 95, 96, 115, 116, 118, 127, 135, 168
Mikhaila 31, 32, 144
Ministerial intervention 42, 45, 52, 53, 90, 111, 125, 133, 137–139, 143, 148, 151, 158, 163, 167, 170, 200, 206
Ministerial request 72, 74, 81, 82, 86, 110, 113, 116, 132, 135, 137, 138, 154, 167, 168
Mortimer, Debbie 148, 149
Mullhead, Judith 74, 81, 82, 89, 145, 146, 159, 160, 163, 166, 168, 170

N

Naldo 35, 36, 56, 62, 63, 139, 146
Nankunda 38–40, 45, 56, 61–63, 67, 73, 75–79 83–88, 93, 94, 104–106, 119–124, 137, 139, 144, 147, 148, 150–153, 196, 197, 199
Natalka 33, 35, 62, 109, 112
Newstart 63, 136

O

O'Connor, Brendan 135, 136
O'Keefe, Serina 157, 170
Olek 33, 34, 50, 60, 62, 63, 68–74, 81, 82, 95–113, 141, 144
Olha 41, 135
Orlando 37, 38, 57, 58, 63, 73, 74, 78, 80, 81, 86, 89, 95, 97, 117, 121, 123, 133, 134, 136, 141–147, 154–174, 196, 201

P

Palmer, M 66, 169, 170, 190
Paola 42, 65
Parliament 7–9, 19, 21, 23, 29, 37, 48, 50, 51, 57, 72, 78, 81, 87, 93, 119–122, 126–132, 135, 136, 147–150, 156, 158, 174–184, 186, 188, 189, 191–198, 202–214
Parliamentarians 19–23, 78, 128, 130, 131, 147, 148, 156, 183, 192, 196, 204, 206, 208, 210–214
Performance Indicators 52, 70
Petitie, Carmel 74, 81, 82, 170
Pilon, Angelina 67, 75, 76, 88, 104, 151
Polina 40, 41, 135, 136
Post traumatic stress disorder PTSD 83, 86, 87, 93, 142, 143
Prime Minister 48, 49, 50, 95, 96, 120, 131, 139, 180, 209
Pro bono 47, 91, 138
Maley, Professor William 153
Protocol 16, 48, 50, 73, 80, 176
Proust, E 166

R

Racial Discrimination Act 175
Rafi 42, 140, 141
Raja 42, 66
Redberrry, Ros 67, 72–79, 82–85, 88, 96, 99–109, 112, 119–124, 151, 156, 196, 197, 199
Refugee 7–11, 16, 17, 21–24, 32, 33, 40–42, 47, 50, 63, 65, 68, 70–72, 80–82, 85–87, 94–105, 11--113, 116, 120, 124, 126, 127, 132, 137, 142, 143, 150–158, 162, 164, 167, 169–172, 175, 176, 181, 183–186, 188–199, 201, 203–209, 213
Refugee convention 50, 80, 164, 189, 199
Refugee Review Tribunal 24, 116, 137, 155, 175, 186
Regina 43, 48
res judicata 125
Reviewer 23, 67, 68, 70–78, 81–90, 93–99, 102–105, 110–119, 120–128, 135, 142, 143, 147, 149, 151–162, 169, 173, 185–191, 196, 197, 200, 202–206, 208, 212–214
Robb 147
Rudd, Kevin 50, 97, 131, 139, 209
Ruddock, Philip 50, 72, 82, 89, 96, 97, 109, 113, 118, 120–124, 127, 128, 131–133,, 135, 138, 141–143, 145, 147, 160, 166–168, 175, 186, 188–190
Rossell, Ngareta 22, 30, 48

S

s48b / 150–152, 167
s417 116, 143, 148, 165, 166
Sabina 31–33, 56, 60–64, 81, 145, 147
Sabrina 42, 140, 141
Sari 42, 140, 141
Sarita 36, 41, 53, 54, 57, 59, 60, 62, 63
Schedule 89, 90
Sergio 51, 57, 58, 61, 63, 64, 93, 139
Senate Select Committee on Migration Matters 128, 143
Set-aside 72

Sporton, Mark 82, 96, 97, 99, 102, 103, 108, 111–113
Srey, Chan Ta 96, 110

T

terra nullius 128, 129, 177, 179, 182, 208
Thouless, RH 113
Thousend, Terry 76, 77, 80

U

United Nations UN 21, 33, 44, 48, 76, 99, 117, 158, 165, 169, 176
United Nations High Commissioner for Refugees UNHCR

V

Valentina 35–37, 57, 61, 62, 64, 139

Z

Zafar 42, 112, 113

www.ingramcontent.com/pod-product-compliance
Lightning Source LLC
Chambersburg PA
CBHW020320010526
44107CB00054B/1912